What Others

For many years the first thing I would turn to in the *Sooner Catholic* was Fr. Monahan's "For the Time Being" column. He always charmed me with the respectful loving humor and the evocative language with which he treated the colorful characters that populated his columns. He taught me to treasure the ways in which God's presence shines through the inspiring foibles of the all-too-human Catholics of Oklahoma!

—Most Reverend Anthony B. Taylor
Bishop of Little Rock

Dave Monahan had a gift for taking a simple event and describing it in a written form that enabled the reader to also experience the event. He had a knack for introducing his readers to a variety of lovable characters. He was such a kind man himself that his story of what happened never demeaned the person. Yet he told the story often "tongue in cheek" in such a marvelously humorous manner that his readers were deep in laughter and waiting to share the story with the next person she/he met.

—Joseph D. Dillon,
Vatican II—A Promise Broken?
Lexington, KY: 2011; with Edward D. Jeep

Sometimes the best way to present something as slippery as *morality* is to wrap it in a story. In the first few paragraphs of "Stepping Warily into Faith, Hope, and Hollywood," Monahan teaches us that responsible motherhood is difficult and that we shouldn't judge others—and we enjoy the lesson. The world needs that kind of wit-wrapped comedy.

These short essays reflect Father Monahan's unique understanding of the meaning of *comedy* in *The Divine Comedy*. Even in the essay about his mother's death, "Present at the End: The Story of a Woman's Death," he shows loss through that comedic filter.

When I taught at Bishop McGuinness High School, Father Monahan was my principal and became my friend. Sometimes I chuckled out loud while reading the essays referring to those school years. But sometimes I felt sad because I miss a man I knew and loved for forty years.

—Judith Tate O'Brien,
Crossing a Different Bridge: An Oklahoma Memoir, (2010)

I highly recommend Dave Monahan's *For the Time Being*.

This collection of Dave's columns is a smorgasbord feast of insightful, delightful, slightly skeptical, and always funny "takes" on the human condition as lived by a man of deep faith, simple tastes, and clear sight. This is a good and most enjoyable read.

—Father Thomas McSherry
St. Patrick Catholic Church,
Oklahoma City, Oklahoma

(Note: Father Thomas McSherry makes the "odd" appearance in the columns as he served seventeen years in the Oklahoma Catholic Mission in Santiago Atitlan, Solola, Guatemala. David Monahan was an enthusiastic supporter of all of those who worked at the Mission.)

If you like to enjoy yourself, join me in thanking Joan O'Neill for producing this collection of essays by David Monahan. This is entertainment at its best: no batteries, no volume control, just the reflections of a man who knows how to tell a story. You'll be disappointed to reach the end of this book, but you will do so with a few more threads woven into your moral fiber and a slightly more coherent view of the universe.

—Doris Hellinghausen
Littleton, Colorado

For years we were treated to the best of humanity in the articles of Father David Monahan. We are fortunate that they have been preserved. These gentle tales are a treasure.

—Father Bill Ross
St. Eugene Catholic Church
Oklahoma City, Oklahoma

Captured moments become unforgettable in Father Monahan's telling. A keen observer, he could grasp the essence of a situation, understand the incongruities, express his observations in down-to-earth language, and make us laugh without ever belittling others.

—Martha King
Teacher 1961-1969
McGuinness High School
Oklahoma City, Oklahoma

FOR
THE TIME BEING

FOR
THE TIME BEING

DAVID MONAHAN
EDITED BY JOANIE O'NEILL

LIFE THROUGH
THE LENS OF
A CURIOUS MIND

TATE PUBLISHING
AND ENTERPRISES, LLC

This book is designed to provide accurate and authoritative information with regard to the subject matter covered. This information is given with the understanding that neither the author nor Tate Publishing, LLC is engaged in rendering legal, professional advice. Since the details of your situation are fact dependent, you should additionally seek the services of a competent professional.

The opinions expressed by the author are not necessarily those of Tate Publishing, LLC.

Published by Tate Publishing & Enterprises, LLC
127 E. Trade Center Terrace | Mustang, Oklahoma 73064 USA
1.888.361.9473 | www.tatepublishing.com

Tate Publishing is committed to excellence in the publishing industry. The company reflects the philosophy established by the founders, based on Psalm 68:11,
"The Lord gave the word and great was the company of those who published it."

Published in the United States of America
ISBN: 978-1-62510-804-3
1. Biography & Autobiography / Personal Memoirs
2. Literary Collections / General
13.10.30

Dedication

In loving memory of
Father David Francis Monahan

1927–2010

- 1953–1958 St. Francis of Assisi Church and Rosary School, Oklahoma City
- 1958–1971 Bishop McGuinness High School, teacher and principal
- 1966–1978 St. Robert Bellarmine Church, Jones / St. Theresa Church, Luther
- 1970–1974 Superintendent of Catholic schools
- 1974–1994 Founding editor of the *Sooner Catholic* newspaper
- 1979–1994 Epiphany of the Lord Church, Oklahoma City
- 1994–1995 Sabbatical
- 1995–1997 Sacred Heart Church, Mangum, with mission of Sts. Peter and Paul Church, Hobart
- 1997–2002 Pastor, St. Catherine of Siena Church, Pauls Valley, with mission of St. Peter Church, Lindsay

Acknowledgments

My deepest gratitude to each of the following for their unique contribution toward bringing this collection of columns to its fruition:

- Cara Koenig, *Sooner Catholic* newspaper
- Father Tom McSherry
- Bryce and Mary Helen Edwards
- James P. Kelley
- Judith O'Brien
- Jeanne Devlin
- Carolyn Leonard
- Carolyn Merritt
- Lauren Kloiber
- Mary McIntosh
- Peg Slater
- Rose Braun
- Sheila Mueller

—Joanie O'Neill, Editor

Table of Contents

Foreword..21

Introduction..23

Chapter 1: Editor's Favorites................................27

Woman in the Ditch Was Barely There 29

If I Ain't out by Then, I Probably Ain't Comin' Out....32

He Was Pumping Iron, Man! 36

Carp and the Young Priest Were Birds of a Feather 39

Misadventures of a One-Language Man 42

Of the Brief Boxing Career of a Panicky Pugilist 46

A Cry from Prisoners of the US Camping System 49

I Know Where You Can Get a Used Bicycle for $10......51

Sure and the Man Can't Organize a Two-Car Funeral 54

Chapter 2: 1977 59

Where Father Carlin Was, Things Happened.............61

Chapter 3: 1979 63

The Health Club...65

Two Amsterdam Women...67

Pilgrimage to a Village 69

Women in My Past...71

Chapter 4: 1980 73

Mountains as Suddenly as Spilt Milk........................75

How John D. Cherry Eliminated the
   Good Guys in Row 61...77
Personal History in a Catalogue of Scars...................................79
If My Father Were Still Alive, He Wouldn't Be Now.................81
The Art of Celebrating Christmas without a Tree 84

Chapter 5: 1981 87
At Gift Wrapping It's the Beginning of the End........................89
In a Republican Year Visit the Old House in Watonga 91
This Week an Old Friend Retires 93
She Possessed a Look That Froze Evil in Its Tracks...................96
An Easter Mix of Alleluias and Acts of Contrition 99
Announcing the Crooked Tooth League of America...............102
Whatever Happened to National Return Books Week? 105
How I Discovered the Inventor of the Beer Can 107
"Jail House Rock" Served with Salad 110
The True Confessions of a New Car Buyer 113
I mean I was Mao Tse-tung on the Long March......................116
I Stepped out of the Car, Slammed the Door, and… 119

Chapter 6: 1982 123
Red Smith: A Talented Bleeder and
   "a Pretty Good Speller"..125
What Is So Comforting as a Celebrity's Boo-Boo? 128
If You Want to Become a Little Nutty Work in a
   High School for a Decade 130
The Great Rubber Gun Wars of the Summer of 1934............134
Sweat, Laughs, and Glory at the PGA Tournament 136
The Old Order Changeth, but Only With
   Some Timely Assistance...139
Surprised at "No-Surprises" Inn..142
He Who Drinks of the Nile Will Surely Drink Again 145

Chapter 7: 1983 149
Before Nicklaus Was, Snead Slammed.................... 151
Pepper Looked Young in Comparison 154
How Could Joe Survive Cosmic Punch?................... 157
Joe the Hermit Put Teddy Roosevelt in His Place 160
Wasn't I Fred Astaire Dancing Up the Staircase to God? 163

Chapter 8: 1984 167
Brother Cold Comes Slip-Sliding through the Cracks........... 169
Something That's Going around May
    Be around the Next Corner 172
Particles of Americana on Night Flight to San Diego 176
In Era of Affirmation, Bitter Sips of the
    Waters of Contempt 179
Moving: It Shakes You up, Causes Tired Blood................ 183
If You Think the Little You Have Is Safe,
    Don't Bank on It... 186
The Nurse in Room 122 Said,
    "He's Ready to Go Home".................................. 189
Something Insidious Is Happening
    Right under Your Feet 192
Even in a Golfing Eden, Beware of the Snakes................ 195
How Long Did Nannie Doss Cook in Your Kitchen? 198
Plodding into New Year in My Wolverine Work Shoes........... 202

Chapter 9: 1985 205
Why He Gets Cold Feet Just Thinking about It 207
Murdered Priest Left Memories Wrapped in Laughter.......... 210
Twisting Down the Hog Back Road to Easter 213
Is This Man's Hair Afflicted with Amnesia?.................... 216
When I Saw This Telephone Pole Pass Me... 218
Summer Camp: A Time to Learn to Appreciate Home 221
Tired of the Heat? Try an Old-Fashioned

Swimming Hole 225
Route 66 and the Case of the Tired Truck.......................... 228
Hitchhiking Is a Theological Problem for Me 232
State University's Game Proves to Be Memorable Event 235

Chapter 10: 1986.. 239
Confession of a Banana Caramel Addict 241
Flagged Out at Northwest Expressway and Rockwell 244
A Limp Salute to the Texas Sesquicentennial 247
Sweetie Pie Is Seventy-Five and Still on His Pedestal 250
Like a Bulldozer Running Full Throttle into
    Mound of Lard 253
The Four Worst Spoken Words in the English Language 256
Your Choice: A Brooding Lincoln or a Muddy Grant 260
Stepping Warily into Faith, Hope, and Hollywood 263

Chapter 11: 1987.. 267
A Seven-Course Feast of Laughs for a Condemned Man 269
Being an Account of an Exodus to the Promised Land 273
Pre-Match Prophecy: May the Worst Player Win! 276
On a Tired Evening, Twenty Years of Rock 'n' Roll................ 279

Chapter 12: 1988.. 283
You Are Responsible for the Life in Your Aquarium 285
In 1945, There Were 144,000 Bald-Headed Women 288
    "Today Nothing Will Upset Me,"
Said the Principal to Himself 292
A Thousand Soft Drinks Wore Bicuspids to Nubs................... 296
Whatever Happened to Characters in the Priesthood?........... 299

Chapter 13: 1989.. 303
You May Yet Be Able to Save Your Nose 305
When the German Sisters Spoke, People Listened.................. 308

Presenting the 1989 Restaurant Lighting Rating......................312
Golf at Its Nadir at Mc&M International Competition...........315
Confessor Gasped, *"Ego te Absolvo"*......................................319
My Motto: Talk Softly but Carry a Big Magazine...................322
Webster States Kook Is an Alternative Form of Cuckoo..........326
What Has Jimmy Mastered That Creates the Urge to...?.........329

Chapter 14: 1990...333
The Case of the Befuddled Burglar and Chaos Security...........335
I Did a Forty-Six-Year Back-Flip and
    Landed in a Defensive Crouch 338
Not Even a Twitch of Weak Will to Write Tomorrow..............342
Nichols Hills Never Had It So Bad as That Holy Week...........345
'y Ballou Reporting from the
    North End of the Water Hole 349
I Left With All the Firmness of Will of a Jellyfish...................352
Girl B Runs up Staircase to Appeal to Supreme Court 355
The Official Asks, "The Purpose of Your Visit?"
    "Cerveza!" 358
Veteran Golfer Unnerved by Opponent's Payless Shoes 361
An Odd Duck in a Pond of Many-Hued
    Protestant Birds 364
Charlie and Me: The Story of a Painful Collision Course........368
Golf Games Melt in Water at Fall Match Play Classic.............372
School Boy Happens upon a Delightfully Bloody Book...........375

Chapter 15: 1991...379
Is It the Fault of the Irish That Catholics Can't Sing?.............381
After Forty-Six Years in the Rough, a
    Golfing Game Reborn!...385
ANTI's Motto: Nothing Good Will Come of It 388
I Looked Up and Wondered Who That
    Elderly Gentleman Was...392

This Moses on I-40 Didn't Wear a Long White Beard 395
Center of Guatemala City Offers Rich Variety of Noises 399
Testimony of One Lured by Siren Call of Sweet Sleep 402
"I'm from Oklahoma!" She Yelled to New York Cop 405
Present at the End: The Story of a Woman's Death 409
Will Someone Please Call the National Enquirer? 412

CHAPTER 16: 1992 415
Is There a Man with a Pint of Old Crow in His Jacket? 417
Packed with 620,000 Batting Statistics 420
That's the State of Things at 1015 Rosario Lane 423
Father Harold Never Heard about Passive Resistance 427
A Sudden Onset of Eire Ire in Front of Cathedral 431
Not So Fast, New York! No First for You 434
On Eating Breakfast Regularly with the Wizard 437
Dick Descended Culturally from Chopin,
    Debussy, and Bach 440
A 100 Percent Chance of Rain during the Game 444
Of Intersection Thieves and Heavy-Footed Tailgaters 447
Before Sending a Cat to a Jesuit, Read This 450

Chapter 17: 1993 453
Father Hugo's Advice: For Venial Sins, One Alleluia 455
And Now a Tribute to the Unknown Baseball Player 458
From Zero to Sixty in What Seems Like
    Eight Seconds Flat 461
The Oh-Dear! and What-the-Hell
    Schools of Kite Flying 464
The Thing Was Called a Sentimental Journey 467
But It Is Raining and Nobody Else Is on the Course! 470
Chomping One's Way through a Mountain of Junk Food 473
Driving Down the Left Lane of Life in Merry England 477
The Day the Theory of Tickets Failed the Test 481

That's the Way It Used to Be 484

Chapter 18:   1994...487
Wash Is Done...Gone the Socks...Down the Drain 489
Afterword 492
Other Books by This Author...496

Foreword

During Father David Monahan's twenty years as editor of the *Sooner Catholic* newspaper for the Archdiocese of Oklahoma City, it was my great privilege to serve him and observe him.

In conversation, Monahan rarely revealed much of himself, for he was always far more interested in others. In fact, he would probably be embarrassed at how much—*collectively*—these stories reveal about him. Behind his wonderful sense of humor, we come to see the inner beauty of a man whose priesthood and humanity were seamless.

These essays, bequeathed to me in Monahan's will, also go a long way toward proving the notion that the Irish love a good story and have a great gift for telling them, something Monahan did often, laughing at the punch line with the same enthusiasm in the fiftieth telling as in the first.

Once, after relating one of these gems about a colorful priest from the past, he laughed and said, "There were a lot of characters in the priesthood." Then, becoming introspective, he added in surprise, "I'm probably one of them!"

In a time when the Catholic priesthood worldwide is suffering because of the repeated sins of many of its membership, Father David Monahan's columns reflect a healthy reminder of the goodness of most priests and the true greatness of some.

Introduction

The idea for this book was originally Monahan's. He had brought a few of these columns with him to the 1987 Catholic Press Association convention to review during the inevitable free time at such events. He would choose the best of the best and see if he could interest a publisher in such a collection.

The keynote speaker scheduled on the last day of the convention was Jimmy Breslin, Pulitzer Prize-winning journalist and author. Convention organizers panicked when, at the last minute, they learned Breslin couldn't make it. Monahan was tapped to fill in for Breslin.

Overheard in the elevator after the event: "I don't know who that fellow was, but I'm almost glad Breslin didn't show. He was great!" He had, of course, drawn from his own material, the stuff of which he'd hoped would be worthy of a book someday.

This is that book.

While the *Sooner Catholic* was published every other week beginning in 1974, Monahan's columns didn't begin to appear until 1977 and then only sporadically. The first one, April of 1977, was dubbed "A Column of Nonessentials" and covered several topics. It wasn't until 1978 that "For the Time Being" became a regular feature. And still they each covered several topics. None of them had titles. By early 1979, "For the Time Being" became more focused, covering only one topic in depth, each one suitably titled.

Monahan brings to each of these stories his unique slant on life based on the many hats he has worn. He wore more than most priests, his experiences extending outside the scope of the usual parish priest. In addition to pastoral duties, he also taught school, both elementary and secondary, and served as high school principal during the turbulent Civil Rights Movement. Monahan's most recognizable hat is probably that of writer and editor of the *Sooner Catholic* because the newspaper was sent to every Catholic household in the archdiocese and beyond.

In addition to priest, educator, and editor, Monahan was an ardent devotee of sports, a historian, and political enthusiast. He knew and loved every back road and obscure cemetery in Oklahoma and any historical figures buried there. With such a varied background plus his keen observations of human nature, we see in these stories a gentle man wrestling at times with his conscience, admiring his heroes, revealing his love of sports, admitting to and overcoming prejudices, his ineptitude in all things technological, describing interesting characters he had met along the way, and his competitive nature when it came to golf.

In these pages you will meet an amusing and colorful cast of characters, some familiar, some not, but all of whom teach us something about life through the lens of the author's keen observation. We meet the man who knew the inventor of the beer can; Gooch the not-so-panicky pugilist decades after retiring from the ring; Joe the hermit in his concrete bunker atop a hill surrounded by "great chunks of silence."

Then there are the more familiar names: Joe Louis, Red Smith, Danny Kaye, Barry Switzer, Hosni Mubarak, Sam Snead, and Chuck Yeager. And we see the human side of some colorful priests including the eccentric saintly priest who gave away everything, including his bed and who "shambled about unkempt, hung his Mass vestments on the wings of a plaster of Paris angel next to the altar and kept his Roman collar together with a paper clip."

There are coming-of-age stories of school, family, and summer camp where he "shuffled through the camp 'activities' with quarts of melancholy running down the inside walls" of his body. And there are two essays describing his embarrassing effort to sing the extremely difficult "Exultet" at the Easter vigil, an attempt so humiliating and mortifying that he was still agonizing over it almost twenty-five years later and wrote of it yet again six years after that.

You don't have to be Catholic to enjoy these stories. There are some we can all relate to—aging, receding hairlines, crooked teeth, noses that are too big, ears that stick out, homesickness, travel, and piles of unanswered mail—and he has an amazing ability to say so much, so cleverly, about such simple, mundane things.

What sets these stories apart is the unique character of the man who wrote them, his goodness, humility, and sense of humor peeking out of each essay.

It is with immense sadness now that many of the stories he loved telling were not written down before his death. And of those he did commit to paper, many had to be omitted from this collection in the interest of length. Place names, unless otherwise noted, are in Oklahoma.

We hope you enjoy reading them as much as we enjoyed selecting the ones to include in this tribute to Father David Monahan.

And so we begin with Eva, the nearly naked woman in the ditch.

CHAPTER 1

Editor's Favorites

Woman in the Ditch Was Barely There

March 1983

This is the fourth anniversary of my nighttime encounter with The Woman in the Ditch. I am sincerely grateful that the intervening period has not been spent gazing at the insides of the walls at Big Mac. The whole incident has given me a new appreciation of people with peculiar alibis.

A post-midnight telephone call formed the first link in the chain of events. John was dying, a parishioner and a friend. I dressed and drove to Baptist Medical Center.

Having done what I could for John and his family, I started back to the rectory preoccupied with the whole mystery and nastiness of death. My route took me south on Grand Avenue where it transforms into Interstate 44.

There was a car in the ditch dividing the highway. It was wedged east and west in the ditch which ran north and south. As I slowed to take a look at the car, I was startled by the sight of a woman standing in the ditch next to the automobile. Her total costume on this chill March night was a pair of red bikini panties. The God of the unexpected had struck again.

I stopped. The area was empty of open stores, service stations, or even passing motorists. There was nothing to do but to help the damsel in distress. I scrambled into the ditch. She was thirtyish and was swaying as though the ground were shifting under her feet. Her first words, which proved to be an exact statement of fact, were: "I'm crazy drunk."

The engine of the car was running, and I turned it off. In the backseat were her purse, her eyeglasses, and a blanket. I wrapped the blanket around her, and together we emerged from the ditch leaning into each other like a couple in the last hour of a dance marathon. Somehow I flopped her into the passenger seat of my old Maverick.

"Where do you live?" I asked.

She began to tell me, but then slurred, "Take me to my boyfriend's."

"You don't need to go to your boyfriend's. You need to go home."

She didn't answer.

I put my car in gear and started south on I-44. "If you won't tell me where you live, I'm going to take you to St. Anthony's Hospital," I said. "You might be hurt and not realize it."

This sane proposal was met by a gusher of profanity describing St. Anthony's, me, and my forebears down to the tenth generation in not altogether laudatory terms. We proceeded.

Only three blocks from my goal, a traffic light stopped us at Northwest 10th and Classen.

Eva (the name had tumbled out along with the obscenities) decided she was going to abandon ship. The Maverick had a tricky indoor latch, and I hoped she couldn't work it. But she did. The right door opened, the dome light came on, the blanket fell off, and I grabbed Eva's left arm to try and keep her in the car. At this moment another vehicle came to a stop behind us.

Imagine the scene. A middle-aged man wearing a Roman collar restraining a young woman in her birthday suit from leaving his automobile at 2:30 a.m. I was hoping that I would do well on the lie detector test.

"If you'll close the door, I'll take you anywhere you want to go," I said, making Chamberlain at Munich look like an unshakable fortress in comparison. We drove north on Classen Boulevard, certain that swirling red lights and a SWAT team would blockade the road ahead, she trying to extract her boyfriend's house number from her pickled brain.

Her first fix on the guy's address turned out to be approximately in the middle of Belle Isle Lake. We tried again and again and then once more for Romeo's illusive habitat. At last she recognized a truck.

"Is this man married?"

"No."

"Does he live by himself?"

"Yes."

I decided to give it a try. Leaving Eva in the car, I walked to the front door and rang the bell. Nothing. I rang again. Somewhere inside a light shown. The door opened. A tall character in blue jeans but no shirt stared at me.

I went into my act like a nervous Girl Scout cookie seller. "My name is Father Monahan from Sacred Heart Church, and I was driving down Grand Avenue when I spotted this car in a ditch and a naked woman standing beside it, and I picked her up, and the only address she would give me is yours, and her name is Eva."

His groaned response: "Oh, God."

I knew salvation had arrived. Before that bozo could organize himself and slam the door, I had Eva, her blanket, her glasses, and her purse on his porch. He opened the door for her, God bless him.

As Eva staggered into the house, she turned and said sweetly, "You are a beautiful man." The beautiful man watched for the police all the way home.

If I Ain't out by Then, I Probably Ain't Comin' Out

February 1983

Priests' funerals are different.

Three decades back as a just ordained priest, I made my way to Our Lady's Cathedral for the funeral of the distinguished Father Urban de Hasque. I distinctly remember meeting one of my senior brothers of the priestly fraternity immediately after the Mass. He raised his glass and called out merrily, "Have some bourbon on Urban!"

You're right if you think that the period of grief was rather short. You're wrong if you judge that long-ago greeting to have been cynical or to be an example of priests' calloused approach to life and death. Quite the opposite is true.

There is no denying that tears are rare among those wearing albs and stoles at one of their own's final rites. There are exceptions— Stanley Rother's funeral was certainly one, but the prevailing practice is more on the side of laughter than of blubber.

It has been my experience that there are few, if any, genuine hypocrites in terms of faith among priests. They believe in that eternal life that they preach. So when a priest plays out his allotted run on his old stage, his colleagues are apt to celebrate his closing production with a proper try at reflection and prayer followed by a wee taste of the spirits and an overall sense that another performance of a lifetime has been given good marks by the only critic who counts.

And paradoxically, priests, with no families, are members of a wider if less emotionally intense family: fellow members of the

local clergy. That kinship is felt most keenly at ordinations and
funerals. Especially at funerals there are family recollections and
a touch of sentimental nostalgia and a pride in the life lived (and
possibly a wandering thought or two on a lower plane—Will I be
next? Who will get his pastorate?).

The late January funeral of Msgr. Raymond Harkin was a
good example of a priest's funeral. One must note that the joy of
the event, which seemed to gain momentum as one part followed
the other, was mainly the gift of the delightfully colorful man
who had died.

Good things began to happen at the wake. Father Tom
McSherry reminded us of Msgr. Harkin's "special language."
Father McSherry said that shortly after he was assigned as
associate pastor at St. Joseph's Old Cathedral, Msgr. Harkin
told him, "The head honcho wants to see you at the big house."
The translation proved to be, "The bishop wants to see you at
his residence."

Monsignor's "special language" included his habit of using a
person's middle initial for a fitting adjective that was "not always
complimentary," Father McSherry said. So the associate became
Thomas "G for Gypsy" McSherry and the former Archbishop of
Oklahoma City was John "R for Roman" Quinn.

On a more serious side, Father McSherry pointed out Msgr.
Harkin's "special fondness" for those who were "a little odd, a
little weird, those on the edge of things."

Father McSherry concluded by remarking, "Each of us has
come to know God's love, God's kingdom, and God's humor
through Msgr. Harkin."

The next morning's Mass of Christian Burial at the Old
Cathedral brought together a collection of worshipers that only
Msgr. Harkin could have assembled. Besides the family members
and a large group of priests (perhaps eighty to ninety from all
parts of the state and beyond), there were the kids from St.
Joseph's Children's Home, a row of old-time lawyers, here and

there a priest who had left the active ministry, Ho-Ho the Clown disguised as Ed Birchall, Catholic Church dissidents of the right and of the left, Louis Eichhoff smilingly shaking hands with the priests in procession, former Extension volunteers, longtime chancery office do-it-all Margaret Novitski, and more.

Father Louis Lamb preached the homily in a voice made husky with emotion. He described his friend, Msgr. Harkin, as "an encyclopedia of knowledge," "a railroad buff," "an advocate for the underdog," and "a man of prayer."

Altogether the homily wove its way nicely from monsignor's love of the church to his concern a week before about the odds on the Dolphins and Jets game.

The verbal high spot of the funeral Mass was added quietly at the end by Archbishop Salatka. He revealed that Msgr. Harkin had left not a will but a page of instructions. Then the archbishop read from the instructions. "Hope to have one hundred dollars left for fifty Mass offerings," monsignor wrote. That was followed immediately by the comment, "If I ain't out by then, I probably ain't comin' out, or I never got there." The mourners laughed and applauded.

At the chapel of Resurrection Cemetery, priests jabbered with one another until the casket was carried in. The short service was concluded by a gentle, moving singing of "May the angels lead you into paradise, may the martyrs come to welcome you...."

The casket was borne outside, where the wind was chill and the ground muddy, to the grave. Pallbearers, priests, and family members formed a tight-packed L with backs to the north and west, a kind of reverse phalanx against the fierce wind. Viewed from the open sides, it was a scene to remember: two lines of solemn faces pinched with cold framed around the casket in the ultimate human rite.

Afterward there were drinks and dinner at the Center for Christian Renewal. An out-of-state priest-friend of Msgr. Harkin took the floor to sing one of monsignor's favorites "They

Cut Down the Old Pine Tree." Father Martin Reid followed with "Danny Boy." Finally, Bishop Charles Buswell of Pueblo, buoyed by the spirit of the event, sang a parody written when he and Msgr. Harkin were made monsignors. It was that kind of time.

People went away glad that they had been there.

He Was Pumping Iron, Man!

January 1983

Yesterday at the Y, I was staggering back to the health club after doing my twenty tiny laps when I met David Winkler. David is a barrel-chested former marine whose hobby is weight lifting.

He said that he had been away from the weights awhile and that now he could bench press only 315 pounds. Smiling, David asked me what I could bench press. "About nine and a half pounds," I replied, "if I have an assistant." We both laughed, partly in unstated recognition that nine and a half was a lot closer to the truth for me than 315, and I went on my way.

That chance encounter set my memory in motion, recalling a few instances of Roman Catholic clerical weight lifting. Names have been changed to protect my health.

When Arnold Schwarzenegger's name was still broader than his neck, Father Dee P. Culture surreptitiously entered an Oklahoma City sporting goods store and began to browse through the racks of weights. He chose that bar because it reminded him of a baton, and this weight because it resembled a cymbal, and so forth.

At the end of the shopping spree, the priest realized that his buying power had outrun his lifting power. He was certain that he was incapable of lugging the weights out the door. Assuming his most dignified but perhaps slightly flushed pose, Father Culture said, "Would you please carry the weights to my car?" There was never any tangible evidence that he managed to remove the weights from the automobile once he arrived home.

Then there were Father Muscles and Father Fatso. I shared a rectory with this twosome during the era when Charles Atlas was powerfully lifting cold cash from the pockets of ninety-seven-pound weaklings.

Father Muscles had been forever on body-building programs, but then he discovered weights. It wasn't long before our living room became the unofficial gymnasium. If one listened closely, one could detect the sighs of the ill-constructed floor as it anticipated the stresses of the late afternoon lifting sessions. He was pumping iron, man! Pumping lots of iron!

As converts are wont to do, Father Muscles sought adherents to his cause. I kept my door closed and tried not to breathe loudly lest I attract attention, but Fatso was gregarious and open to adventure and willing to take risks and all that.

So it happened that Muscles enlisted Fatso in the cause of pumping for pulchritude. The strong one painted golden visions for Fatso of clothes being altered and of difficulties locating bathing suits suitable for a middle-aged man with a steel-like abdomen. Fatso's tailor was put on emergency standby.

One afternoon I walked in upon that day's lifting session. Muscles vibrated with verve and enthusiasm, but Fatso, poor Fatso. He stood there all pale and saggy in his boxer underwear shorts. Across his shoulders was an iron bar with two tiny weights, the size of vending machine pies, one on each end. Hanging from his lower lip was a half-smoked cigarette. His lusterless eyes spoke as clearly as if his lips had formed the words: "My steel-like abdomen hasn't arrived yet, and I don't think it's coming."

A few nights later, it was about ten o'clock, I heard the beginning of a commotion from the "gym." Three-at-a-time up the stairs bounded Muscles. He was hysterical, but I couldn't tell whether it was laughing hysteria or sobbing hysteria. "I've just measured Fatso. You know what his measurements are?" I shook my head. "Forty-three, forty-three, forty-six," Muscles hollered and fell on the floor in a fit of convulsive giggles.

Fatso being the senior priest in the house, the "gym" disappeared overnight from the living room and only telltale creaking from Muscle's room gave hint that weights had ever entered the place.

Having come this far, it would be cowardly of me to conclude without confessing that I, too, was a onetime closet weight lifter. In today's drug culture terms, it might be said that I experimented but I was never a really heavy user. Being as mechanically inclined as an amoeba, I even had trouble getting the blankety-blank weight to stay on the bar.

In John Irving's popular novel, *The Hotel New Hampshire*, weights are lifted intermittently from page nine to page 450. The central character's grandfather, Iowa Bob, says about pumping iron, "You've got to get obsessed and stay obsessed."

Thank the good Lord that I never got or stayed obsessed about the weights. Otherwise, two decades of that torture would have found me sitting here either a 250-pound mass of deltoids, pectorals, and biceps scaring little children at every flex, or more likely I would be my normal mushy self, angered that I had invested twenty obsessive years in a bad bargain.

Carp and the Young Priest Were Birds of a Feather

July 1983

"Pares cum paribus," croaked the old Vincentian priest. The ancient seminary professor was trying to enculturate us rude offspring of mid-America with a taste of Cicero. Not so much out of a love for the classics but more from sheer terror of Father Duggan, my memory tells me that "pares cum paribus" means, in loose translation, "birds of a feather flock together."

This issue of the *Sooner Catholic* makes a stout attempt to humiliate Father Thomas Wade Darnall by painting him a hero. That being the case, I thought it appropriate to decorate this nook with a tale of one of Father Darnall's heroes—Dominican Father George Carpentier. Remember: *pares cum paribus.*

As a background to our story, let me say that it was a close call whether Father Carpentier was greater as a saint or as an eccentric. Certainly he was substantially both.

In the middle part of this century, Father Carpentier was pastor of St. Catherine's Church in Guthrie, a parish in those Jim Crow days that served black Catholics in Logan County. As a saint, the Dominican priest lived in stark poverty, smoldered with zeal to share God with others, and trusted divine providence absolutely. As an eccentric he shambled about unkempt, hung his Mass vestments on the wings of a plaster of Paris angel next to the altar, and kept his Roman collar together with a paper clip.

Surprisingly Msgr. Gustave Depreitere took a liking to the Logan County Dominican and was one of his benefactors. I say surprisingly because the two priests were nearly total opposites. Msgr. Depreitere was aristocratic, modulated his life to the precision of a Swiss clock and bordered his existence, not with splendor, but with material appurtenances of high quality. Father Carpentier mumbled when he spoke, habitually held his head down, and loosely rolled to one side as though something had snapped in his neck, and saw little difference between one hundred dollar bills and toilet paper except that the latter was more practical.

At the time of our tale, Father Darnall served as an assistant to Msgr. Depreitere at St. Joseph's Old Cathedral. The younger priest became acquainted with Father Carpentier during his frequent visits with Msgr. Depreitere at the downtown Oklahoma City church's rectory. Father Darnall sopped up the wisdom of the two elderly gents as they worked their way through long table talks.

Father Darnall came to realize that "Carp" was a genuine diamond, covered in crusty inelegance but with pinholes of splendor shining through. He helped the oddball holy man when he could. I recall driving to Guthrie with Father Darnall to see Carp and witnessing a quick tuck of a bill (it looked like a fifty) into the old fellow's pocket.

One Holy Week I helped with priestly chores at the Old Cathedral. After the liturgy, we sat down in the rectory's well-appointed dining room for supper. Father Carpentier was there, immediately to Msgr. Depreitere's right. There were five or six others of us including Father Darnall.

The tablecloth was up to Msgr. Depreitere's standards, so white that it spoke of kings and queens and tended to carry one's mind back to the Transfiguration. The best china was in place, and the silver seemed to lie at military attention. Altogether the ordinary perfection of the monsignor's dining environment.

Well, Carp was mumbling a blue streak, but with head down and wobbling around, when he was passed the mashed potatoes. He scooped an enormous spoonful of the potatoes, flipped his wrist, and plopped a mound of the vegetable some six inches from his plate—smack dab on top of the virginal tablecloth.

As though having witnessed a meteorite whistle from the sky to burrow into Harvey Avenue, we all stared at the potatoes while our minds made a hasty recount to check the validity of our vision. I should say all stared except two: Carp neither missed a syllable of his lecture nor noticed his faux pas, and Msgr. Depreitere squinted at the white horror while trying to force his ninety-year-old eyes to see clearly what they had never seen before.

I can still picture the monsignor's eyebrows working up and down in agitation and Father Darnall covering his mouth with his napkin as he shook with silent laughter.

At last, Carp spotted the errant spuds. Did he faint in red-faced humiliation? Did he fall at his host's knees and beg mercy? No, no. He simply reached out with a tiny teaspoon and began transporting the potatoes to his plate. It must have taken twenty trips with the spoon. He never stopped talking, and he never said "boo" about it. I think it was an amazing display of humility.

Father Carpentier and Father Darnall. *Pares cum paribus*, even if the one had feathers a bit more askew than the other.

Misadventures of a One-Language Man

August 1984

Doing an issue on Hispanics in Oklahoma reminds me of my destitution in the use of languages. My lingual poverty is so stark that I don't carry a dozen usable Spanish words in my communications wallet.

But my linguistic indigence extends well beyond Spanish. I possess neither tongue that speaks nor ears that hear French, German, Russian, Polish (sorry, Holy Father), Chinese, Japanese, or any other organized human method of verbal communication. I humbly admit that I seek the counsel of others for translations of Pig Latin.

My single-language life has not been developed without blame on my part. The Catholic Church has struggled to move me into a wider world of speech and hearing but the results never got much beyond "*In nomine Patris, et Filii, at Spiritus Sancti.* Amen."

I was provided with six years of Latin—four in high school and two in college, two years of Greek, a year of Hebrew, and a year of German.

Latin I could read a little; German had possibilities, but once the course stopped, I stopped. Greek and Hebrew remained dark mysteries to me, like intriguing Mayan temples covered with vines that I never summoned the wherewithal to attack.

As a one-language man, I have wandered the earth, hugging the shores of English-speaking nations, remaining mute and smiling a lot when washed up on lands of "foreign" tongues.

When out of my element the resulting misadventures often have been disconcerting, embarrassing and even a little funny. Some examples:

- When Archbishop John R. Quinn came upon the Oklahoma scene, he greeted me one day in a friendly fashion with a comment of several words in Latin. My learned reply: "Huh?"
- I stepped onto the streets of Paris in 1965. It was the first time I had ever been in a place where a language other than English prevailed. I sauntered up to a vendor and tried to buy a newspaper. My English opening was countered with a long stream of French. I got rattled, retreated from the newsstand, and felt shrunken in this swarm of "others." I quickly made my way back to the hotel.
- Once I traveled to Rome with my aunt Agnes. We Englished our way successfully around the Eternal City until one afternoon when we went shopping in a large department store. Aunt Agnes picked out a sweater but wanted to buy it with a credit card. After much gesturing and facial contortions and one-syllable utterings, I was made to understand that I should stand where I was while the clerk took Aunt Agnes to another area to complete the transaction.

    After fifteen minutes examining other merchandise, I began to look around for my aunt. After thirty minutes, I started to inquire about her from other clerks, but never the twain—Italian and English—did meet. At forty-five minutes, I was on the ground floor vainly trying to communicate with a woman at the information desk. Ascending once more to my original post, I was wondering how I could explain to my family about losing Aunt Agnes forever in a Roman department store.

Panic wasn't setting in, it was in. I strode through several floors and numerous departments looking this way and that. I went to the ground floor again. Skittering up and down the aisles, I thought I would call the police if only I knew how to call

Suddenly from above—the department store had an open center portion—I heard, "David!" I looked up several floors and spotted Aunt Agnes leaning over a railing and waving.

So the Monahans were reunited. It wasn't the same emotion as the Iranian hostages meeting their families again, but it was close. It seems the department store had wanted to see my aunt's passport before they accepted her credit card, and she had traveled several miles to our hotel to fetch it.

- On my original journey to Santiago Atitlan, Guatemala, Father Ramon Carlin and I walked up the steeply inclined streets from the boat dock to the rectory. As we passed thatched huts and small stores, the Tzutuhil people would look up, smile, and say something that sounded to me like "It's a watch." Father Carlin said it meant hello. I began to repeat what my ears were hearing. At least it brought good-natured giggles.

- I was superintendent of Catholic schools here in the early 1970s. For our diocesan teachers' meeting one year, I invited the distinguished Maryknoll editor and writer Father Miguel d'Escoto (now for better or worse foreign minister of Nicaragua) to deliver the keynote address. I introduced him phonetically as Mig-well. When Father d'Escoto was allowed the microphone, he didn't hesitate to set the record straight. He was Me-gale. Sitting there red-faced, I recalled the late Father Hugo's advice: "If you are going to mount a pedestal, make sure you don't wet your pants."

Conclusion: To any incoming high school students who may read this, sign up for Spanish I, and don't look back.

Of the Brief Boxing Career of a Panicky Pugilist

August 1985

I don't know how Sugar Ray Leonard got his start, but my boxing career began when I was six.

My father apparently had visions or desires of a manly son who, as the saying of that particular period went, was handy with his dukes. So at Christmas I tore open a good-sized package to find therein two pairs of boxing gloves.

At first I found boxing to be a delight. Frank P. Monahan, my trainer and manager (and daddy), was brash enough to mix it up with me. He couldn't move too well, as he fought from a kneeling position. I circled him with mayhem in my heart and the big gloves on my fists. *Bam! Bam! Bam!* My blows found their mark. His were feeble in comparison.

It was a glorious pugilistic Christmas day. Someone got out the Kodak and snapped a picture of me in the backyard—a young gladiator in a fighting stance with gloved hands cocked for the kill and displaying the confident smile of someone who knows he is too good to be defeated. I had a perfect record until that evening.

What happened that night was, of course, my manager's fault. He tried to bring me along too fast. It put a crimp in my championship plans.

The trouble started when Bill Brown came by the house. He was a year older than I. Unfortunately he didn't know the primary rule of boxing at Monahan Square Garden: I was supposed to win.

We put on the gloves. *Wham!* Bill busted me right on the snozzola. *Wham!* He did it again. Wait a minute: Bill's got the script backward. *Wham! Wham!* The last blast evidently struck the nerve that controls the tear ducts. I began to cry. My corner threw in the towel. A TKO was declared eighteen seconds into the fight.

Bill went home thinking boxing is a fun game. I, having retired to the comfort of my mother's arms, had the sudden insight that boxing is dehumanizing, something below the dignity of civilized people. I announced my retirement from the sport. No one was going to find me punching at age seven.

The years pass. Boxing is a spectator sport for me. My father hauls me to various boxing matches. I learn that when you sit in the front rows of professional fights, you get spattered with a mixture of sweat and blood sent flying as the blows land. I see Joe Louis, before he was champion, clobber three opponents—each one led into the ring like a steer dumbly approaching the slaughterhouse knife.

At fourteen I was a lethargic member of Troop 34 of the Boy Scouts of America. I had bargained on things like square knots and sleeping in tents, but I hadn't perceived that scouting was to lead me back into the ring.

I can't recall the preliminaries too well, but one night found Troop 34 of Christ the King Church visiting Troop 12 of St. Francis Church. The purpose of the meeting: a boxing match. With a graphic picture of Bill Brown still in my mind, I was doing my best to pull a disappearing act. No luck.

The heavy hand of fate, in the person of my scoutmaster, fell on my shoulders. My opponent was to be Gootch Ruskoski, a tall, spindly, likeable boy. In me he faced a 115-pound dreadnought (more dread than nought).

A scout leader slipped the gloves over my hands and cheerfully laced them for me. He stepped aside, and there, on the stage of the parish hall, stood only Gootch and me.

Right reason and cool thinking had nothing to do with what happened next. Propelled by sheer panicky terror, I attacked

Gootch with wildly flailing arms. The sweet science of boxing went out the window. It was kill or be killed.

Somehow one or two of the blizzard of blows landed on Gootch's anatomy. He retreated. I pursued. I remember hearing one of the adults present laughing at the sight of this scrawny runt and his windmill offense. The fight was stopped. I was declared the winner—a classical case of what a ton of fear and strong doses of adrenaline can do.

What brought all that to mind was a recent note from one Albert S. Ruskoski, distinguished Certified Public Accountant in Tulsa. He recollected the fight and signed the letter "Gootch." Thanks for the memories.

A Cry from Prisoners of the US Camping System

July 1986

Attendance at summer camp can change one's character. A boy or girl, having survived a week or two at camp, returns home with much the same emotions as a rescued POW. Never again will that lad or lass gripe about the home environment with the same wholehearted enthusiasm as before the camp experience.

There are many awful things about camp—food prepared by cooks with doctorates in the infinite variety of uses of Kool-Aid and Van Camp beans, mattresses inherited from the doughboys of WWI, mosquitoes trained to hover one inch above campers' ears at night, bullies, chiggers, counselors with hearts of brass, mournful hoots of owls at dusk, reports of large snakes seen slithering under the floor of your tent, etc.—but worst, by far, is homesickness.

Even as this bit is being written hundreds of thousands of American boys and girls, prisoners of the US camping system, are clinging stubbornly to the memory of air-conditioning as their T-shirts sop up perspiration and one hand pierces the other with a needle meant to assemble beads into a belt. *Ouch!*

Home, oh sweet home, dream these camping wretches. They think, *What I wouldn't give to smell chocolate chip cookies baking while I loll on the sofa in the dark coolness of our home and my mother glides toward me holding out a giant glass of iced tea. But here I am, smelling only the canvas of this tent in the middle of purgatory, and some idiot outside is screaming for us to line up for a nature hike. Which will break first: my mind or my heart?*

Once upon a time, deceived by some Technicolor propaganda, Bob Beltz and I left Tulsa on the Frisco Railroad to travel to St. Louis and Camp Don Bosco. We were, I think, eleven years old.

Camp Don Bosco was, in its day, a good idea. In reality, however, it was something less. The camp featured tiny cabins and an infinite number of rocks. The creek, which wended its silvery way past the camp in the movie, proved to be a trail of dry rocks, bordered by banks of rocks, surrounded by many acres of more rocks.

Rocks or no rocks, Camp Don Bosco for me was one long ache of homesickness. Appetite vanished. I shuffled through the camp "activities" with quarts of melancholy running down the inside walls of my body. When my mother and my aunt Agnes appeared to deliver me from the jaws of homesick hell, at the close of the two-week camping period, no Iranian hostage ran forward to freedom with more passion.

Then there was the seminary. Eighteen years of life in loving warmth, then a long trip to a foreign land (almost) and into an institution operated with all the personal attention of, say, Alcatraz.

The one saving grace was the presence of other forlorn Oklahomans, a straggling band on our way, we hoped, to the Promised Land.

About the second day, one of the Okies began to say to me (and to other Oklahomans), "You look homesick."

Third day's greeting: "Gosh, you look awfully homesick."

Fourth day's message: "I never saw anybody look so homesick."

The fifth day he was on board the Frisco Meteor with a one-way ticket to Egypt.

I Know Where You Can Get a Used Bicycle for $10

December 1988

Nineteen thirty-six wasn't the greatest year for a little Oklahoma kid to campaign for a new bicycle. Especially when one considered the state was still wrestling with the Great Depression, our family had lost its home only a year or so before, and my father was drinking too much.

But nine-year-old children are often not deterred by reality. So as Christmas approached, I was busy lobbying for Santa Claus or someone to show up with a bicycle for me. Inside the red-brick rented house at 1128 S. Norfolk in Tulsa, I trotted after my beleaguered mother promoting the idea.

I was willing to negotiate. "Mom, I know where you can get a used bicycle for $10," I remember saying. My mother was gently but sadly sympathetic. She gave no hope.

There is too much haze between here and there to see clearly all the details on that horizon of my life. It may have been the same year, only a few weeks earlier, that I threw a conniption fit when my beloved Notre Dame football team lost to Southern Cal. (The mother-son dialogue: "But the Notre Dame players feel as bad as you do, and they're going to eat their dinners tonight." "I don't care! I don't care!") And it well may have been the same season, when my procrastinating father ablaze with Christmas cheer roared into the driveway with a tree, tall enough for Rockefeller Plaza, strapped to the old car.

As the great twenty-fifth loomed ever closer, I cared not a flip about previous mishaps or Christmas trees. My wee brain (right brain, left brain, forebrain, aft brain, upper brain, lower brain) was totally tense in concentration on a bicycle.

But despair was written six feet high on the red-brick walls. Even I could see that. No doubt, I stalked along the Midland Valley Railroad tracks behind our house and angrily whanged a few rocks off the side of a boxcar or two and sat moodily in the wooden hut in the backyard and wandered aimlessly across the deserted surfaces of the public tennis courts at the foot of the street.

Somehow Christmas morning dawned, even if the promise of my fondest wish had now gone into eclipse. Never a fast starter, I wobbled into the living room. There magically standing at attention, as if it were on the display floor at Otasco or Sears, was an extraordinary green-and-white new bicycle. I was stupefied with joy.

So what if Notre Dame had lost to Southern Cal? So what if Pope Pius XI was flat on his back at the Vatican, lamenting via the radio the horrors of the Spanish Civil War? So what if King Edward VIII had chucked his crown and toddled off with Mrs. Simpson, making grandma cry? The shield of glee, which surrounded that nine-year-old boy in the living room that Christmas Day, was impenetrable. It might have been absolute self-centeredness, but it was real.

Looking back at that morning, I see it all as mystery. Where did my mother and/or father get the money? Or did they get the money? Was the bike bought on time payments? Did they take out a loan? Had my dad gotten lucky on a punchboard in one of his favorite hangouts? Did my parents know they were going to get it all along? Or was the bike the product of my father's impulsive generosity? Or had my mother's heart been broken open by the pounding of my pleas. Or both? Did Aunt Agnes, whose annual Christmas Eve arrival in her Plymouth coupe, loaded with beautiful packages, was a true event, play a major role in this miracle? And how about Helen, my beautiful sister? How did she feel about this bicycle business?

Not too much later than the looking, I sped away on the shakedown run of my new bicycle. I crashed landed at the corner. No harm done. It seems things were loose on the bike, like the handlebars and seat and such. (Daddy was a salesman, not a mechanic.)

However the green-and-white bicycle got to our house and into my hands, it turned out to be a whale of an investment. I rode it from that day until I graduated from high school. That simple machine carried me for thousands of miles around the streets of Tulsa.

I pedaled the bike to school, to church, to basketball practice, to deliver newspapers, and probably to places I wasn't supposed to be. It was a social vehicle—on long, leisurely rides with my great friend Joe Dillon and on visits to my cousins Jack and Mike Egan. That bike gave a kid in a middle-sized American city just the right touch of freedom—the sense that you could go away and come back again without being afraid.

A year ago that holy sister of mine gave me another cherished Christmas gift. It's a framed snapshot. The photo shows lovely Helen with her hands on the shoulders of her little brother, an open-mouthed, squinty-eyed kid with unruly hair and big ears. In the background on the grass at 1128 S. Norfolk is the green-and-white bicycle.

Sure and the Man Can't Organize a Two-Car Funeral

May 1990

I am one of those of whom an old-time pastor might have said: "Sure, and the man can't organize a two-car funeral."

I am a practitioner of the "Muddling Through" school of management. The thing to be done is there, shining clearly in the distance. I run toward it desperately flailing away until, disheveled and sweating, the objective is in my grasp.

Others, who insist on a certain minimum of rationality in their work, calmly assess the situation, concoct a plan, take three crisp steps forward, do a right turn, then a left, seize the ring marked "Goal Achieved," and have fifteen minutes to wash up before lunch. No muss. No fuss. Not a hair out of place.

This flow of consciousness bubbled forth after recalling a certain Frederick Winslow Taylor, "the father of scientific management." A Harvard management expert recently wrote of Taylor that his principle was rationality, his aim was efficiency, and his method was programmatic. In the last category were included observation, standardization, training, and incentives.

The father of scientific management focused on the physical motions of people at work with the fierce determination to eliminate all false, slow, and useless movements. It seems his first famous research centered on the absolute best way to shovel coal.

(As I'm writing this, I realize the elimination of all false, slow, and useless movements from my life would shrink my time to 5- or 6-minute days.)

Professor Taylor's ultimate question is said to have been not the usual—What is the purpose of life? Why does God allow pain?—but rather "What constitutes an honest day's work?"

As a former yardman who spent most of his working day lying on Grandma's floor drinking Coca Colas, let us look at this matter of efficiency. As a dreamy ethnically Irish person, leave us peruse scientific management. As one darkly tinged with the vice of sloth let us consider "What constitutes an honest day's work" even if the thinking along that line brings on heartburn and/or hives.

Scientific Management: Take One

World War I was started because of scientific management. Well, sort of. On August 1, 1914, when Germany was mobilizing with the intention of invading both Russia to the east and France to the west, Kaiser Bill suffered an attack of misgiving and told General Helmuth von Moltke to stop the operation.

The stunned general, whose staff had worked for a decade on the plans to go to war, replied that it couldn't be stopped. The plans, the general knew, were designed in detail down to the number of train axles that would pass over a given bridge at a given time. Eleven thousand trains were scheduled to move several million soldiers to the borders in a deadly efficient manner. Halting this vast process would gum up the works, ruin those precious plans. Von Moltke burst into tears and refused to sign an order checking the movement. On August 4, the war began, an exercise in no wasted motion.

Scientific Management: Take Two

At a reunion picnic in Tulsa, a longtime friend recalled for my benefit how his employing oil company, renowned for being well-managed and awash in profits, actually operated.

In the afternoons, my friend's section of the company sent out for cocktails, doubles I believe, which were promptly but clandestinely delivered through the Prohibition-dry streets of Tulsa. "We were a well-oiled machine," he said.

Scientific Management: Take Three

Father George Carpentier fought the brave fight against scientific management. It wasn't a conscious struggle on his part. It was just that his mode of working would have created severe blood pressure problems for a guy like Frederick W. Taylor.

Father Carpentier would leave for Crescent, say, without the least idea of how he was going to get there from Guthrie. He gave away things others considered essential. His bed, for example. He made do with whatever might be handy—a paper clip for a collar button, the wing of a statue of an angel for hanging up Mass vestments, berries growing wild along a fence for lunch.

The request for an annual financial report by the chancery office would be met by a postcard saying: "Sufficient to carry on another year."

The poor old soul shuffling along the dirt roads of Logan County was neither efficient or managerially rational, only effective, still causing little explosions of courage and charity in souls two decades after his death.

Scientific Management: Take Four

Aunt Agnes did nothing for the major oil company that employed her except work her loyal head off for thirty-five years. She was a dandy executive secretary who made her boss look like a genius.

Then one fine Tulsa day, the New York crowd sent into the office the efficiency experts, smiling and congenial, clipboards and stopwatches in hand. They noted everything Aunt Agnes did. Every motion, every typed key, every step were carefully written down.

Then the company said, "Thank you, Aunt Agnes, for your excellent, consistent work. Here's your hat. Oh, by the way, your retirement pay has been cut in two."

Later that year, Aunt Agnes and I went searching for our family roots in northern England. In County Durham, we came upon the Thornley Colliery—a coal mine to us Yankees. Down below was the "office" of our ancestors. No scientific management there in the old days. Only brutal, dangerous, semi-slave labor. An honest day's work in that place was whatever the bosses could rip out of your body. Maybe it made Aunt Agnes feel better.

CHAPTER 2

1977

Where Father Carlin Was, Things Happened

June 1977

Father Ramon Carlin was a rare person. Where he was, things happened. He both warmed hearts and heated blood pressures. He was a pied piper and an agitator. His life, in the words of the old liturgical rubrics, was a moveable feast.

Hundreds of individuals felt that they knew him better than most of the people in their lives. At Ramon Carlin's funeral scores of friends appeared as if from nowhere: a former football coach at McGuinness High School drove all night from far South Texas to take part; a priest who has left the active ministry flew in from Colorado; the nun who taught Ramon in the first grade, Sister Lucy Kreiser, was there etc., etc., etc. If there had been time enough and means enough, the crowd at the funeral would have been utterly remarkable both in numbers and in diversity.

The *Sooner Catholic* can't let the opportunity pass to share with others at least a few stories involving Father Ramon "Tex" Carlin.

- When he was director of McGuinness High School, Father Carlin ran an "open" rectory—that is the doors were literally never locked and conversation ("sessions" he called them) continued almost around the clock for four years. Slouched in his favorite easy chair, blowing cigarette smoke vertically in that peculiar way he had, Tex Carlin would be instigator, marksman, and target in the endless flow of words. If an argument concerned liturgy, for example, he might grab the telephone and call the world's best authority on the subject ("Sorry to wake you up, Father Diekmann!"). It was not unusual to have the host interrupt proceedings in the wee hours to whip up a pot of his own indescribably peculiar chili. There were times when he simply sessioned all night, showered, and went to school for the day. How he loved to talk! And not just chitchat but about serious subjects ranging from existentialism to teenage psychology and from pastoral ministry to linguistics.

- Visitors at the Oklahoma-staffed mission in Guatemala were surprised to hear the cheery young Indian handyman enter the rectory and say "Hello, fatso!" to the overweight Father Carlin. What many didn't know was that the Indian man could not understand a word of English. He had been taught this phonetically memorized greeting by Father Carlin.

- As a young priest, Father Carlin was responsible for the Muskogee missions on the eastern side of the state. He was forever ferreting out Catholics who had lost contact with the church. At the rural home of one family near Porum, he was accustomed to saying Mass using the grand piano as an altar. He would chuckle when he recollected the early ambitions of the young men in the family: to go to Kansas City and see the stockyards.

- Father Carlin had a way of disarming people who approached him with preposterous ideas by countering with something even more far out. Once the seniors at McGuinness High School tried to convince him that some changes should be made in year-end senior activities. A few hours of dialogue later, the seniors left him in a daze. Among Father Carlin's suggestions were to have the junior/senior prom changed into an afternoon tea dance with a senior dinner held in an exclusive Dallas restaurant after a chartered flight to Texas.

CHAPTER 3

1979

The Health Club

June 1979

If one runs in the gray middle lane all the way, there are exactly 19.25 laps to the mile. And one mile is what I run three times a week on the indoor track at the Central YMCA.

Runners (or joggers, if you will) at the Y are legion. They come in many varieties—the old, middle-aged, and young; the too fat and the lean; the grim marathon types who number their laps with handheld counters, and the casual trotters-for-a-day; the fashion plates with the latest jogging togs and the gray-haired man who consistently wears an undershirt top (add one, slow-moving priest with great and small holes in his T-shirts); and the talkers who run in packs and the solitary contemplators of their pounding feet. And, now, there are two sexes.

The YMCA was sexually integrated a couple of years ago. This integration, as others, did not come about without the pain of change. The new order of things required that swimmers wear bathing suits. Whereupon a small number of old duffers with firm principles about skinny-dipping shook the last drops of pool water from their bodies and stomped out. For good.

The Central YMCA is a haven for hundreds of beleaguered Oklahomans striving to keep at least some faint acquaintanceship with good health in a world tilted in the opposite direction. It is probably a fair statement to make that the oldest, wealthiest, most crotchety, and least physically fit group at the Y are members of the male-only health club.

With the exception of the part about the bank account, I fit right in. I have belonged to the health club for a dozen years.

Two exceptions to the above description of health club members are Wayne Wells, a former Olympic gold medal winner in wrestling, and Walter Thomas, a world class weight lifter.

The health club consists of a locker room complete with exercise equipment at one end and a scale that never works at the other, a television lounge, a massage room, sauna and steam baths, a large whirlpool, and showers.

Within the confines of the health club, there is a kind of democracy of nakedness. It is simply amazing how powerless the powerful look stripped of their clothing. Judges, oil company executives, real estate developers, bankers, lawyers, upper-level movers of state government, (priests!)—they all clump about the health club in their birthday suits reminding one another of the terrible effects of the pull of gravity upon the human body much more than holding others in awe at their station in life.

The health club is not distinguished as a gathering spot to conspire about world revolution. Nineteenth century Republicanism maintains a firm base of support there. President Carter had best not call a town meeting in that hallowed place. There are exceptions. This writer once heard former President Nixon given a fierce verbal trampling in the foggy depths of the steam room.

Last in the health club but more likely first in the reign of God are the masseurs. Willie, Arthur, Chris, etc., knead bodies back to life for their bread and listen to the talk. They are wise men as well as the Y's men—wise enough to work quietly, and wise enough to interpret independently what they believe.

Two Amsterdam Women

August 1979

She was an angry woman. Her eyes were narrowed in spite. Her face contorted with rage. Volleys of Dutch words fired from her snarling mouth. She repeatedly raised her two arms and flung her hands forward and downward in the universal symbol of contemptuous dismissal.

The target of the beleaguered woman's wrath was a small group of men and women singing Christian hymns. They stood beneath a banner that declared Jesus Christ as Lord and Savior. The singers did not respond to the angry woman. They calmly continued their hymns.

One of our group of three priests whispered, "We should applaud them." But we didn't.

What made the scene memorable was the place: the infamous red light district of Amsterdam, Holland. The seething woman was a prostitute—eyelids drooping from the weight of mascara, lips a garish red, hot pants, boots, and lines of too many nights on her face.

Finally, she stomped off, presumably to place herself on sale with hundreds of other women in the doorways and windows of the district.

That was one woman I will remember from Amsterdam.

The other woman from Amsterdam whom I will carry in my spirit for a long time was not home when I visited her. In fact, she left that city forever thirty-five years ago this August 4.

But her spirit never left the address of 263 Prinsengracht, just around the corner from the West Church ("Westerkerk"). The rich person of this silent woman spoke to me and hundreds of others on a July afternoon pilgrimage to her former dwelling.

Anne Frank whispered through the displayed pages of her handwriting. She revealed herself through newspaper clippings, which she had pasted to a wall and remained where she put them. She talked to us about freedom and the human spirit in the bare rooms where she remained in hiding for two years.

And as Anne Frank spoke to us, there was a hush, an abnormal quiet among the many people passing through—looking, touching, recollecting what it must have been like, and searching for a meaning to it all.

Anne had kept a diary. It was found after her capture and kept intact by a family friend. Later her father published it, and we in America know it as *The Diary of Anne Frank*, a literary monument of our century.

So, those were two very dissimilar women whom I met in Amsterdam.

The first represents a "tourist attraction" side of the city— vulgar, coarse, a curiosity for gawkers, a paid package of flesh for customers.

The other stands for simplicity, refinement, innocence, sensitivity, and hope—not exactly what most people identify with Amsterdam. One of the last sentences Anne Frank wrote was, "In spite of everything, I still believe that people are really good at heart."

I found myself in a very judgmental mood about the prostitute. Then as I rode home on the train that evening, I wondered what the war had done to her. She could have been only a little girl then. She too might have her story.

Pilgrimage to a Village

August 1979

The Belgian village of Russeignies is not one of the better known dwelling places in the world. Hardly any Belgians can locate it for you on a map. To Oklahomans, Russeignies might as well be in another galaxy of stars.

Yet, the village of Russeignies gave Oklahoma, and especially the Catholics of Oklahoma, the gift of a great man—Theophile Meerschaert. Bishop Meerschaert, Vicar Apostolic to Indian and Oklahoma territories and first Bishop of Oklahoma (1891 to 1924), undoubtedly was the most important person in the history of the Catholic Church in our state.

So, during my July stay at the American College of Louvain, Russeignies became my destination on a special one-day pilgrimage.

I purchased a detailed map of Belgium. Russeignies was found to be about fifty miles west and a little south of Brussels, near the small industrial city of Ronse.

Away I went on Saturday, July 21. The first leg of the trip was by train—Louvain to Brussels, then Brussels to a city named Oudenarrde. From Oudenarrde, a bus took "the scenic route" to Ronse.

At Ronse's deserted railroad station, I located a genial taxi driver carrying several loaves of French bread. He agreed to drive me to Russeignies, a distance of about six miles.

Russeignies in reality fitted very well the Russeignies of my imagination. It is a tiny crossroads village, dominated by the Church of St. Amandus.

Tucked in neatly around the edges of the church was a cemetery. An elderly woman, hoe in hand, was puttering around the graves. She indicated the home of the pastor.

I rang the doorbell of the rectory. A priest, complete in black suit and Roman collar, answered the door. What followed was a comic opera of non-communication.

He spoke French. I spoke English. Neither of us could use the opposite's language.

After a few futile attempts at jumping the language chasm, I pointed at myself and said "Oklahoma." At that word, the priest's right arm flew out and up. I followed the line of his forefinger. There on the wall was a large portrait of our mutual pride— Theophile Meerschaert.

Using Latin with all the skill of two arthritic carpenters trying to pass small nails to one another, Father Theodore Van Oostuelot and I carried on a dialogue, one word with one gesture at a time.

Father Van Oostuelot led me across the road to the church. The church was built in 1645.

I jotted down a few impressions of the church:

- As in most European churches, there were no pews but rows of plain, moveable wooden chairs. There were, perhaps, 300 chairs. The parish has 640 parishioners (or families, I couldn't be certain which).
- Toward the back of the chair section was a large, coal-burning stove. One could imagine the effects of a sermon on hell on someone seated near that stove in the winter.
- The interior was very dark, not helped at all by the perennial Belgian cloudiness.
- I knelt by the altar and said a prayer of thanksgiving for the life of a little boy who often worshiped there and who was moved to become a missionary to America.

Women in My Past

October 1979

There were about twenty of them. Each was beautiful in her own way, those women in my past. They were women of mystery even to the point of never being seen publicly except in haute couture of basic black.

I spent thirteen quick years with those beautiful women, first with one then another. Finally, the Benedictine Sisters divined that enough is enough. They handed me a diploma. I had been graduated from Marquette School.

This month those Benedictine Sisters are celebrating 100 years as a religious community (begun in Creston, Iowa) and ninety years in service to the people of Oklahoma.

As one who was served by them, more than almost anyone else, I qualify to fetch back a few personal Benedictine memories.

After my mother, Sister Mary Andrew was my first love. Don't ask me why because I can't recall specifics. But she must have stretched the quality of mercy out of shape in shepherding me through not one but two years in the first grade.

Sister Mary Ligouri (now Sister Leona) inherited our exuberant (another descriptive used was incorrigible) class in the seventh grade. She had a neat way of saying no to you with her eyes and an ever-so-slight shake of her head.

Sister Pancratia in the eighth grade smothered our meannesses with an enveloping kindness. She followed the advice to sisters to be mothers to those they cared for four decades before Pope John Paul II gave it.

The nun who leaned forward as she clickety-click stepped down the high school hall was Sister Imelda. One class willed her a set of roller skates to fit her habit of darting through life—all its scenes, all its times.

Sister Mary Edward (now Sister Marie) wondered, wondered, wondered about the boy who kept endless lists of football players and their weights and basketball players and their heights crammed into his messy desk. Why couldn't he learn to conjugate a Latin verb at least occasionally? (Note to Sister Mary Edward: Billy Sims' weight is up to 215 this year.)

Then there was the incident of the school clock. Mother Rita is now in heaven, but I hope this message gets to her: Charlie Skeehan and I did not break the school clock. Do you think a guy who has spent thirty-one years as a Trappist monk would do such a thing? No, Mother, he is not doing penance for breaking the clock.

Wrapping it all up in a package, almost every child the Benedictines taught at Marquette would agree that those women in black gave us room and encouragement to grow, enabled us to have a sense of oneness, helped us appreciate the church's liturgy, and offered us a chance to learn to handle words and numbers. We were a family.

CHAPTER 4

1980

Mountains as Suddenly as Spilt Milk

March 1980

"In the United States there is more space where nobody is than where anybody is. This is what makes America what it is." Gertrude Stein wrote that.

Yesterday, I was in one of those empty but beautiful pockets— Custer County, Colorado.

This week I hauled my old bones out of the furnace in Oklahoma and headed for higher elevations. Presently, I am camped out on the east trail of the Ramada Inn in Canon City.

Thursday afternoon, I cranked up the asthmatic Maverick (91,000 miles toward eternity) and struck out for the sure enough mountains.

South of Canon City is a crossroads named Wetmore. There I turned west on Colorado 96 and began to climb through the front range (the Wet Mountains) one meets as one approaches from the plains.

It's always fascinating how dull and simple mountains appear from a distance only to reveal all kinds of subtleties and complexities as a person draws closer. Pines and spruces lined the upward path. The perfume of those conifers was delightful and somehow, to me, comforting.

As I reached the crest of the Wets, my anticipation grew for what I really wanted to see: the Sangre de Cristo range, a whole line, perhaps fourteen, of mountains at or over 14,000 feet.

As suddenly as spilt milk, the peaks were there on the horizon. As my moving observation platform wound its way downward, the Sangre de Cristos were revealed more and more completely in their green and purple gigantic loveliness, still striped with stubborn snow.

The Wet Mountain Valley, running parallel to the Sangre de Cristos, has two principal towns—Silvercliff and Westcliffe, the county seat. They are not two miles apart. The elevation is almost 8,000 feet.

In the late nineteenth century, this was a silver mining center of such proportions as to cause men to salivate with greed. Silvercliff had a population up to 10,000 with ten miles of streets complete with fire plugs. Twenty-five saloons helped to slake the miners' thirst and water sold for forty cents a barrel.

At the last available count (1970 census) the population of the whole county was listed as slightly above 1,000. Silvercliff probably has less than 100 permanent residents, Westcliffe a few more.

I decided to visit the Lake Camp Ground, up a thousand feet or so toward the peaks. On my way there, I had one experience and one flow of thought that I can recollect.

The experience was the milliseconds passing of a red-winged blackbird between me and the meadows and the mountains. It happened so fast! But the sensation was a perfect lick of color— slash of red, set in jet black, against an ocean of emerald.

The flow of thought went like this: *I come back to this blessed spot about once a decade but a decade or two from now I won't return because I will be gone, and all these brooding mountains will still loom over this valley, but wait a minute, they are wearing down too and I, I am going to be with the forever being of God.*

Sounds sticky pious, but that's it.

How John D. Cherry Eliminated the Good Guys in Row 61

June 1980

When the going gets tough for the Oklahoma Sooners next fall and it's cold and drizzly and Missouri is a touchdown ahead with five minutes to play and OU has the ball on its own one yard line and a weary team is huddling in the end zone, J.C. Watts will not be able to look deeply into the eyes of his teammates and whisper solemnly, "Let's win this one for the guys in Row 61, Section 13, Seats 3 and 4."

Sorry, fellows, but we—Father Philip Bryce and I—won't be there.

It's a long story.

I became hooked on OU football over three decades ago while an inhabitant of a seminary. Other young men at the seminary hailed from such awful places as Texas, Kansas, Missouri, Iowa, and even Nebraska.

Oklahoma had a delightful habit of pounding football teams from those benighted areas into bloody pulps. Oh, sometimes the games would be close for a while, but inevitably Jim Weatherall would block a punt or Billy Vessels would burst off tackle for a long run, and the Sooners would win.

On top of all that, the Oklahoma football team was led into battle by a man who somehow combined the masculinity of a Tarzan with the personification of the Boy Scout Law.

Oklahoma seminarians frequently confused Bud Wilkinson with St. Philip Neri.

So, following Oklahoma football became a habit and a passion. For years, tickets were not difficult to come by. Somebody always had an extra one.

Then came the 1970s. Legions of new fans, many of whom thought Tommy McDonald was the grandfather of Ronald, marched to Norman on Saturdays. It became necessary to buy season tickets. Father Bryce and I began to plunk down our yearly spring check for next fall's entrance to the kingdom of Switzer.

Each year you would get a little packet of material advising that your money and the enclosed form should be returned by such-and-such date. Some years I returned it on time, some years I was a few days late, but always a shiny new slab of tickets arrived.

Last week, however, OU's athletic ticket office struck a blow for cold-blooded efficiency. I was informed by mail that my ticket request was four days late and thereby null and void.

The second paragraph of the cheery note read, "If you wish to be put on the permanent season ticket waiting list, please write to our office and we will make a notation that you were once a season ticket holder."

Thus we joined the ranks of Nikita Khrushchev and China's Gang of Four as non-persons in our world. The ticket office could have had the decency to send us two signs saying "Once a Season Ticket Holder" that we might wear around our necks during the coming autumn.

The last lines of the letter from OU stated, "Have a good day, but *drive carefully*." One has to interpret this parting message as an encouragement to avoid semi-intentional suicide.

The letter was signed with a genuine rubber stamp signature of John D. Cherry, Athletic Ticket Manager. I have a suggested new title for Mr. Cherry: Grim Reaper of Procrastinators.

Go-o-o-o-o, Cowboys!

Personal History in a Catalogue of Scars

September 1980

It was early in the morning. Too early. I stared into the bathroom mirror. The figure in the glass looked wary. Gravity was clearly winning the long struggle against firm facial tissue. Even eyelids were sagging at half-mast.

Perhaps to acquire a less discouraging view, I tilted my head back, and there, along the ridge of the right side of my chin, ran a fine white scar. That scar, I reminisced, was contributed on the floor of the gym at the St. Louis Preparatory Seminary over thirty years ago.

Scars. Curious things aren't they? Each one has its story and all the tales are personal. Once we are marked with a scar, we bear it in season and out. Sometimes we would rather not have a scar, but it is ours and no one else can claim it—as unique to us as our fingerprints.

My wandering mind spent the remaining shower time that morning cataloguing my scars. My collection is found to be modest in number and style but revelatory—character irks, my mother called them.

That slanted one, high on the forehead over my right eye, is the result of desert warfare. Sometime below the age of five, I was playing in the sand with a next-door neighbor, Edwin Hanna. The matter of contention is now lost in the long interval of time, but Edwin settled the issue by getting there "fustest with the mostest"—a sand shovel embedded in my dome.

The little beauty of a scar below the left eyebrow is now mostly covered by intertwining growth of five decades of wrinkles. That one was born at a summer's evening softball game. I was catching. Someone else with a flying elbow wanted badly to cross home plate. As I recall, the blood ran down my face very decoratively and won much sympathy.

Another scene. It is pure white winter. I am on a golf course, sledding, not slicing. With all the exuberance and none of the prudence of a twenty-one-year-old, I attempted to use the side of a sand bunker as a kind of sled jump. The result: body airborne for hundredths of a second, face scarred forever where the sled cut an irregular hole just below my lower lip.

Then there are the wages of sin. On my right hand, between the thumb and forefinger (almost where the Bic pen fits as I write this), runs a scar of about one-half inch. By golly, that little rascal has been there for forty years.

It seems that one evening, as my conscience reminds me, a group of boys entered the entrance hallway of an apartment across the street from Marquette School in Tulsa. Someone simultaneously rang all the doorbells in the apartment.

We ran smack into the arms of an enraged resident of the apartment who was approaching the entrance. Breaking free like terrified jackrabbits, we bolted into the night. I can still hear the man's heels hitting the ground behind me.

Veering south, just past Temple Israel, I began vaulting fences. It was one of those wire fence prongs that claimed an ounce of my flesh.

There are more but the shaving and the showering are completed. I only wonder if I have any scars for the sake of the Gospel. I wonder.

If My Father Were Still Alive, He Wouldn't Be Now

November 1980

If my father were still alive, he wouldn't be now. The presidential election would have done him in as surely as it ended Jimmy Carter's political life.

Word of the 1980 American election probably has filtered through to that heavenly mansion where my father carries on an animated discussion with Casey Stengel.

"Ronald Reagan has been elected president of the United States," softly announces an angel.

"That actor! What does he know about being president?" growls my father.

"Now, now, Frank," counsels Francis of Assisi, who happens to be passing by. "Think of my day. We had to put up with Otho IV and Frederick II. The president-elect can't be all that bad."

God's Little Poor Man is rewarded with a baleful look, a technique that my father perfected by turning down his chin and staring at the world through the border of lowered brows. The look always communicated an unmistakable meaning: disagreement mixed thoroughly with utter disgust.

It is safe to say that Frank Monahan in his later years was disdainful of Richard Nixon and Ronald Reagan. In earlier days, Herbert Hoover would have joined the list. Nixon, my father seemed to dislike on general principles. With Reagan, it was always "That actor!"

My father lived as a man on the outside. Most of our family members were in the oil business and politically equated

Republican. As an oil field supplies salesman, he had to keep his opinions under tight rein as he stepped from one "damn Roosevelt" conversation to the next.

Even about the church, my father stood apart as a sometimes scathing critic. Among other reasons why my father's Hall of Fame featured Harry Truman as its centerpiece, was Mr. Truman's ability to blister the privileged and articulate the feelings of marginal people.

The Great Depression had knocked my father to his knees when he was in his midthirties. I preserve fragments of memories of those days:

- Standing on Boulder Avenue in Tulsa with my father to watch the New Deal parade of soldiers in World War I uniforms;
- Looking at the National Recovery Act's Blue Eagle glued to a pane of glass by our front door;
- Watching my mother's tears (What was my father feeling?) as some men explained that we would have to move out of our home, a house that had been a wedding present from my maternal grandparents.

The Depression had much to do in the making and unmaking of my father.

An experience immediately before the Depression—the defeat of Al Smith for the presidency—also was embedded in my father's soul like a plank of rough wood that was plunged in and broken off.

He professed to believe that America would never allow a Catholic to be elected president. He assumed an attitude of resigned defeat prior to the 1960 voting. However, on election night, he followed the counting of ballots with an obsessive fervor previously reserved only for the World Series.

Then came the Dallas shooting. The bullet that blew apart John Kennedy's head continued its fatal trajectory straight into my father's heart. He was dead six months later.

The Republic should be aware that my father died convinced that "that actor" could never be a decent president. In the interest of fairness, however, let it be known also that he didn't consider Sandy Koufax to be much of a pitcher.

The Art of Celebrating Christmas without a Tree

December 1980

I must confess to an absence in my life that may qualify me as un-American or, possibly, un-Christian. Of the twenty-seven Christmases I have observed as a priest, I can recollect a genuine Christmas tree in my place of residence only once.

Two years ago some good people of Sacred Heart Parish stealthily decorated my room with an honest-to-goodness tree. My first reaction to that sparkling symbol of Christmas was similar to the cry of the hero in *A Thousand Clowns*: "My God, I've been attacked by the Ladies Home Journal!"

What is worse, I remain unconverted and unrepentant. No surge of desire for a Christmas tree has driven me forward this year to repeat the Sacred Heart experience. I have no sense of remorse—not even imperfect contrition—for trees that might have been.

My Christmas treeless celebration of the Lord's birth is probably fairly typical of Roman Catholic priests. As in other areas of life, priests' modes of keeping holidays tend to be different.

I was chatting with a group of priests the other day about Christmas presents, or lack of, received by pastors serving small missions. One fellow, who had been an assistant pastor in a large place, recalled his first Christmas at a much smaller parish unaccustomed to a pastor's presence. His one and only present: a shirt.

Another told of a single gift he had received at a Yuletide: a jar of homemade piccalilli.

My own favorite was a small wrapped gift from a kindly older woman handed solemnly to me before Midnight Mass. I took the package home and tore off the wrapping. It was a ballpoint pen with the name of a local funeral home printed on the side.

(The above examples certainly are not the norm for parishioners' generosity to their pastors, but they do illustrate the point that priests' Christmases tend to be different.)

Do priests, then, at this time of the year become one big mixture of the Blabs compounded of one-part Scrooge and two-parts pragmatism with a dash of Brezhnev bitters? Not at all.

In the midst of the Christmas season whirlpool into which we all get sucked, priests seem to undergo a precious alchemy. It's the public worship of the Church that does it, I think.

Both the Advent celebrations of the Eucharist and frequent ministerings of the Sacrament of Penance are the key factors.

This happens in spite of things. A priest may have had his nerves rubbed raw by some difficult persons approaching the Sacrament of Penance. He may have been depressed by the apathy of many parishioners toward his efforts to make Advent meaningful. He may be so tired by December 15 that if he could wish the next day to be January 16, he would do so.

On the other hand, most priests are moved quite deeply by the honest, humble approach of people to the Lord in the Sacrament of Penance. This does happen more often before Christmas than at other times.

And the liturgy of the Eucharist has a way of working its spirit into the fiber of one's soul. "O come, O come Emmanuel" kinds of repetitions do make a dent.

The result is that whether it be Midnight Mass at the Cathedral or an early morning celebration at a tiny frame mission, there is a very special sense of God's tender love—Christmas tree or no Christmas tree.

CHAPTER 5

1981

At Gift Wrapping It's the Beginning of the End

January 1981

My story begins as western Oklahoma joins the dark side of planet Earth on Christmas Eve. I push my way through the west doors of Montgomery Ward's in Penn Square. In my arms are a load of six books, unwrapped.

People inside the store fall into two categories. There are the Ward's employees—moving in slow motion, faces reflecting the season's exhaustion, bodily systems winding down from full speed to dead slow. The only salvation they are capable of appreciating at the present will arrive when the store closes at 6:00 p.m.

Then there are the others, the last-day, last-minute shoppers. Four out of five are male. Five out of five register symptoms ranging from frenzy to absolute panic. Facial tics are in; serenity is out. Processes of decision-making are short-circuiting; instincts to buy now and examine later are the prevailing mode.

It is the deck of the floundering Titanic, the last moments on the beach at Dunkirk, the restrooms at halftime at Owen Field, all bundled into one unruly package on this early evening of December 24. In the distance a chorus sings "God Rest Ye Merry Gentlemen."

And here am I heading for Gift Wrapping with my books and a crumpled list of seven more presents needed before this joint closes down. It is 5:15 p.m.

The young women in Gift Wrapping are standing ankle deep in discarded patterned paper. Their practiced hands work surely but deliberately. The few customers stare fixedly at the wrapping actions like spectators in an operating room mesmerized by the elaborations of open-heart surgery.

I hand over the books, mutter "I'll be back," and start a half lope for Men's Wear. The voice of impending doom speaks, "Attention, customers. The store will close in thirty minutes."

The next fifteen minutes is a blur. Three sweaters are selected and paid for—*Bang! Bang! Bang!* The clerk asks which church I belong to. The answer and my Roman collar encourage him to violate store policy in pronouncing judgment on my personal check.

Then, on to Women's Wear. A gentle saleswoman has no difficulty interpreting my anxiety. She sells me four gifts for four nieces in four minutes.

Now I'm on the escalator bound once more for Gift Wrapping. The voice: "Attention, customers. The store will close in fifteen minutes."

At Gift Wrapping, I find that it's the beginning of the end. There are no more boxes, no more energy, no more time. People are being turned away. One man tries charm, tries sarcasm, tries humor, tries pleading, but ends with a handful of wrapping paper, a few spare bows, and good wishes.

The crew agrees to do my books but not my latest purchases. We are all becoming giddy. If we had a bottle of champagne, I am not certain it would not be broken over the cash register.

At last I march away with a sack of wrapped books, two bags of unwrapped gifts, and a strange sense of elation that I am the next to the last customer in Gift Wrapping at Montgomery Ward's for the entire 1980 Christmas season.

In a Republican Year Visit the Old House in Watonga

February 1981

It is fitting to commemorate the new Republican administration with an Oklahoma Republican column. The locale of this tale is the Blaine County seat—Watonga. The story concerns a simple visit to the home of an Oklahoma territorial governor Republican Thompson B. Ferguson.

T.B. Ferguson was appointed governor of Oklahoma Territory by President Theodore Roosevelt. The Oklahoman's term of office ran from November 30, 1901, to January 6, 1906. Before, during, and after his time in office, Ferguson published the *Watonga Republican*. He had arrived in that city with the opening of the Cheyenne and Arapaho lands in 1892.

It was sometime before Christmas when I drifted into Watonga, realized that I had an extra couple of hours, and decided to visit the T.B. Ferguson home. A modest sign on the highway pointed the direction. I had a vague recollection that Ferguson had been a territorial governor.

The governor's home proved to be a white-frame, three-story house at the corner of Weigel and 5th Street. The yard is bordered by a white picket fence. Leaves covered the ground, fallen from good-sized native elms probably planted by Ferguson himself.

The house is distinguished by a large turret built into the front of the house (the glass in the windows of that section is curved). A wide porch extends across the front of the house. It was a mighty high class place when it was built in 1901.

I was met at the door by Lillian Cronkite, the assistant curator. She is white-haired and gracious. I signed the guest book, the only visitor that day.

Mrs. Cronkite made the tour worthwhile. She knew the history of the house and also talked freely of her own background as a wife and mother on a nearby old-time Oklahoma ranch. The J.B. Cronkite ranch became the greater part of the present Roman Nose State Park.

To the nosy questions of the *Sooner Catholic's* editor, Mrs. Cronkite admitted that the Oklahoma Cronkites are cousins of that broadcaster fellow, Walter, who hails from St. Joseph, Missouri, (even though Walter's family dropped the H or our folks added it).

T.B. Ferguson died in 1921. His wife, Elva, continued to publish the newspaper until she sold it in 1930. Her maiden name was Shartel. The street in Oklahoma City commemorates Elva Shartel Ferguson's brother.

On the second floor, I spotted an old copy of *Cimarron* by Edna Ferber. My guide explained that in the 1920s, the author came to Watonga and lived for a time with the late governor's widow. Elva Ferguson became the model of the pioneer newspaper woman heroine of *Cimarron*.

The house held still another journalistic connection that Mrs. Cronkite brought to light for me. It seems that the wife of Walter Ferguson, one of the governor's sons, was the well-known newspaper columnist Lucia Loomis (Ferguson). For decades she wrote a widely distributed column "A Woman's Viewpoint" syndicated by Scripps Howard.

All in all it was a pleasant way to spend part of a peaceful, late-autumn afternoon. The Ferguson Home was an unexpected pleasure, but the genteel Mrs. Cronkite was the greater treasure. Stop by and let Walter's cousin-in-law talk you through the house.

This Week an Old Friend Retires

March 1981

This week I will attend the retirement of an old trusty friend. The ceremony will be brief. There won't be a lot of hoopla, not so much as a going-away present for my old friend.

The act of retirement will be close to me, closer even than under my nose. Indeed, it will take place on my nose. Along about Wednesday, a solemn P.M. Wolfley will slide my old eyeglasses off my face and replace them with a 1981 model.

My old black-rimmed glasses are a little gray from sun and heat. There is evidence of plastic fatigue. Thin lines of Oklahoma grit are wedged between lenses and frames. But they are comfortable, like one's favorite chair or personal bed. Somehow over the years they have conformed to the contours of my face.

For someone who has worn spectacles for forty years, each change of equipment becomes a good-bye time-a-gram of sadness as we part from a never-failing service.

If one really needs them, eyeglasses become almost a part of one's body. Every waking hour they are on your face. When asleep they are placed carefully no farther than your arm's length.

Once, I was asleep on the upper floor of a house exploded by a tornado. I lunged for the bathroom and made it just as my bedroom disappeared into the storm. It was truly a case of fractions of a second between life and death. Only later did I discover that I was wearing my glasses. They had been placed on a table next to the bed.

A number of times I have taken baths or showers, realizing only when the view became a bit murky that the old specs had not been removed. Temporarily at least, your eyeglasses do become a part of your body as much as a nose or an ear or a tongue.

My new glasses will be E15 (Eyeglasses number 15 in my life). I have no doubt E 15 will prove to be as loyal and obedient as its predecessors, but I can't let E14 go without a round of recollections.

Today I wrote a list of some of the highlights I have witnessed in the past four years with E14's essential assistance:

- Billy Sims' wild breakaway dash against Nebraska in the fourth quarter of the 1979 game at Norman;
- The view out the attic window from the very place in Amsterdam where Anne Frank watched during the family's long months of hiding before the Gestapo came crashing in.
- The black-and-white TV picture of the man "from a faraway nation"—Karol Wojtyla—walking onto the balcony of St. Peter's after his election as Pope John Paul II on October 16, 1978;
- The green-on-brown panorama of the serpentine joining of the Ohio and Mississippi rivers from the 30,000-foot platform of a 727 over Cairo, Illinois;
- The mind picture from reading Bruce Catton's description of Abraham Lincoln's walk through Richmond the day after its capture by federal troops—April 4, 1865—with black people massing around the Great Liberator and crying "Glory, glory, glory."
- The perfection of my newest nieces and nephew—Anne, Carrie, and Travis.
- And hundreds of dazzling Oklahoma sunsets—guaranteed no two alike—seen over Resurrection Cemetery:

So much for E14. There are sentimental attachments, but the remorseless reality of the ever-changing river of time demands I turn loose and go on to the new prescribed lenses.

The whole thing is a tiny lesson in the need to change.

I could choose deliberately, willfully to keep grand old E14. That choice would include seeing reality more unclearly, with greater blur than necessary. It would be one way to distance myself from this beautiful but cantankerous world. I suspect many of us do that in more important ways than keeping obsolete eyeglasses.

With the donning of one's latest eyeglasses, there is the bother of an eerie day or two when the whole world appears to be an inch or two out of kilter.

Then there is the uncomfortable sensation, like a young woman in her first high heels, that everyone is staring at the different you in those strange glasses. Actually the only one who notices is some four-foot-ten-inch altar boy who yawns as he makes his observation.

Okay, Mr. Wolfley, let's try that new pair.

She Possessed a Look that Froze Evil in Its Tracks

March 1991

Said the old Jesuit teacher as he pushed away from the breakfast table, "It's time to hack away at the ever-growing jungle of ignorance."

Said the no-nonsense pedagogue to the frightened beginning teacher on the first day of school, "Don't smile before Christmas."

Said Sister Mary Andrew to God as she made her way to the first grade room in September 1933, "Lord, let the Monahan kid make it his second time around. I don't know whether I could take him three years in a row."

Looking back on my undistinguished but inordinately long scholastic career—twenty-one whole years in the receiving end of the classroom plus painful parts of perhaps nine more—I figure I have as much right as the next bozo to choose a few of the better teachers I have experienced.

Let's start with Sister Mary Andrew Vanderpool. She was in her youthful third year of teaching when I appeared on the scene in 1932 for my original run at the first grade hurdle. My old mind is a blank about specifics of the two years I was with her except for odd recollections—Jack Hilditch was too big to fit into his desk seat, and I believed two of my classmates to be Jay O'Millions and Martha Savior (later clarified to Jay O'Meilia and Martha Sager).

But there remains a definite sense of approval of Sister Mary Andrew. Love in the first grade. As far as I was concerned, I would have remained her pupil for all the grades ahead.

A decade or so later, I came under the tutelage of Sister Mary Edward Mundell. She was (and is) an impact maker.

She was the possessor of a look that froze evil in its tracks. A slender woman of no particular physical attributes to reinforce "the look," Sister Mary Edward could quell incipient riots, irrational rages, and stubborn defiance by one long, level look. The look was usually followed by calm well-formed questions or declarative sentences that dissolved recalcitrants into puddles of head-bobbing compliance.

Meanness had nothing to do with it; personal authority had everything.

Sister Mary Edward coaxed me through four years of Latin. I sang of arms and the man in my translations of the Iliad with all the soul of a harpist whose real abilities were in tire repair.

She became a genuine friend to her students, one who kept in touch. Today she has a long trail of admiring former pupils rapidly passing her in the aging process. And she still owns "the look."

Somewhere in the late 1960s, I found myself strolling about the University of Oklahoma campus in the summers, keeping one-step ahead of the baying certification bloodhounds of the Oklahoma State Department of Education. I was required to take a course in business administration. I enrolled.

My vision of a professor in business administration was The Man in the Gray Flannel Suit. The first day, our motley group sat uneasily in the classroom, not knowing one another and a little on edge about what to expect.

The door opened, and in walked a fellow wearing a sport shirt hanging out at the waist, red socks, and slightly disarrayed hair. Something tells me he was smoking a cigar. It was Dr. Don Woolf.

The doctor was one smart cookie and an A+ teacher. Blinking his eyes as he chattered away, handing out challenging assignments, throwing out clues on available resources, and delightfully leveling those of us who carried preconceived notions of the subject, Dr. Woolf gave us our money's worth and change.

Still pursued by the certification gang, I fled one summer to Carroll College in Helena, Montana. I needed credits in English so I enrolled in a course on Shakespeare.

The professor's name was Hank Burgess. He didn't hold a doctorate, but he possessed something more precious: a large family. And that summer at least he worked a second job in a convenience store to keep his little ones in food.

But what a great teacher! He was in love with William Shakespeare. He had immersed himself in the great man's living literature. We students would read a Shakespearean play, say Henry IV. The next day Professor Hank pulled out of us what we had learned. In the process, he provided his own wonderful insights that made the play sparkle and intrigue. His enthusiasm and competence swept us off our feet and left us eager to read more of Shakespeare.

I still remember Cordelia speaking to her dad, old King Lear, about her inability to express her feelings for him: "I cannot heave my heart into my mouth."

Finally, let me mention Dr. Robert Christin, a professor of literature at Notre Dame University. I heard him speak once. He said there were thousands of writers in the United States, but only the work of a few would endure. One of those, said Dr. Christin, is Walter "Red" Smith, sports columnist.

The next morning I began reading Red Smith, and I haven't stopped yet.

An Easter Mix of Alleluias and Acts of Contrition

April 1981

We were two boys as eager as springtime. The date was April 20, 1946, that year's Holy Saturday. We made our way—ran a little I'm sure—the half mile or so from the grounds of St. Louis Preparatory Seminary to the highway: Route 66.

Charlie Skeehan and I were going home for Easter. That curvy ribbon of concrete was our golden road to Oklahoma. We planned to use our thumbs to get there.

Our Holy Saturday had begun with an early, early liturgy that was long, long. The liturgy and, let us hope, the Holy Spirit had stuffed us brim full of alleluias.

For more than three months there had been only a weekly few hours outside the seminary grounds to break a demanding, highly regimented lifestyle. So, we were two elated young men, eighteen and nineteen years old, headed for the Promised Land (spelled T-u-l-s-a).

At this point, thirty-five years away from that Holy Saturday, I can recall only a few details of the trip but lots of half-memories and impressions.

I do know that the trip required fourteen separate rides and was stretched out over a period of twenty-one hours.

One recollection remains most vividly.

By Saturday afternoon we had reached Rolla, Missouri, some 100 miles west of our starting point. We were strolling along US 66 beside what appeared to be a golf course. Some children were running here and there collecting Easter eggs. We needed rides—eight hours already used and over 300 miles to go.

An old car veered onto the shoulder of the road and skidded to a stop. Being naive and inexperienced and a little desperate to get moving, we jumped into the backseat without sizing up the situation. We should have looked twice.

As the car roared away with us in it, Charlie and I became instantly aware that both the driver and his partner in the front seat were absolutely, totally drunk—as inebriated as one can get and keep functioning minimally.

Our benefactors had a bottle of green something that looked like Wildroot Hair Oil (maybe it was). The driver had the fixed notion that it would be hilarious if he could make his companion fall out of the car by driving extremely fast and then slamming on the brakes. When the driver did this, the door on the passenger's side would fly open and the partner—Wildroot bottle and all—would come close to tumbling out. The act was repeated many times.

Now this was being done, mind you, on US 66 when it was two lanes and everybody in America was trying to celebrate the end of World War II by driving to California on that narrow highway. When the intoxicated driver hit the brakes, the cars behind us went into ditches, passed in no-passing zones and skidded every which way.

Talk about terror! Charlie and I set the North American record for the most Acts of Contrition recited in ten minutes' time. Finally, the fan belt broke. The car stopped. We excused ourselves.

After that, almost anything would have been better. We did a lot more standing around; rode in the back of an open truck; hitched a ride with a salesman and his girlfriend at Conway; trudged through Springfield in the dark; were driven to a motel outside of Joplin where a cursory assessment indicated that emphasis on the virtue of chastity seemed to be on the decline;

and mercifully were offered a ride from Galena, Kansas, in an hour after midnight.

About 5:00 a.m., the good guys from Galena deposited us on East 11th Street in Tulsa. We walked wearily but happily through Tracy Park and down Newport Avenue to our homes.

Out of those twenty-one hours of madness, I got one face badly blistered by sun and wind, plus a delicious vacation. It was an Easter to remember.

Announcing the Crooked Tooth League of America

April 1981

One of the least-noted social phenomenons in our peculiar society is the growing legion of perfectly straight teeth. I mean, just look around—on the streets, in purple mountain majesties and above the fruited plain—everywhere there are row upon row of regular, gleaming choppers, aligned with the precision of the ranks on the West Point parade round.

The difference between those under 0 and those on the gray side no longer has anything to do with radicalism and traditionalism. The difference now is who has straight teeth and who has crooked ones.

I am here to warn you that straight teeth may be the death of America! Consider the following in the blinding light reflected off the snowy walls of the perfect teeth of millions of younger Americans:

- Straight teeth, emitting their laser-like beams are burning neuroses of inferiority on the souls of those whose origins date to BBBRDEAC (Before Braces Became the Right and Duty of Every American Child). People who are BBBRDEAC never smile in photographs and talk with either hand in front of their mouth or speak in muffled syllables through closed lips.
- Straight teeth are undoubtedly one more step down the road to Big Brotherism. What does Big Brother want? Why, of course, Big Brother wants us all to look the same,

as the Chinese in their baggy unisex outfits. Big Brother couldn't trick us into the baggy suits' mold, so he subtly began the movement to straighten teeth. Some scoff at conspiracy theories, but don't forget that dental schools have been highly subsidized by the federal government.

- Straight teeth are the underlying cause of inflation. Otherwise thrifty parents, after their first peek at junior's crooked teeth, begin to sling—then shovel—money at the problem. The nation no longer chooses between guns or butter—straight teeth clearly have the priority over the two lesser items.

- Straight teeth are the white-stair steps to the throne of a new elite in America—the orthodontists. Clad in their white smocks, braces in hand, the orthodontists have climbed tooth by tooth to the top of the heap. Lesser modern gods—astronauts and physicists and even rock singers—are prone to fall down before the orthodontist, those who alone control the wires to social acceptance.

Whereas all of the aforesaid is obviously true, be it hereby known that to save the United States the author of this article is establishing the Crooked Tooth League of America. The time is past due to bring the crooked toothers out of their closets.

My credentials as founder of the Crooked Tooth League are established by one upper incisor that bashfully has lingered a step behind the others and by a row of lower incisors that are tilted toward Amarillo.

Those who proudly bear a Crooked Tooth League membership card will have *prima facie* evidence of their unity with survivors of the Great Depression and the general run of the earth's afflicted. No one will question whether a Crooked Tooth League member belongs to the human race or is a descendant of Adam and Eve.

The Crooked Tooth League plans to set forth as a nonnegotiable demand that at least half of all the mass media ads show people with crooked teeth. Presently, Alfred E. Newman is our sole representative.

Furthermore, the League will demand that April 30 be set aside each year as "Smile a Crooked Smile Day." The League is convinced that there is some profound human connection between smiling one's crooked smile and W.H. Auden's admonition "Love your crooked neighbor with all your crooked heart."

Whatever Happened to National Return Books Week?

June 1981

Father John C. McGinty is a man of opinions. Of course, everyone has opinions, but Father McGinty is blessed with a greater than average bundle of them, and he is not loath to hold ones that fly in face of your ordinary, run-of-the-mill opinions possessed by the majority.

Father McGinty and I sit next to each other in the priests' dining room at the Center for Christian Renewal. Consequently, I have heard a wide and colorful variety of his views. For example, I recall the hilarity around the table in the mid-1960s when he stated firmly that Richard M. Nixon would someday be elected president of the United States. (This was the period when Richard had removed himself from being kicked around anymore.) We all agreed it was a good joke but a ridiculous opinion.

Another of Father McGinty's favorite convictions is that something needs to be done about people who borrow others' books but do not return them. He thinks priests are particularly villainous in this respect. Now and again, he has suggested that the *Sooner Catholic* enlist in this struggle on behalf of despoiled book owners.

So, here goes.

Before grabbing my first stone to heave at the dirty book pirates, I look cautiously around my office to ascertain who might be flinging rocks back at me.

Egad! Against the east wall I spy three large books—a bound volume of 1947 *America* magazines, a hardback copy of Carl Sandburg's *Abraham Lincoln*, and *The Encyclicals and Other Messages of John XXIII*. Somehow these books are marked as property of the library of the Center for Christian Renewal. "Anybody is liable to make an oversight," I say to myself.

Uh-oh. Behind my chair on the floor are two more books— *Land, Wood & Water* by Robert S. Kerr and *The Water Hustlers* by Boyle, Graves and Watkins. There must be some mistake. The Belle Isle Library cards in these books distinctly read Date Due—April 9, 1981. I rationalize. Either their rubber stamp was set for the wrong month or I have been terribly busy. Then, a little voice insists, "If you have five books belonging to someone else in your office, how many more do you have in your house?"

I go home to see what there is to see about possession of unowned books. Stacked around my favorite reading chair are five books about Central and South America (all due at Belle Isle Library on April 8, 1981), a companion copy of *Abraham Lincoln*, also due at the Center's library, a volume on Soviet oppression in Lithuania borrowed from Archbishop Salatka, *The Little Prince* loaned last Christmas by Sister Martha Mary McGaw, a book on papal elections from Father Philip Bryce and, worst of all, a George MacDonald Anthology that I gave to someone else, who in turn handed it back to me to read, and which has never been returned.

Mea culpa, mea culpa, mea many times *culpa.*

At this point, I abandon plans to be the founder and leading promoter of National Return Books Week. It would be like W.C. Fields drunkenly taking the field at the head of the forces for alcoholic prohibition.

Instead of being a champion of justice in the borrowed-but-forgotten books camp, I shall contritely return the fifteen books in my possession that have been whimpering in the night for their rightful owners. If you see a haggard figure in sackcloth and ashes begging forgiveness before the Belle Isle Library, blame it on Father McGinty.

How I Discovered the Inventor of the Beer Can

June 1981

I have been sitting here for thirty minutes in room 140 of De Grasse Hall at St. Gregory's College trying to get a usable idea for "For the Time Being." I just finished a can of Dr Pepper. While idly examining the metal tab from the can, I recall a man I met a number of years ago.

On a Saturday morning, I was driving east on the Northwest Highway. A little west of Portland Avenue, there was an elderly fellow trying to push a shopping cart, top-heavy with plastic bags, along the muddy shoulder of the road. The wheels stuck. The shopping cart turned over and spilled its contents in the mud and the grass. I pulled over to help.

The older man said that he was taking the empty beer cans to a center down the road where he could sell them. We agreed to load the smelly bags with the cans in the trunk of my car and to come back for the cart later.

We drove away toward the aluminum can collection point. The old gentleman began to talk. Our brief conversation—only a few minutes in length—proved once more that everyone has a personal story to tell.

He was unkempt and, as I recall, unshaven. A real stereotype of a bum. He said that he was a retired professor of engineering from the University of Oklahoma. Recently he had been working in a bowling alley. He was broke. That was all stated matter-of-factly. There was no appeal made for money.

The grizzled professor discovered that I was a priest. Briefly he stated his philosophy of religion. His opinion was laced with reverence.

We discussed the beer can business. Offhandedly, he said that he had taught engineering to the man who invented the beer can. You know, I believed him. I still do. There was some edge of intelligence, of understated integrity, that moved me to accept his story.

Occasionally, over a period of months, perhaps a year or more, I would see the old professor struggling with his shopping cart and beer cans along the highway. He was fitting into my world nicely as a genuine character, a familiar but eccentric figure, a person who lives his unique life without giving a tweet what other, more proper, folks might think. Those kind of community characters add a little salt to everyday existence.

I can think of two other community characters who salt my life with a distinct but subtle flavor.

One is The Runner. This man plies the median on the Northwest Highway. He runs with short steps as though his feet hurt. Sometimes he runs with a small dog on a leash. Other times he runs with a transistor radio to his ear. Always he runs. I have seen him in dust storms and in sleet, in fifty-mile-an-hour winds and in road-buckling heat.

The Runner moves with grim intensity. He pays no heed to the four or six lanes of traffic moving on each side of him. It's as if The Runner was running there before the highway was laid or the cars began to roll. The last time I saw him his t-shirt carried the legend: This Space for Rent. A real community character.

Then there is Brother Paul. He is the bearded one you can see on North Robinson. He stands there like a mute bird feathered with signs—signs hanging off each arm, signs covering his torso. Brother Paul's signs carry but one theme: heaven and hell, salvation and damnation.

I met Brother Paul once, in a discount store. He talked gently and sensibly, thus undercutting my notions of his religious fanaticism. Be that as it may, Brother Paul is another true community character.

In our plasticized age, I value the old professor and The Runner and Brother Paul over a thousand fast-food restaurants or a mile-high stack of designer jeans or an infinite number of television game shows.

"Jail House Rock" Served with Salad

July 1981

"Your lo–ove is lifting me higher!" So the young woman wailed in the dining room of Roman Nose Lodge on the evening of July 5.

Her song startled me. I had eaten in this establishment many times but never before had music with my meal. The song itself always had been interpreted by me as rather sexually explicit. Yet here it was being earnestly baptized by a Christian rock group. Yes, a Christian rock group. I should be so lucky.

Was this kind of performance in a state-owned resort possible only in Oklahoma? Was this George Nigh's idea of a joke?

I appreciate music as a means of religious expression, even the mod forms, but to be force-fed a religious experience in a public place (compounded by the amateur hour quality of the music) is more than I can take with a smile.

My trip to the dining room had been preceded by a pleasurable fifty-six minutes watching *60 Minutes*. There had been a pre-supper cocktail. I chose my copy of *Dust Bowl* by Donald Worster for table reading.

I would, I thought, while away the dinnertime by vicariously reliving the tragedies and triumphs of the Okies who went West in the 1930s. Instead, I was swallowed in a vibrating black cloud of noise pollution (albeit "Christian") produced by the descendants of the Okies who stayed behind.

To reach the salad bar and partake of it, one had to slog through the audience at tables and pile one's plate full of the goods of the earth while directly facing the Savior's Six (or whatever their name was). The ensemble's centerpiece was an enormous conglomeration of shiny blue-and-white percussion instruments under the control of a slight male, who might be a soul brother of Francis of Assisi, but who somehow impressed me as the sinister operator of a vile machine of torture.

I scurried back to my appointed place.

"Jail House Rock" was served with the salad. I distractedly crawled one paragraph forward in the book. It was paragraph three on page 48. It began with the words by Woody Guthrie "Lord, I'm going down this road feeling bad." Appropriate.

As I chomped my way through a piece of ham and a baked potato, the presentation varied. Between songs there were exhortations to give oneself to the Lord. The musical director-evangelist really used the word *really*, really too much. I mean it was really, really overdone.

One number had all kinds of catchy lyrics about people who couldn't save you. For example, one verse was something like "Old Mohammed ain't gonna be callin' you home!" Being partly paranoid, I forgot about the ham long enough to cup an ear to learn if the pope would be included in the cast of characters with no salvific force. The pope didn't make the scene.

To those who aren't attuned to this brand of hokey evangelism, I wondered what the reaction was. At the table next to mine was a guy in a tank shirt drinking a glass of beer. His tired, lined face was expressionless as he listened. My hunch is that the unsolicited Christian rock stirred anger against the very persons and values being promoted. Does Jesus need enemies when He has friends like this outfit?

I downed a chocolate sundae as we musically pounded our collective path through the book of Revelation.

Near the cash register sat a small wicker basket with a $10 bill and a $20 bill in it. The cashier explained it was for contributions to the music group. I remarked that the seed money was rather much and that I would have contributed to a payoff to keep them silent. The cashier did not reply. I went out for fresh air.

The True Confessions of a New Car Buyer

October 1981

The following is the true confession of a new car buyer. To verify the facts of the story, you may check with God at the Last Judgment.

I detest buying automobiles. Besides the pain of signing on as an indentured servant to a loan institution for a period of years, there is an uncomfortable catch 22 operating in my psyche concerning the whole process of purchasing a car.

My psychological problem is composed of two elements: First, I harbor the prejudice that car salespeople are not to be trusted. (This prejudice, in turn, has a double root: my father was a salesman who frequently informed me of the machinations of other salesmen; and, once in my youth, a grizzled car dealer leaned into my face and said both sadly and solemnly, "All car dealers lie.") Secondly, prolonged conscious nursing of that prejudice makes me feel distinctly guilty for not being open to my brothers in the flesh.

In any event, I had succeeded in stalling the purchase of a new car over a period of months. I said inwardly that I will wait for a super deal, that I can't afford the present interest rates, that my gutsy Maverick will last another year, that I will do it next week, that I don't have time to take care of this matter now, etc., etc., etc.

All this time the Maverick was spewing oil over the Oklahoma City streets like a hemorrhaging elephant seeking a place to die. When I attempted to run the air-conditioner, the engine vibrated to a stop. I had worn a hole in the floorboard with my heel. And one could see the sky near the rear door crease where the fabric was tearing away.

Something happened on Wednesday, September 23. On a lonely hill of my cerebral hemisphere, a bugle sounds the call to battle.

I dress in my $19 black suit. I drive resolutely to the Speed-O-Matic Car Wash. Having sent two winters', three springs', three summers', and two falls' grime down the drain, I proceed straightaway to Fred Jones Ford. (Somehow I have kept intact a feeling that Fred Jones is an exception to the rule in the car industry.)

My salesman is Weldon King. He is a quiet, polite man, but I am seized by the notion that Weldon, a la the Cure of Ars, can read my timorous soul like a book. We look at an EXP, a Mustang, and two dusty Escort station wagons. He casually mentions that the cheapest Escort available is in the body shop getting "a scratch" repaired. I leap at the bargain like a starving cat happening upon an overlooked tuna fish salad.

Weldon and I go for a ride in the Escort. It rides along smoothly enough. My guide tells me of his involvement with the Baptist Church at Mustang. We return to home base with the fenders undented and the gears unstripped.

Weldon looks at my old Maverick. He climbs into the front seat and emerges with a kind of a grin. "Is that the true mileage?" he says. It certainly is, I say, except for the fact that the odometer cannot accommodate the first digit of the 112,629.

Then comes the figurin'. Inevitably you are seated in a small room mindful of an antechamber to the Gulag Archipelago. The salesman looks at numbers, lots of numbers. He consults small but fat, well-thumbed books. He frowns and taps on his adding machine. Meanwhile, you are seated there like a convict waiting for the sentence to be read. There is nothing for you to do while the figurin' continues. You look at the photos of the salesman's children. You try to study a painting on the wall, but it is too close for your regular lenses and too far away for the bifocals.

At last Weldon gives me the results of his arithmetic, and I trudge down the hall to the finance officer's place of business. He is a blocky man with a heavy thatch of gray hair. His name is Tom Nickerson. Tom doesn't use fat, well-thumbed books. His magic tool is a shiny computer. It's like having a direct line to Henry Ford's grave. Ask it a Ford question and one gets a Ford answer. Tom asks the magic box about financing the Escort. The machine hic-coughs an answer: it will cost $1,922.84 in interest over 48 months. I succeed in holding back the tears.

Saturday morning I return to pick up the new car. All is anticlimactic. Tom Nickerson has me sign numerous papers, which, for all that I read them, could have made me a member of the Mafia or the owner of the Red Dog Saloon. What the papers actually do is seal a four-year sentence of car payments.

I meet Weldon King's Saturday surrogate, Whitey Lane. I hand him the Maverick's keys. He turns over the Escort's keys. That's it.

As I drive away, it enters my mind that American happenings as solemn as buying a new car should be suitably ritualized. Perhaps in the future, the new owner could sit behind the wheel and say, "For better or for lemon, and definitely for poorer, I take you Escort for my lawful automobile. I promise to be true to my payments in good times and in bad." Then the one taking Whitey's role would say, "I pronounce you man and car. Go in all your pieces, and I hope you make it safely off the lot."

I mean I was Mao Tse-tung on the Long March

November 1981

Alberto Salazar won the New York City Marathon on October 25 and set a new world record for humans running twenty-six-mile, 385-yard races.

Mortal joggers can better appreciate Salazar's nearly incredible feat of completing the marathon in 2 hours, 8 minutes, and 13 seconds, when they use their calculators to determine he averaged less than five minutes a mile over the course. He ran his seventeenth mile in a remarkable 4 minutes, 33 seconds!

However, it seems that the huzzahs accompanying Salazar's triumph this past weekend have turned the world's attention away from another of humankind's constant assaults on the barriers of distance and time: D. F. Monahan's heel-and-toe walk from Guthrie across Logan County to Edmond Road in Oklahoma City. Distance 25.5 miles, time 21.5 hours.

Hark! Did we hear a snicker? A titter in the shadows by some insensitive pocket computer operator who holds aloft Monahan's rate of walking at one point 1.19 miles per hour? Hold the merriment please, until, as P. Harvey would say, you've heard the rest of the story.

It seems that last spring, the editor of the *Sooner Catholic* dashed off a note to Father Thomas Boyer, Archdiocesan Inspirer of Youth, to the effect that pilgrimages—a venerable tradition among Christians—be added to our Church's youth programs.

Before summer had been properly laid to rest, there I was, on Friday, October 23, standing, with eight other brave and/or imprudent people on the steps of St. Mary's Church in Guthrie poised to begin a "Cathedral Walk" from Oklahoma's first cathedral to its second, St. Joseph's Old Cathedral in downtown Oklahoma City.

How quickly the idea had evolved into the act! There was nothing to do but to clamp on a brave face and march into the setting sun. I did. I strode through and out of Guthrie—arms swinging, head high, with confident, tight smile—like Alec Guinness playing the British colonel in *Bridge over the River Kwai*. I mean, I was Mao Tse-tung on the Long March, Hannibal over the Alps (minus elephants), Daniel Boone through the Cumberland Gap and Casey Stengel to the pitcher's mound— all rolled into one middle-aged priest wearing his trusty black Wolverine work shoes.

That night we walked over nine miles to Harmony Community Church, almost due west of Guthrie. We stepped through a tunnel of rural darkness under a roof of stars and occasionally, as we reached high points of ground, surrounded by a shimmering but distant necklace of ground lights.

We slept at the church. I should say some slept at the church. This old sinner, wrapped in his sleeping bag, found the floor as hard as the church pastor's heart was soft in allowing us to spend the night there.

The remainder of the Great Walk resumed early the next morning and might be catalogued thus as an adventure in the well-known state of semi-trance experienced by marathon runners.

Some recollections of the ordeal:

- Wind blowing dust strongly from the south as we limped down the dirt road that masquerades as Western Avenue in Logan County.
- A crisp, clear vision of Sacred Heart Church at Navina across a couple of miles of wheat-green prairie.
- The interesting variety of stares given by passersby at us bedraggled marchers.

- The sweet dispositions and thoughtfulness of the members of our band.
- The strange traveling pains in my legs, which glided from left big toe, to right instep, to right calf and finally took up permanent residence all along the back of the right leg.
- The arrival of my rescue car at 4:00 p.m. and my gallant, cheery wave to the troops I left behind as I headed for a tub of hot water.

P.S. By Monday, I could move painlessly again, as long as I walked backward.

I Stepped out of the Car, Slammed the Door, and...

December 1981

It was an early November evening when my car rolled to a stop outside Stormy's Pizza on Noble Avenue in Watonga. I had been roaming around Blaine County all afternoon on *Sooner Catholic* business, and it was definitely time to eat.

I stepped out of the car, pressed down the door lock knob, and slammed the door. Simultaneously with the sound of the door closing, my psyche crashed somewhere in the depths of my innards as if I had swallowed a chocolate-coated cannonball. I checked my jacket pockets and my pants' pockets. Nothing. Could it be? Leaning close against the side window, I could make out my key holder resting on the front seat. Yes, I had locked myself out of my beloved Escort!

It was like St. Paul's description of the Last Judgment: "Just when people are saying 'peace and security' (or lusting after a Stormy's Pizza Supreme), ruin will fall on them with the suddenness of pains overtaking a woman in labor, and there will be no escape."

I stood there on Noble Avenue blinking in the gathering dusk, a man instantaneously beyond the pale of the great American driving public. In the click of a latch, I had become an alien, wheelless in a radial-tire culture, cut off at the knees in a society on the run, locked out of Ford's Family of Fine Cars.

At last I wobbled down the street seeking salvation in the corner service station. I told my story to the service station crew—a man with moustache and sad eyes, a boy in greasy outfit.

They were sympathetic, but, they said, the Ford agency was closed for the evening and there was no locksmith in Watonga.

I trudged back up the street with a borrowed coat hanger. It proved to be no contest, like trying to break out of Leavenworth by using a cornbread stick to saw the bars. You see, the automobiles of our era have been so constructed that the age-old coat hanger action no longer works. Honest but absent-minded folks can no longer burgle their own cars.

I returned to the service station for more sympathy but no practical suggestions. I handed over the mutilated coat hanger. No explanation was necessary.

Then, in a brashness born out of desperation, I dialed the home of the Watonga Ford dealer (the number remains written on the back cover of *Prize Stories of the Seventies from the O. Henry Awards*, which I was carrying). A small voice answered. I asked for Oliver Hursh. "Daddy!" When an adult male came to the telephone, I poured my pail of woes into the line. Without hesitation, he said he would meet me at my car in a few minutes.

I paced the darkened sidewalk along Noble Avenue for fifteen minutes. It was getting colder. I exhaled steam. A husky, shortish man came striding out of the shadows. It was Oliver Hursh. We shook hands.

Oliver allowed that this new model of automobile might foil his best efforts at opening the door. Using a thin metallic "device," he popped the lock open in about fifteen seconds. I was elated. I wanted to pay him, but Oliver said, "No! No!" I thanked him. He walked away. And that was it.

Seated at last in front of a glass of beer in Stormy's and waiting for my pizza, I reflected. Would a Ford dealer in any place but a small town leave his house at dinnertime to rescue some anonymous sap dumb enough to lock his keys in his car? I doubt it. What prompted Oliver Hursh to be so generous? I don't know.

I never met the man except for those few moments of that chilly evening on Noble Avenue. However, on the Last Day, if

Oliver stands in need of a boost, there will come one voice from a back pew, "Remember, Lord, that night in Watonga!" Oliver Hursh converted me into a cockeyed optimist about the human race for the next week.

CHAPTER 6

1982

Red Smith:
A Talented Bleeder and
"a Pretty Good Speller"

January 1982

Red Smith once wrote: "Creative writing is easy. It's done in little drops of blood."

I first met Red Smith two decades ago during a lecture on American literature at Notre Dame University, and I learned of his death yesterday over poached eggs and bacon at a Holiday Inn in Lawton. In between, Walter Wellesley "Red" Smith graced my life with frequent touches of excellence, wit, and insight.

The lecture at Notre Dame was delivered by a handsome professor of English by the name of Dr. Robert Christian, if my memory is correct. The man of letters told us in all seriousness that of all the writing being done then in America little would survive the years, but part of that which would endure was being produced by a sports writer, Red Smith. The lecturer said that one had to be decently educated in order to appreciate the many classical allusions in Smith's work.

Well, I was hooked even before I tasted the bait. Here was an opportunity to read "that which would endure," and it would be about sports! That summer I began to read Red Smith in the *Chicago Sun Times*. His column was the peaches and cream of the season's breakfast table.

Red Smith soon was assigned an honored place in my private pantheon. His pedestal was in the vestibule between those of JFK and Bud Wilkinson.

Oklahoma was not Red Smith country (although in recent years the *Daily Oklahoman* occasionally ran a column by him). Smith addicts had to search for fixes in out-of-state newspapers, magazine articles, and infrequent books of the Best of Red Smith. I recall buying a secondhand volume of that variety in Chicago's Loop. But I persevered, finding and consuming just enough scraps of Smith's meaty stuff to keep me plugging along for more.

Then one sunny September afternoon, I had the good fortune to shake hands with my hero. The meeting took place in the press box at Owen Field in Norman. Oklahoma was playing Syracuse. I was in the press gallery out of the kindness of Harold Keith, who used the excuse that I wrote a sports column for the *Oklahoma Courier* to seat me there.

Harold engineered the introduction. I told Red that English teachers at McGuinness High School pointed to his columns as examples of good composition. "That's frightening," he replied.

Now Red Smith is dead. A memorial Mass is to be celebrated at St. Patrick's Cathedral. Tributes will splash on the casket like spring rain. Probably none will reach Red Smith's standards for eloquent use of the English language.

Some examples of praises sung in his lifetime:

- Morley Safer on *60 Minutes*: "The keenest of all the observers of the games people play."
- Roger Kahn in the November 1979 *Notre Dame Magazine*: "I assume he can write a tortured sentence, but I cannot remember reading one."
- Jim Murray of the *Los Angeles Times*: "He was more than a sports writer. He was a writer."
- A.M. Rosenthal, executive editor of the *New York Times*: "I get depressed sometimes editing this paper. But whenever I get down, I say to myself, 'Wait a minute. I hired Red Smith.'"
- Ernest Hemingway in his novel *Across the River and into the Trees* described his main character in a hotel room in

Venice: "He was reading Red Smith, and he liked him very much."

The ultimate accolade was a Pulitzer Prize in 1976 for Distinguished Commentary.

Red Smith was a testimony to the contribution made by any one person who does a single thing well. He could appreciate the apple grower and the furniture maker and the plumber who knew his craft and practiced it with extraordinary care.

When one opened the newspaper to Red Smith's column, one expected and constantly got a polished nugget of English that reflected precisely many angles of the human condition that happened to be attached to sports. If one observed closely, the traces of a talented bleeder were evident.

What Is So Comforting as a Celebrity's Boo-Boo?

January 1982

Few things are dreaded more by most people than to pull a boner in public, as for example, the father of the bride treading on the train of his daughter's wedding gown thus causing a backward lurch just as the groom extends his arm.

On the other hand, hardly anything is as comforting as a genuine, public boo-boo by a well-known person. A great army of golfers felt true kinship to professional Gil Morgan last August when, in full view of North America, he shanked a shot at a ninety degree angle in the midst of a championship playoff. Ah, bliss! If Morgan can mangle a golf shot like that, we think, whereof do we poor hackers have to be ashamed?

One might dispute the Christian ethics of it all, but the reality is that when the Big Boys stumble, the lesser runners in the race are encouraged to go forth and do, even if they too catch their tootsies in the cracks of life's sidewalk.

I recall taking a tour of a theater that was the creation of the architectural genius Frank Lloyd Wright. When Mr. Wright designed a theater, the hoi polloi didn't serve only as an audience but also as a tour group. The great American architect was the ranking expert at combining beauty with function. If anybody knew how a building should be planned, it was good ol' Frank.

As I recollect, our tour group wound through the theater, emitting oohs and aahs at the appropriate features as indicated by our guide. Frank Lloyd Wright had thought of everything. We were dazzled by his graceful marriage of form to function.

Then we arrived at the dressing rooms, which were located directly behind and somewhat above the stage. Our guide limp-handed us inside one of the dressing rooms, all the while chattering about the whys of this or that Wright characteristic. The far side of the dressing room opened into a small bathroom. On the door to that bathroom, in large letters that conveyed the unmistakable notion that this was urgent business, was tacked a sign that read: *Don't flush this toilet during performance.*

God bless you, Frank Lloyd Wright.

Other notable boo-boos salvaged from my eroding memory:

- A year or two ago, *Time* magazine carried an advertisement, aimed at Oklahoma readers, which misspelled about every third name on a long list of Oklahoma towns and cities. A real boost for all editors.

- Once, I saw the rector of a seminary present to his seminarians a Bishop Treacy. The rector trumpeted a long list of accolades about Bishop Treacy—"A man who...A bishop that...," and then he completed the florid introduction with "I give you Bishop O'Connor." There was silence, and then a burst of laughter as the rector melted into a small puddle. We always liked that rector.

- Somewhat further back, Msgr. Don Kanaly served as master of ceremonies for an appearance in Oklahoma City of America's holy woman, Dorothy Day. The monsignor reviewed Miss Day's many accomplishments and the rare qualities of her person, both of which were difficult to exaggerate, then stated solemnly, "It is my pleasure to give you Mildred Stone." (No doubt, Miss Stone founder of St. Thomas More Book Store appreciated the Freudian-slip compliment.) Msgr. Kanaly accepted the chuckles with good humor and relieved the tensions of other ecclesiastical hosts for a spell.

If You Want to Become a Little Nutty Work in a High School for a Decade

April 1982

If you want to have nerves that vibrate like a tuning fork at the first syllable galloping out of a teenager's larynx, try working in a high school for a decade or so. Worse yet, become the principal. As Sam Levenson so aptly put it, "Insanity is hereditary; you can get it from your children."

Being as this is an issue of the *Sooner Catholic* with the theme of youth, this former youth, and onetime high school principal is sitting here at his desk and reflecting on a period of his life a couple of decades back when he crept daily into McGuinness High School hoping for the best and expecting the worst.

Some recollections:

On Frustration in Promoting the Intellectual Life (or Feelings after Hacking Persistently at the Jungle of Ignorance only to Have the Jungle Win)

The second prize in this category goes to a nameless social studies teacher staring blankly at a map of Europe drawn by a sophomore during an examination. The map revealed the Euphrates and Rhine rivers intersecting at right angles in the middle of France. No indication was given as to whether it was an underpass or an overpass that allowed this marvelous geographical concept to function.

First prize was an entry that reduced a teacher of freshman English to a heap of sobs and hysterical laughing. On a test, the teacher had requested Thelbert to change the following to the passive voice: "John shot the rabbit." Thelbert's written answer, done in a firm hand, which flowed with confidence, was, "The rabbit shot John."

On Heartbreak

Frankie was a loner. He had light-colored hair, front teeth that protruded, a harried look, and no friends. Naturally one day he disappeared—not only from school, but from home, city, state, and what have you. All interested parties consoled one another with the notion that the lost sheep soon would return to the fold.

Days went by. Frankie's locker was opened in a search for evidence. We discovered a broken heart. At first we were puzzled by notations inside the covers of Frankie's books. The notes stated that the books were presents from "Your friend, Harry." There were also warm, encouraging letters from "Your friend, Harry." Finally it dawned on us that all of the writing was Frankie's. In his loneliness he had invented a friend. The poor little guy.

When Frankie returned with trembling chin and embarrassment at what he had done, he was shocked at the warm enthusiasm and even tears with which he was welcomed. We had come to know who had been wronged.

On Courage

Here was this high school boy, terribly twisted in arms and legs by an atrocious disease, planted in the midst of a field of hyperkinetic, toe-tapping, lip-flapping, almost mindless teenagers. He was dependent on a wheelchair and someone to push it. To watch him eat lunch was a study in determination as the food traveled tortuously by way of a crippled arm to his mouth. And sometimes he wasn't given that opportunity, because he had been left forgotten in the last classroom during the heedless rush to the cafeteria.

It would have been so easy for Greg Burns to have stayed at home and to have wedded himself to a television set. But he was at school smiling and taking part. Gradually we began to see Greg clearly—that the most obvious thing about him was an overdeveloped heart. He gave lessons in courage every day. It was later that he gave lessons in art.

On the Inevitable Pleasant Surprise

Experienced parents and teachers come to this wisdom: When all is lost with young people, when a point has been reached at which the older person slumps in his or her chair and frankly admits "There is no hope for this rotten kid." Sometime later comes the inevitable pleasant surprise. Now I know there were Hitler and Stalin and the Los Angeles rapist etc., etc., but with most despaired-about teenagers, sooner or later comes the pleasant surprise.

Tim was a case, a character and a problem. One of my last vivid memories of Tim was a high school dance at which he, in a conflict over a girl and perhaps tipsy, locked a student's head under his arm and rammed it through a large plate glass window. Fortunately, no one was hurt seriously. Tim was told never to set foot on McGuinness property again under pain of arrest.

Not long ago, I was sitting in Chi-Chi's restaurant waiting to get a table. Tim walked in. The earth had spun through twenty years since the head through the window business. We shook hands. I asked him what he was doing. He said he was a lawyer doing legal aid work in the Bronx. Then he said something to the effect that "Some bad boys turn out okay." God bless him. The inevitable pleasant surprise.

The Great Rubber Gun Wars of the Summer of 1934

June 1982

In a nation gone bananas over firearms, it seems odd that one cannot buy a good rubber gun these days.

A what? A rubber gun, an invention of some unknown and poor but gifted American child of the 1930s.

I hadn't thought of the merits of the rubber-gun culture in years, until yesterday at Belle Isle Library when I spotted an elongated paperback book titled *The Great American Depression Book of Fun* by John O'Dell.

The Great American Depression Book of Fun was not published by the Humpty Dumpty Press, but rather by the distinguished company Harper & Row.

I was attracted by the cover illustration, which depicted six little boys in a rubber gun shootout in an old barn. I opened the book and learned that the first chapter's title is "Rubber Guns and Cowboys." Next, I discovered that the author is an Oklahoma native of my era, having been reared at Fort Gibson in the Roosevelt years.

The mere mention of rubber guns snapped loose a whole explosion of pleasant memories. I was hooked. I checked out the book. My left elbow is resting on it as I write this.

Now some folks, no doubt those without superior educations in the literary classics or lacking real comprehension of the science of physics, still may be asking, "What in the heck is a rubber gun?"

Well, a rubber gun was a homemade contraption of two pieces of wood fitted together to form the shape of a pistol. To the back of the handle was attached a clothespin. Rubber bands cut from old automobile inner tubes were clamped in the clothespin and stretched forward to encircle the end of the gun. In combat, the gunman pressed the clothespin to release the rubber band that, in turn, flew with deadly accuracy for all of ten to twelve feet.

More realistically, a rubber gun was a magic instrument that, combined with an ordinary imagination, allowed little boys hours of delight. Who cared if there wasn't much food in the house, your dad was out of work, and the temperature was hotter than Hades?

John O'Dell sets his narrative in the summer of 1934. I spent that same summer in short pants, no shirt, and bare feet, fighting rubber gun wars all through the forts and castles, the canyons and mountain ranges that can be seen on a clear day in the 1200 block of East 20th Street in Tulsa.

The bad guys and the good guys all came out of one batch of kids—real ornery hombres and swashbucklers—Hugh King, Edwin Hanna, Billy Garrett, the Pickards, Betty Hindman, Jane Garrett, and maybe Arnie Rubin, Mary Hindman, and my sister, Helen, to name a few of the gang.

Then late in the afternoon, Mr. Garrett might load a half dozen of us in his car and head for Riverside swimming pool. Riverside was filled with well water. The water reflected a sickly rusty iron color, but it was cold. And one little spot where the water entered the pool was fit for polar bears. We loved a quick, breathtaking plunge in and out of there.

One airless stifling night that summer, my father lugged our mattresses outside and simply threw them on the grass. We slept there in complete cool bliss lying on my back and counting the shooting stars. He wrapped in worries about ways and means to pay the family's bills.

By next summer, we were gone—the house a victim of the Great Depression. There were no rubber guns in the new neighborhood.

Sweat, Laughs, and Glory at the PGA Tournament

August 1982

What is it that would move tens of thousands of Adam and Eve's sons and daughters to plunk down $18 or more to spend a day tromping several miles through dust and high grass under a sun and humidity combination marvelously equipped to reduce human bodies into puddles worth 98¢ each (or whatever the going price is for our basic chemical composition)?

Golf!

More specifically the 1982 Professional Golfers Association's Tournament at Southern Hills in Tulsa this month.

It was great. None of us ever sweated so much in our lives, nor was ever a cohort so thoroughly fleeced at the hot dog and beer stalls. But it was great.

Allow me to explain myself with a couple of examples.

No other spectator sport has the degree of up-close involvement of the onlookers as tournament golf. I mean, man, you're right there, only a few feet away from a sun-flushed Jack Nicklaus as he swats a tee shot, or you hurry along stride for stride with a Mark Hayes as he walks toward a green straining to discover exactly how close that last four iron brought him to the hole. The crowd at each green becomes a kind of community. The packs following specific threesomes exhibit a tribal loyalty.

Professional tournament golf is also dead serious. One can note the pain of concentration tightening the lines of the players' faces and observe the golfers' meticulous care attendant to each swing of a club. And the silence of the grave is the spectators' gift to each player as he putts.

However, within this tight-lipped, familial affair some very funny, human things occur. I saw one of the unreported best the first day of the tournament.

Sitting beside the par three sixth green on a campstool was a well-groomed woman wearing the uniform dress of a female tournament official. Her task was to call in the scores for that hole as each of the threesomes completed the sixth.

Rex Caldwell struck his shot from the sixth tee. To his consternation the ball missed the green, bounced once and landed like a gift from heaven in the woman official's lap. She started to stand up. "No! No!" cried the marshals working the hole. She sat back.

Caldwell, a loose-limbed guy with a moustache and a reputation for independent thinking, strode onto the scene. "Now, honey," he said to the woman whose skirt had become a cotton trap, "you sit real still while I swing."

Then Caldwell laughed, deftly picked the ball from her lap and told her to move the campstool so that he could drop the ball at that spot according to the rules. The dropped ball disappeared into the high grass of the rough. The golfer bent to examine it. He straightened up and called for a rules official.

"I think the ball has landed in a hole made by one of the legs of the stool, and I should get another free drop," he said. Then followed the kind of scrupulous study ordinarily reserved to astronomers and biochemists. At last, the rules official told Caldwell to play it as it lies. The player's muttered retort, "I would rather have played it out of her lap."

He selected a wedge, took one, two, three short, crisp practice swings, addressed the ball, swung again, and watched with us as the ball skittered across the green and dropped into the cup for a birdie two.

A roar of whoops and cheers followed. Rex Caldwell turned to the gallery and raised both arms aloft in a victory V framing a face full of delight. He kissed Miss Score Reporter on the mouth and strode away in triumph to the seventh tee.

Most spectators at golf tournaments have played golf, and many have tried their luck recently. So the golf fan can appreciate the amazing skill of the tour professionals. When that artistry is combined with a go-for-broke spirit it is a combination worth savoring, which brings us to Tom Weiskopf at the fifth hole in the second round.

The fifth hole at Southern Hills is an extremely long—614 yards, par five, which begins on a hill by the clubhouse and takes a left turn toward the green that seems to be situated just short of the Los Angeles city limits.

The hole is so long that nobody even tries to reach the green in two swings, with very rare exceptions. I saw one of them.

Tom Weiskopf is both tall like a poplar and sturdy like an oak. He has a classical golf swing and the wonder is that he has not won more tournaments. He had played badly on Thursday, and he needed a good score on Friday to stay in the running.

I was sitting behind the fifth green watching the incoming players through binoculars when I picked up Weiskopf's group at the turn in the fairway. I had been stationed there an hour, and none of the great ones—Nicklaus, Floyd, Kite, etc.—had attempted to get to the green in two.

Weiskopf's partners' second shots landed some 100 yards short of the green. I saw Weiskopf reach into his golf bag and draw out a wood. He was going to try it.

The faraway, white-capped figure swung. I watched the ball soar and grow larger as it came straight at both me and the flag. It seemed as though the ball was aloft for thirty seconds, like a satellite that had escaped—the normal course of gravity. Then it fell about two yards short of history into the trap guarding the green. It was a noble effort.

Weiskopf blasted out of the sand and tapped in his putt for a birdie four.

The Old Order Changeth, but Only With Some Timely Assistance

September 1982

It had to happen sooner or later. The old order changeth. So, last Friday I observed the retirement ceremonies of my T. Raymond Higgins wristwatch and strapped a square, flat digital to my left arm.

It was no small item to consign the T. Raymond Higgins Bulova to the drawer of my nightstand. That old wristwatch had ticked off twenty-nine years of my life (10,585 days, 254,040 hours, and 15,242,400 seconds—for the statistically minded).

The Bulova dated to the football season of 1953, when T. Raymond Higgins discovered that the assistant pastor in his parish possessed no timepiece. Perhaps in an effort to get me to the church on time, the generous Mr. Higgins simply handed over the "self-winding, anti-magnetic, water-tight" Bulova. I have a vague memory of the presentation taking place on the north side of St. Francis of Assisi Church.

Whatever the details of its origin, the T. Raymond Higgins Bulova traveled along on my wrist when I celebrated Mass in a Roman catacomb and in St. Theresa's Church at Luther, when I counted the seconds to the end of another school day at McGuinness High School and when my mother went sweetly through death to God. And in the middle of the night, I read the illuminated dial of the Bulova to see how ill or well I fared in terms of sleep lost or still to come.

Finally the Bulova died of congestive spring failure, and I took myself to T.G.& Y., plunked down $23, and purchased a genuine Timex digital watch. The backside of the timepiece reads "assembled in Philippines," and the imitation leather strap bears the label "England." Apparently only my wrist was made in America in the new arrangement.

The personal import of this old-watch, new-watch business has to do with my wary and losing approach to modern life. For some time I have had the sense that modern living is leaving me behind, like a scene from a science fiction film in which an old meteor-pocked moon recedes rapid into the background as the modern hero's spacecraft rockets away to fresh adventures.

Leave me confess:

- I have never played a single computer game. I wouldn't know an Atari if one sat down to lunch with me today. My impression is that all computer games are built on the elemental human urge to destroy things, even blips on a screen.

- My ears have never been able to decipher more than one consecutive word of rock music lyrics. Frank Sinatra I can hear. Everybody else, from Chubby Checker onward, might as well have been howling in Chinese for all my enlightenment or provocation.

- I talk gently to computers but walk at a distance from them, even in my office. My theory relative to computers is summarized thusly: "Remember, you can never tame a wild animal." Photos of innocent children at school in the clutches of computers cause me chills and a nervous stomach.

- A modern hair dryer has never blasted my thinning strands with its dragon's breath. I remain a member of an endangered species Henry Bellmon is another who clandestinely carries and uses a pocket comb. Our mark of membership is hair plastered in perfect grooves like an aerial photo of a cornfield.

- Somehow the style of my clothes runs a decade or so behind the mainstream. Occasionally, I am so far arrears in the fashion world that I'm nearly caught from behind by a fad making a return appearance.
- For shame! For shame! I have never mastered the art of typing. I face the world of journalism without the twentieth century tools of the trade save for my trusty BIC pen and yellow legal pad.

So, the $23 Timex digital is a personal breakthrough of sorts—a testing of the cold modern waters with one gnarled middle-aged toe, so to speak.

Who knows, perhaps tomorrow I'll buy one of those thin gold chains to wear around my neck, and the day after that get myself a perm, and… Why is my guardian angel laughing?

Surprised at "No-Surprises" Inn

October 1982

This is a sad tale of a "no-surprises" Inn chockfull of unexpected happenings, of pretensions that didn't work, of culture shock, and of an irascible non-au courant middle-aged man muddling through.

The scene is a Holiday Inn in Warren, Pennsylvania, a small city built at the confluence of the Allegheny and Conewango rivers and on the edge of the beautiful Allegheny National Forest. My sister, Helen, and I checked in there one evening this past August.

We sat down in the Inn's dining room about 9:00 p.m. Lights were low; candlelight shone on pure white tablecloths; conversation in the room was muted, and the bill of fare was long and complicated. This certainly was not Oklahoma City's Big Beef Bar-B-Que. One had the unmistakable impression that the Warren Holiday Inn was putting on the dog.

I forget now what I ordered, but I recall that the salad was tasty, very good indeed. Suddenly the waitress set a round scoop of something in front of me. I peered through the gloom attempting to determine the essence of the dish.

"What is this?" I asked.

"Sherbet," said the waitress.

"I didn't order any sherbet."

At this point, my sister gently interjected, "It's to cleanse your palate."

"Cleanse my palate?"

"Yes."

"Oh."

Palate cleansing was obviously not high on my list of priorities. No, that's inaccurate. What was plain was that palate cleansing was outside my experience. Imagine that, a fifty-five-year-old man who had never been to the palate cleaners.

It was slightly humiliating to be revealed as a bumpkin with a virginal palate, but it was mostly irritating to be a victim of a backwoods restaurant's attempt to be high-hat. However, I dutifully consumed the sherbet, thus qualifying my taste buds for the next course.

About the time I spooned the last bit of Holiday Inn palate cleanser into my mouth, I noticed people beginning to slide back large room dividers. On the other side of the dividers were dozens of young people plus the makings of a rock band. The lights went up. The blue-jeaned aliens began to invade our space.

The swift shift from quiet candlelit supping, complete with palate cleansing, to the rock culture nearly stripped my psychic gears. Our table had been transported from dinner at Antoine's to Saturday Night Live.

Then somebody must have said something ugly to the band, because they began to play. All atoms within 100 yards of ground zero commence to vibrate. The floor vibrated, the plates vibrated, and, I'm sure, even my palate vibrated.

Like people with amputations, who momentarily continue to try and use the departed limbs, my sister and I went on speaking to one another. At least I was trying to talk and her lips were moving although no decipherable sounds were reaching my ears. Soon, we simply hunched over our food and stoked it away in personal silence while being buffeted by a storm of sound. It was really living.

On our way out, I made note of the local Holiday Inn softball team sprawled over nearby chairs, their table already covered by a forest of beer bottles. I was tempted to ask if they cleansed their palates between Budweisers.

Returning to my room, I learned that the air-conditioner had taken the night off, probably zapped by the electrical storm downstairs. Came the dawn and the telephones—all of them at the Inn—were out of commission.

I went to breakfast. No newspapers were available. Of an innocent waitress, I inquired, "Do I cleanse my palate after the cereal? Does the rock band play during the morning hours? Is the odor from the refinery always so strong when you have to sleep with your windows open? How long will it take to get out of here?"

He Who Drinks of the Nile Will Surely Drink Again

December 1982

We, gentlemen and gentlewomen of the Catholic press, were trying to appear nonchalant as we waited our turn to meet Egyptian President Hosni Mubarak in Oruba Palace.

A distinguished elderly general had been given the task of keeping us company. Realizing that we were Roman Catholics, but not understanding that our group's probably combined Latin vocabulary totaled twenty-five words or less, the general enunciated, in Latin, an Egyptian aphorism.

His words had scarcely been uttered when the general grasped the fact that the Latina lingua had made a nonstop run in and out of thirty-five pairs of American ears. He translated for us. "He who drinks of the Nile will surely drink again."

The general smiled. It was a nice way of saying, "We hope you come again." Our lips pulled back in grinning appreciation, but further down in our anatomies the mere mention of drinking of the Nile unleashed thirty-five green billiard balls, which rolled coldly around the walls of our tummies seeking a way out and not finding it.

We weren't exactly ill, but one had to keep in a perfect state of balance or that billiard ball began to roll—sometimes picking up speed as it climbed the walls of one's stomach like motorcycle riders inside those wooden bowls at the State Fair, and other times swooshing down the bobsled run of one's small intestines. You get the sensation. Egypt has a way of doing that to weak-willed westerners. It's included as part of the price of the tour.

In any event, during my recent seventy-two-hour adventure in Egypt, I had to walk carefully and turn slowly—no tilting, jumping, or hard laughing allowed—else the green billiard ball began to roll.

So, that's the situation with me as we approach the next two true tales of horror.

I had made a firm resolution not to ride a camel. Then we were told that the camel ride already had been purchased. Who am I to fritter away a freebie? Our guide sent us on our way with the firm advice, "Only $1 tip to the camel drivers!" Our mission was to ride a few hundred yards up to the base of the Great Pyramid of Cheops.

Quicker than I could make a rational decision to forget the whole thing, the beast rose from the sand and we undulated forth. My thought processes were of the contemplative order of those who daily ride the stately ships of the desert: "Oh my God, I am heartily sorry…where's the seat belt…forget the camera and hold on with both hands…look at those cowards on the bus…."

Oddly enough, I did not fall off. My camel did veer sharply once, but the driver (actually a walker leading with a rope) was obviously a devotee of Teddy Roosevelt: he spoke softly and carried a big stick, which he promptly applied with vigor to the dromedary's schnozzola.

At the end of the ride, before my feet touched the ground, the hand of the camel driver was in my face. A thumb rubbed against a forefinger and a middle finger in the international sign for "gimmee."

"Five," he said.

"One," I mumbled.

"Five!" he repeated.

I gave him the one and walked away convinced that more enmity toward the Holy Roman Church and the United States of America had been built on the banks of the Nile.

The guide said that if a person was afflicted with claustrophobia or heart problems, he should not attempt to enter the Great Pyramid of Cheops to see the king's burial chamber. What the guide didn't say was that only Green Berets or successful conquerors of Mount Everest were fit to make the trip.

How can I describe it? Imagine all the people at your favorite shopping mall squeezed together in a passage four feet wide by three feet high, going up hill, with two-lane traffic—one up, one down.

In the first segment of the duck walk, I wondered why the descenders were glistening with sweat. My body soon told me why. Climbing upward while squatting has that effect.

Finally, we arrived at the goal: the burial chamber itself. It had all the mystique of the boiler room at the Center for Christian Renewal—gray stone walls. On one was written the Arabic equivalent of "Joe Bob loves Debi." For this, 100,000 men had slaved twenty years to stack 1.5 million gigantic blocks. Old Cheops had a great sense of humor.

One thing to say in favor of the climb into the Great Pyramid: for the next twenty-four hours, my legs trembled so badly that I was barely aware of the green billiard ball rolling across the floor of my stomach, except when it dropped with a thud into side pocket.

CHAPTER 7

1983

Before Nicklaus Was, Snead Slammed

April 1983

Last week that American institution labeled Samuel Jackson Snead announced it was going out of business. No more pursuit of golfdom's silver grail. Nor more teeing it up on dewy mornings so fresh that the twosome in front might be Adam and Eve. No more squinting under that straw hat to judge whether it was 150 or 155 yards to the flag. No more mashing 1 irons so hard that calls were placed to the Society for the Prevention of Cruelty to Titleists. No more signing autographs for ten-year-old boys sent running to him by their granddads who themselves were a generation younger than the signer. And, thanks be to God, no more nervous perspiration over four-foot putts.

Before Jack Nicklaus was, Sam Snead slammed golf balls for a living. As far back as 1937, Sam had stuffed the US Open trophy 71/72nds into his pocket; but it fell into the creek on the last hole, and forty-six years later, the young man from West Virginia still hadn't placed that hunk of sterling silver on his mantel.

Sam Snead shot a 79 in the opening round of this year's Master's tournament during Easter Week, and he didn't bother to try a second day. He said he would just go on down the road. So at age seventy, the amazing athlete closed the book on his professional career.

If you've read this far, chances are that you either like golf or have heard of Sam Snead or recall that he's the guy who wears the porkpie straw hat. Let's get acquainted a mite better with the old Slammer.

William Howard Taft was president, Henry Ford was turning out Model Ts, and the Titanic was still settling on the bottom of the Atlantic when Sam Snead was born on May 27, 1912, in Hot Springs, Virginia. God blessed little Sam with uncommon rhythm in his feet and strength in his arms. And he grew to manhood in a place and time when one could become mighty shrewd just by whittlin' and observin'.

When the Depression squeezed till it hurt, Sam gave up the sports of hunting and fishing for the business of professional golf. From his first tournament try at the Hershey Open in the autumn of 1936 to his last on April 7, 1983, the man won eighty-four Professional Golfers Association Tour victories against an army of exquisitely skilled competitors. That is a record unlikely to fall in the foreseeable future. Only Nicklaus with sixty-nine victories is within hailing distance, but Nicklaus's own reluctance to play often and his advancing age are combining to put more and more distance between his triumphs—three wins in the past four years, one in the last two tour seasons. At thirty-three, Tom Watson has required twelve years to cut twenty-eight notches in the handle of his putter.

Although the Slammer never quite took the US Open (he did manage four second places in the event), he won three Master's titles, three PGA Championships, and one British Open.

Beyond the regular professional tour, young-old Sam has finished first in a barrelful of senior professional events—for example, six times in the PGA Seniors Championship.

After reaching his seventieth birthday, he averaged 72 strokes per 18 holes in 32 rounds on the 1982 professional seniors' tournament schedule.

He seemed to snicker at arthritis and to save his best sardonic stare for the presumption that stiffness is inevitable. In his upper sixties, he could stand in a doorway and kick the frame overhead, and he could pluck a golf ball out of the cup without bending his knees. There were rumors that mom and dad had mixed silly putty in his genes.

As a qualified sports nut, I have my own memories of Sam Snead. From a tarnished set of Sam Snead Championship Wilson irons in my golf bag; to a chance observation of him in the coffee shop of Milwaukee's Pfister Hotel some twenty-five years ago; to trudging in the gallery beside a cursing, profane Snead during a dreadful round in Chicago, I have a number of tenuous human connections to the eminent retiree.

My favorite recollection of Sam dates back to a time when he was a youngster of only sixty-one. I was on vacation by myself; and for want of something better to do, I stopped to watch one round of the Quad Cities Open, one of the least distinguished tournaments on the tour. Those pros who play at the Quad Cities are those who have chosen not to participate in something called the British Open. Lo and behold, in 1973 there was Sam Snead at the Quad Cities. He must have heard that the pigeons were plentiful for the hunting on the banks of the Mississippi.

I followed Sam that day as he played. Unlike most tournaments in which he took part, there were only eight or ten of us who walked with him. Hence it was a rare opportunity to study at close range a marvelous golfing antiquity and to be touched by his celebrity.

That afternoon we formed an ad hoc community, a kind of moveable forum with Sam as the centerpiece and main speaker. Occasionally he would break off the conversation to knock the bejabbers out of the ball. We talked about politics and the economy and fishing and Sam's habit of burying his money in tin cans in the backyard. Sam even talked to his golf ball as he addressed it, "Come on, honey, go straight down the fairway."

On that lovely sunny day in Coal Valley, Illinois, we were elated to converse with a legend, and the Legend was satisfied to have at least a few pay attention to his presence. It was grand.

Pepper Looked Young in Comparison

May 1983

There is a man who calls often to an Oklahoma City radio talk show with this mode of action: "Hey! You know what?" he yells. Then follows a kind of philosophical proposition that, if not an absurdity, at least runs counter to conventional wisdom. An example: "Billy Sims doesn't know how to run with a football." This is followed by: "You know what I mean?"

If the caller were to pick up his telephone this week, he might say: "Hey! You know what? David Monahan is older than Abraham Lincoln. You know what I mean?"

Holy cow! Older than Lincoln! What's that guy talking about? Sorry to say, good reader, the caller would be almost correct now; and as of next Wednesday, as true as mortals can be. Here are the melancholy facts. The great Civil War president, who was born on February 12, 1809, and died on April 15, 1865, lived to be fifty-six years and sixty-five days old. God willing, your humble columnist will be fifty-six years and sixty-six days old on May 11. Oh, my goodness. Older than the man the nation called Father Abraham.

I am reminded that growing older is America's most popular but least favorite sport. Everybody participates, painfully.

Some suggestions of gray have caught me off guard recently:

A month or two ago, I spent a night at Fountainhead Lodge. The designer of yore, no doubt a youth cult member, had loaded the dressing and bathroom area with multiple mirrors.

For me it was a chamber of horrors. Every slack muscle, every line grooved by weariness and anxiety, every ounce of flab, every gleaming square millimeter of deforested scalp, and every battle lost to the twin tugs of time and gravity were on exhibition. If I turned just the right way, the images were repeated like the long gray line at West Point—all with bald spots. Claude Pepper looks like John Travolta in comparison.

This week I sat myself down at a Denny's restaurant. The waitress handed me a menu. The first item my eyes fastened on read: "Senior Citizens' Specials. Available for persons 55 years and older."

I don't recall what the specials were—probably milk toast and Sanka or a prunes and all-bran salad. But I do remember halfway expecting the hostess to offer to assist me to my car.

A short time ago, I sallied forth to play golf for the first time in 1983. For three days in a row, I pounded golf balls with ineffective enthusiasm.

The incontrovertible fact is that I have a shorter walk each year from the tee to the spot where my drives stop. Mind you, I'm not hitting them straighter; consistently, just fewer yards.

Even my golf clubs are older. This year my entire collection of clubs is observing its silver anniversary in my service—and they were second hand when I bought them at Lake Hefner.

All of this somehow reminds me of a particular visit to my grandmother Monahan. She was about ninety then, and a broken hip had imprisoned her in a hospital room for some time. But Grandma's mind and spunk were still intact. Occasionally she would try to walk and almost succeed, unmended hip and all.

On this day, Grandma perched on a well-padded chair next to her bed. She leaned toward me, and, in a tone indicating that this was a matter of confidence, said, "I'm getting old, David." It was a revelation. Not about her age, but on her whole approach to life.

So here I am, a quarter of a century away from the time my grandmother felt she might be "getting old," bellyaching about too many years' wear on my bod.

Yes, it's time to brace up and to begin to think young again. Still, older than Abraham Lincoln... You know what I mean?

How Could Joe Survive Cosmic Punch?

July 1983

August 1982, Arlington National Cemetery. I was making my way down the slope from the Tomb of the Unknown Soldiers when I spotted a name on a grave marker I hadn't expected to see: Joe Louis.

Somehow it moved me to come upon Joe's grave. Here in the midst of the Kennedy brothers and John Foster Dulles and James Forrestal and the Unknowns and scores of Congressional Medal of Honor recipients and umpteen generals and admirals and more than 183,000 other men and women who had served in the nation's armed forces was a sharecropper's son and a prizefighter, the Brown Bomber, Joe Louis. He had been buried there only because of the direct order of President Ronald Reagan.

Why honor Joe Louis? He was an uneducated man who had gone through money like a chainsaw through soft pine. He never paid a monumental income tax bill due the Internal Revenue Service. He became addicted to cocaine for a period in his later life. He was married three times.

Nevertheless, Joe Louis was a special man—quietly generous, humble, uncomplaining. When Joe died in 1981, Red Smith wrote: "Dignity was always a word that applied to him. Dignity and candor."

Beyond that he carried awesome lightning and thunder in his fists—at the top of the heavyweight hill for twelve years, twenty-five title defenses, and retirement as an undefeated champion.

Beyond that he was a kind of double symbol: to blacks a flicker of hope in the gloom of mean segregation; to all Americans in the miserable 1930s a sign that this nation was still home to the best in the world.

My memories of Joe Louis are these:

At age eight or nine, I was hauled by my father into the smoke-clouded chamber of Tulsa's Coliseum to witness this wonder man from Detroit. Joe was not champion yet, but the wave of his celebrity as a puncher had swept at least as far as Tulsa.

It was an exhibition bout. Men chewed on their cigars, plunged grasping hands into popcorn boxes, and waited for the slaughter to commence. That night Joe fought three men and dispatched each one in the first round.

I recall my impression that Joe, standing quietly in his corner, appeared very compact with heavily muscled shoulders and upper arms. I was a little disappointed. My expectation was that he should have been larger to fit the image that had run before him.

When the bell rang to start each round, Joe moved straight across the ring to his opponent. There was an explosion of crisp blows and the opponent, most probably mentally prepared for the fall, crashed to the floor. Joe walked back to his corner while the carcass was removed and the next victim propped into place opposite.

On June 22, 1938, Joe Louis was matched against Max Schmeling at Yankee Stadium. Though Joe had won the heavyweight championship a year earlier, Schmeling had knocked out Louis two years before this 1938 fight. Beside the drama of two great fighters clashing, there were the added incendiary factors of Schmeling, a German national, representing a system that acclaimed Aryan superiority over "inferior" races, such as black, and of a substantial body of American bigots who relished the thought of a white man, any white man, knocking Louis's block off.

I attended this fight too with my father, but via radio in a hotel lobby in Pampa, Texas. Even in Pampa feelings were running high. People leaned forward, turning their good ears this way or that, to pick up the voice from New York.

We didn't listen long. In a total of 124 seconds the Brown Bomber decimated Schmeling—three knockdowns and out! Joe Louis really became champion that warm night, including a solid two votes from Pampa by a traveling salesman and his son.

Finally, I remember the ballyhoo of the challenge by Lou Nova for Joe's boxing crown. The promoters described Nova's development of utterly fearsome new weapons in boxing—the Dynamic Stance and the Cosmic Punch. (It seems that the mystic secrets of the Dynamic Stance and Cosmic Punch had been pirated from the Orient.) Teenage boys in Oklahoma cringed at the thought of Joe Louis having to face those invincible instruments of destruction.

A reporter asked the champ how he planned to deal with the Dynamic Stance and the Cosmic Punch. How could he survive? What in the world would he do? Said Joe: "I think I'll try a left hook."

After proper demonstrations of the Dynamic Stance (pretty) and the Cosmic Punch (powerless), the old-fashioned hook whistled out of left field and collided with Mr. Nova's skull in the sixth round, and a kid in Tulsa learned a bit about interpretation of the English language as spoken by fight promoters.

Joe the Hermit Put Teddy Roosevelt in His Place

October 1983

So you think you have strange neighbors. The other day I was sitting in the farm home of Doyle and Mary Burrows and children way out in the rolling prairie of Roger Mills County.

In the course of guzzling tall glasses of fresh raw milk and chomping Mary's home-baked cookies, the conversation turned to a character who lived in the neighborhood of the Burrows' farm some years ago. His name was Joe Mulbacher (spelling open to correction), but those thereabouts accurately labeled him Joe the Hermit.

The talk turned loose a train of memories for me. As a teenager, I had been in the area one Sunday; and after Mass at Cheyenne, I was taken to visit Joe the Hermit. My escorts were Father Cecil Finn, who cared for the mission from Elk City, and Miss Minnie Slief, who was to the Catholics in the vicinity what Peter was to the universal church—a rock upon which etc., etc.

To form a decent picture as background for this tale, let me tell you just a bit about Roger Mills' geography. The county's border is the same as the state's. There are about five citizens for each of the county's 1,140 square miles. Altogether the county's population is the second smallest of Oklahoma's seventy-seven counties. Cheyenne, the county seat, is home to less than 1,000 hardy folks. Big sky. An ocean of hilly harsh land. Great hunks of silence. An environment that pressures people more than the ordinary to become noble or mean or peculiar (or perhaps a bit of all three).

Forty years ago we rolled out to Joe's hilltop place, west of Cheyenne. From there one could look down into the valley of the Washita River at the exact site where in 1868 Col. George Armstrong Custer's troops massacred the men, women, and children in Black Kettle's camp, including the venerable peacemaking chief himself.

We came first to a perimeter of barbed wire, mostly come apart, which Joe the Hermit had used to protect himself against an invading German Army—in World War I! It seems Joe, who was a native of Eastern Europe, carried a lifelong fear of the German military. (The truth is that if Germany had won World War I, the German occupation would not yet have reached Joe's spot in Roger Mills.)

On the crest of the hill was the hermit's dugout and the famous man himself.

I can't recall Joe's appearance with the exception that he was generally wild looking, complete with beard, I think. He wore heavy boots but said that he preferred to walk barefoot. However the "Rooshian" thistles had put at least a temporary stop to the shoeless act, he said.

But if the image of the man has gone foggy, his home and its trappings remain clear. The dugout was more of a concrete bunker than anything else—all constructed by Joe. In the dugout was a concrete stove, and on the roof was a concrete bench; and here and there were concrete statues (something of a scandal in those days because they depicted nudes—male and female—in what doll manufactures now term an "anatomically complete" condition), and even his water buckets were lined with cement.

As I write this, I recall that one of the statues, according to the hermit, was of Teddy Roosevelt. Apparently I was too young to be startled by the sight of the former president standing there au naturel on the brim of this Roger Mills hill.

Joe's bed was a piece of canvas hanging from the corners by four ropes fastened to the ceiling of the dugout. On the canvas was an assortment of blankets, which seemed to me to have been three-feet thick. The hermit allowed that from time to time he would crawl in there and stay for a day or two.

Miss Minnie told us that Joe would make rare appearances in Cheyenne to buy supplies. She also said that good ol' boys from town would make less rare forays to Joe's place seeking a kind of ultimate hideaway for their card games and perhaps a wee bit of gambling. We also learned that Joe was a victim of America's insatiable hunger to celebrate the quirky, once being hauled to New York City to appear on the "We the People" radio program.

Doyle Burrows stated that despite the hermit's reputation for being on the wifty side, Joe was the first person in the area to terrace his fields in order to hold moisture and prevent erosion, and he built a kind of crude underground system of tunnels and pens to allow care of his animals without exposure to bad weather.

Joe the Hermit is long gone from his hill—gone we hope to meet God and to shake hands all around with the likes of Custer and Black Kettle and departed Friday night card players and, maybe, even old Kaiser Wilhelm.

The stuff he built is so tough that it's still up there amidst the jackrabbits and the tumbleweeds, with the exception that some puritanical iconoclasts seem to have lopped off offending parts of the statuary. If some cold night Teddy the Roughrider takes it upon himself to come roaring down that hill screaming "Charge!," he'll do it as a eunuch. That's progress for you.

Wasn't I Fred Astaire Dancing Up the Staircase to God?

November 1983

My first involvement in the business of prayer turned me into a thief.

It happened this way. About the age of five, having been duly instructed by my good mother in the Our Father and the Hail Mary and the Sign of the Cross and thus impressed with the importance of prayer, I entered one weekday into the darkened mystery of our parish church in Tulsa.

Lo and behold, I discovered the pews and the racks attached to them to be a treasure trove of prayer books and rosaries. *This was the very stuff of which grownups' prayer was made*, I thought. Immediately I applied the well-known moral principle of "Finders keepers, losers weepers." Arms loaded and pockets bulging, I managed to stagger the several blocks to our house.

The astonishment on my mother's face when I proudly displayed the holy booty signaled to my wee psyche that something was amiss: the gold in my hands had turned into Limburger. There were rapid movements of Buster Brown-shod feet back to the church. Restitution of prayer aids was made in full. (To this day only God knows how many pious old ladies were driven half-batty searching for their very own prayer books always before left safely in the exact same spot in the same pew.)

The next scene of action is St. Louis Preparatory Seminary. Here prayer was a top item superseded only by emphases on obeying the rules, keeping a low profile, and learning to cope with the sophisticated boys from the big city (some of whom had traveled as far as the western boundary of St. Louis County).

At first the encouragements and opportunities to pray more and better bounced off me like bee bees off a battleship. However, gradually my resistance was eroded, and the dimmest of lights glimmered in my brain allowing me to make out the message: prayer may be right and fitting for a seminarian.

Then I read this book about St. Philip Neri. It described the Roman holy man's ecstatic moments in prayer and how his rib cage was battered out of shape by his wildly pounding heart during those trips to the high country of prayer and how St. Philip had to work hard to be distracted from prayer so that he could get on with daily work.

I sopped it up like an Oklahoma wheat field greeting rain after a long drought. My Irish imagination helped. Wasn't my heart burning with fervor at Holy Communion time? Wasn't I clicking through the stages of prayer with the ease of Fred Astaire dancing silkily up a wide white staircase?

The weeks rolled by and the "ecstasies" faded, and I found no trouble at all in achieving distractions, and the seminary authorities did not roll in an X-ray machine to measure any undue battering of my rib cage.

A few years later someone handed me a Roman breviary and with scant sentimentality said, in effect, say it, pray it, read it, or chant it, but do it daily for the Church until death do you part from it. The priest's prayer book, by informal tradition, is called "wife."

So, my wife and I started, hand in volume, up the twisting road of priestly existence. We had communications problems. I spoke English. She knew only Latin. We sought counseling in the confessional to resolve our conflicts. The word came back: "Be faithful to your commitments and say five Our Fathers and five Hail Marys for your penance."

After a decade or more of so-so dialogue with my wife—some breathtaking moments of high flying but much more time spent cruising on automatic pilot—help came from an unexpected source, the Holy Spirit.

Only the Spirit could bring together a couple of thousand Latin-oriented hierarchical codgers in Rome and convince them to let the boys back home pray the breviary in their own languages. He did. And we do.

The wife and I have gotten along better ever since, not quite in absolute sync but at least we understand each other now. On a scale of ten, my prayer life has zoomed from a drab two to the sparkling heights somewhere between three and four. I may not be a Himalaya of prayer but perhaps I'm hovering at the Mount Scott elevation. Praise God for the vernacular.

Finally, twenty-five years ago this month, I was privileged to listen to a perfect prayer. It was uttered in a northeast corner, fifth-floor room of St. John's Hospital in Tulsa. A slight woman, who had lived through a lot of pain and practiced a library of prayers, was dying. The feeble patient was completely rational. She spent several minutes slightly fibbing about the goodness of her daughter and her son. Then a rush of agony hit her, and she cried out, "Jesus, help me!" Not long afterward, having been embraced by Him in Communion, she was healed by Him forever.

Yep, that was the same woman who sent her acquisitive son scurrying posthaste back to church with his load of purloined prayer books. Now she had given her own ultimate short course in prayer to her children.

Finally, finally, life and prayer go on. Life bears little resemblance to the cigarette and beer ads, and that book on St. Philip Neri won't catapult one into a life of union with God. (Although the next physical I get, maybe I should ask the lab technician to check one last time for a bent rib cage.) But life without prayer would be odd indeed, filled with gray grotesquerie and really unfit for human habitation.

CHAPTER 8

1984

Brother Cold Comes Slip-Sliding through the Cracks

January 1984

Cold. That is the topic of this here essay. Cold as in Alaska. Cold as in shivers. Cold as in icy feet in bed.

This is being written during the Great-End-of-1983-Freeze-Up. Moments ago I donned my nightly in-the-house-freeze-up footwear: one pair of all wool sox inside of a pair of those booty things (knit sox on top and "leather-like" vinyl on the bottom, made in Taiwan), and all that inside my sturdy black galoshes. Not fashionable but comfortable. Parisian couturiers might dub it the "Battle of Stalingrad" look.

The chill wrapped around my humble dwelling tonight has that quality that sportswriters fasten on certain baseball pitchers—sneaky fast. I'm sitting here theoretically warm, thermostat set on seventy, the heating unit wheezing its darnedest. Yet Brother Cold comes slip-sliding through the cracks around the doors and gliding quietly through the window connections to work his way through the fibers of my sweater into my old skin. Cold.

This evening, however, I have prepared a new defense. I have decided to fight cold with cold. I am going to run through the video of my mind scenes of coldness past times so frigid that the present uncomfortableness will seem to me like Harmon County in July.

June 1969. Clare Castle, County Clare, Ireland. I am registered at the Castle Guest House, which is described in an Arthur

Frommer travel guide as probably "the most unusual guest house in Ireland."

My room is a box within a box within a box. Mine is one of twenty bedrooms carved out of what was formerly a British barracks. The barracks is in turn surrounded by a decaying 900-year-old Norman castle. Yards outside the castle walls flow the dark waters of the River Fergus.

Tonight my bedroom is on the top floor of "the most unusual guest house." The room has king-sized dimensions, of a big king. It is drab, dark, and dusty—something like the nonoperative loft in an inelegant warehouse. And there is no heat.

I climb into bed. The blankets above me form a covering some eighteen inches thick, but it's no use. My feet are cold. My nose is cold. Hypothermia is closing in for the kill.

Psychologically I am being assaulted by water gurgling through pipes in my room. The gurgling is not the sound of a brook bubbling but of ice water gurgling. It's like living in the coils of a refrigeration unit. The gurgle is not constant but often and irregular so that one begins to tense for the next gurgle passing overhead. Where the gelid gurgle is coming from and going to I'm not aware but imagine that it may be caused by the ghost of Michael Collins applying the cold water treatment to a person of Irish descent who has dared to stay one night in a British barracks.

November 1975, the south end zone at Owen Field, Norman. Father Tom McSherry and I are seated on the bare boards of the old bleacher seats. The temperature is well below freezing. We are watching Oklahoma University do battle with Oklahoma State through the pain of northern gusts intent on dropping the wind chill to degrees heretofore created only in a laboratory.

At halftime we decide to seek refuge behind the south stadium wall. I know I'm walking because I can see my feet moving; but feeling has retreated upward to the level of my Adam's apple, and frost is forming in my throat. I would take off a glove to eat popcorn, but I hate to look at gangrenous flesh. We agree that it's a honey of a game. What's the score?

Winter of 1978 is the kind they will fondly remember in Aspen and Vail. In Oklahoma it bids fair to be only painfully recalled, and the recollections will be of cold and snow, and cold and ice, and cold.

I choose this time to move to Jones in eastern Oklahoma County where for a number of years I have cared for St. Robert's Church. My residence is a small one-bedroom frame house. I am informed that it has been a farm house around which more modern homes have been built. Ironically the house is situated on Hawaii Street.

To say that the house on Hawaii Street is not quite airtight is a gross under-exaggeration. Combine that fact with the heating system—one small open stove for living room, kitchen-dining room and bedroom—and one begins to get the ache of it all.

When bedtime comes for this middle-aged bachelor, I really dress for the occasion: thermal long johns top and bottom under flannel pajamas, two pair of all wool sox, gloves, and stocking cap.

The open fire is turned off. I climb into a sleeping bag on my bed. Above it are heaped a mighty stack of all available blankets. It's kind of warm in here, but you can't turn over. I imagine I'm a prehistoric mammal being preserved face up in a glacier. For amusement I blow steam from my mouth, but sometimes that doesn't work when the blankets are pulled over my head.

Dawn will find a non-Superman moving faster than the speed of light as he dresses.

Now, that feels better. Or does it? The cold remains, the one ugly, blue, physical reality of this evening. I struggle to imagine how Norman Vincent Peale would deal with this situation. I have it. I thank God I'm not an Eskimo.

Something That's Going around May Be around the Next Corner

January 1984

When a fourteenth century serf was being hauled feet first out of his hut in the midst of the Black Death, his next door neighbor probably said, "It must be something that's going around."

Think of other instances. When the Abraham Lincoln's Grandpa Abraham was a successful target for an Indian bow-and-arrow artist, do you suppose Grandma cried out, "It must be something that's going around." Or when the smoke had cleared in Chicago after the St. Valentine's Day massacre, was it a curious passerby who peeked into the garage and whispered, "Geez, it must be something that's going around." Or when the Oklahoma football team was poisoned en masse in Chicago the night before the Northwestern game a decade or two ago, was it not a teary-eyed gambler with a bundle bet on OU's opponent who choked, "It must be something that's going around."

So it's completely in keeping with a long tradition that only yesterday in the *Sooner Catholic*'s office, Joan O'Neill—cough, cough, cough—was looking at me through watery eyes and saying, "It must be something that's going around." And I replied—acho-o-o! aaacho-o-o-o! Sniff, sniff—"Yeah, it must be something that's going around."

(At this point, dear reader, you would be well advised to hold this column at arms length, because in the composition of it considerable something-going-around effluvia from the aaach-o-o-os came to rest on the old yellow writing pad.)

There is no doubt that this is the something-that's-going-around season. Half of the living one meets in hallways and on the streets is sneezing, hacking, popping lozenges, blowing noses, gobbling aspirin or grimly slouching along in a something-that's-going-around funk.

When something that's going around entwines you in its feverish clutches, it's not a heck of a lot of fun. Existence seems to be colored in a smogish gray. Things don't taste right, if you can stir up the embers of appetite enough to chew and swallow. Pulsing headaches motivate you to snap at Dan Rather for saying "Good evening" and to make threatening gestures at Johnny Carson for smiling too much.

Your head knows, kind of, that a day will dawn soon when the something-that's-going-around will have skedaddled, but a more elemental part of you feels as though you will never be well again. This latter sense is especially keen when you have those periodic sensations of a live Maine lobster crawling around inside your tummy and occasionally pinching the abdominal walls out of plain orneriness. Then there are those mystery twinges in the small of your back that makes you wonder if John Riggins somehow stomped across your prone form while you were sleeping last night.

Treatments to alleviate something that's going around vary. One good woman, who works in an office near ours, swears by the following medicinal formula: Pour eight ounces of raisins into a wide mouthed jar. Add one pint of gin. Fasten lid to jar, and shake vigorously. Unfasten lid. Pour contents through a sieve into a large glass. Sit down. Grab glass and chugalug medicinal contents. (If you are Irish, yell "To hell with the queen!" after downing the medicine. If your name is Kennedy, yell "To hell with the queen!" and throw the glass into the fireplace. If you are of another ethnic descent and/or name, simply yell.) The kind woman down the hall guarantees that this treatment will make you feel decidedly different.

More conservative types visit doctors' offices, where, in crowded waiting rooms, you may exchange with the kind gentleman sitting next to you Type B of something-that's-going-around for Asiatic something-that's-going-around.

If treatment can bring relief, prevention can eliminate the whole something-that's-going-around mess. Two qualities of mind help in prevention—prudence and sheer terror of being blindsided by something that's going around.

Catholic churches are sometimes the scenes of prevention in action. One recalls the proper professor of literature in the state who was the lone Sunday inhabitant of the church balcony so that you-know-what couldn't get around to her.

And, of course, there are those who perform delicate side steps around communion cups.

(One can only speculate how a modern prevention oriented Catholic would react after presenting a newborn for baptism to the late Father Edward Van Waesberghe. Father Edward routinely collected the salt to be placed on the infant's tongue by scraping a little off the cattle salt block he used as a doorstop in the sacristy.)

But if the doggone something that's going around already has gotten around to you this winter and nothing that doctor or witch doctor or gin merchant has manufactured can seem to make it let go, then what are you going to do?

Have the right attitude, of course.

A) Practice a stiff upper lip and all that.
B) Focus on the old adage that there's nothing more pleasant than being a little sick, unless you're too ill to focus.
C) Reflect on the community of human sufferers, about five billion of us, to which you are now joined as a full-fledged brother or sister.

D) Let your mind play with Sophocles' thought "Wisdom comes through suffering."

E) Or take a long look at that cheap crucifix on your bedroom wall. There's a fellow that really got pinned by something going around. The good word is that He parlayed it into Something Super Special That's Still Going Around. His Something even makes sense of that stinky little something going around these winter days.

Particles of Americana on Night Flight to San Diego

February 1984

The front range of mountains was off to our left. The sun, dropping behind the jagged outline of those crags, shot daggers of light into our cabin. It was then that I struck up a conversation with Cleo Toran.

Cleo and I had been sitting next to each other for an hour; but aside from an initial nod, we had not spoken. We were aboard Frontier Airlines' Flight 515 to Denver from Oklahoma City on January 24.

He was black, kind of bug-eyed, short, middle-aged, and sported a blue, knitted cap.

Cleo said that he was reared in Van Buren, Arkansas, not a particularly encouraging environment for a black child in the 1930s. It was not surprising to learn that he had vacated the Land of Opportunity upon reaching manhood. Destination: Chicago.

In Chi Town, he became a tailor. Gradually he developed his own tailoring company, which specialized in alterations for department stores. His business required lots of cleaning, and this need evolved into his own cleaning company. He described how he learned to cut overhead by taking courses in plumbing and boiler repair.

For Cleo it was three decades of capitalistic expansion. But when his blood pressure expanded to 200 over 100, he quit and went home to Van Buren.

The end was only the beginning for Cleo. He returned to his original love affair with the trumpet. (Here he interrupted his story to point to an oblong case housing his instrument under the seat in front of him.)

He was now a professional jazz musician, Cleo said. He plays with some of the best in America. This evening he was on his way to Portland.

Cleo obviously wanted to tell his story. Listening for fifteen minutes gave me a whole new measure of this little man next to me.

At 6:00 p.m., Frontier's Flight 697 for San Diego lifted off Colorado pavement, did a left turn, and headed west. Looking down from our mechanized magic carpet, I could see that Denver's downtown was laid out cattywampus to the rest of the city (or more probably vice versa). Bright amber lights defined the major streets and dimmer blue ones were spread between—fudge cake gridded in caramel and sprinkled with mint candies. American cities do sparkle at night when seen from the angels' angle of vision.

My body occupied Seat 13A. One empty seat away was a tall man in two parts of a three-piece suit, his jacket being stored above. He wore horn-rimmed glasses and held a *Sports Illustrated* in scoop shovel hands remindful to me of western Oklahoma wheat farmers' grippers. Altogether my seatmate was of the Clark Kent cut—mildly disguised strength wafting pleasantly of the natural virtues.

When supper was served, he set his gift bottle of wine to one side then tried to give it away to me, to the greenish, pale man in the next seat ahead, and finally found a taker in the stewardess.

I think it was over the food that we began to talk about the Super Bowl and drifted from that into the great common topic: weather. It was only a few tales of snow and ice until the subject was him.

Sure enough those banana-like fingers grew out of the soil, a potato farm in southern Idaho. He explained to me how the production of potatoes had been increased markedly through a better scientific understanding of the beginnings of the plant. He said he lived now in Salt Lake City where he worked as a certified public accountant.

The gentleman in 13C inquired what I did for a living. I said that I was a Catholic priest on my way to Southern California for a week's vacation. My priestly identification completed the thawing process between us, but not in the way you might think.

His name was Ray Westergard, he said. He was a Mormon and had recently served a stint as a Mormon bishop in his home district around Bountiful, Utah. As a younger man, he had spent more than two years in Switzerland as a missionary.

I asked about the Mormons' self-operated welfare system. Ray said that as bishop, he was responsible for meeting the welfare needs of all in his district, mostly Mormons but also a number of "nonmembers."

Ray and I were still chatting when our 737 made its final approach to Lindbergh Field. We watched the city's gleaming buildings glide by our window at eye level on the port side then quickly the light was reflected off the dark waters of San Diego Harbor. A woman could be heard saying, "It's so beautiful."

Cleo Toran and Denver. Night flight to San Diego and Ray Westergard. Particles of the better half of the American experience: spunk, achievement against the odds, pristine strength, religious freedom, goodness, and beauty. God had provided a nifty send-off to my midwinter R and R.

In Era of Affirmation, Bitter Sips of the Waters of Contempt

March 1984

Among people of goodwill affirmation is in. Folks are more sensitive to the need of shoring up one another, of reassuring that one's ship is not sinking.

For priests affirmation often comes in small packages of "Good sermon, Father," or "We appreciate what you do for us," or "Thanks for being understanding."

Believe me, those affirmative statements are important. In an age of affirmation there remains a lot of determined denunciation. The old wrecking ball of heedless words is swung frequently at the stone-facade psyches of priests.

Some personal examples of non-affirmative actions:

As a newly ordained, I was assigned to Oklahoma City's St. Francis of Assisi Church. Life there had its ups and downs for me much the same as for an assistant pastor anywhere in these United States. I put genuine effort into preparing my sermons. They were short and, I hoped, to some point. Once in a while a parishioner would make a positive comment on a sermon. It made my week. I began to gain confidence and to see myself as competent in the pulpit.

There was an old, apparently foreign-born parishioner at St. Francis. Let's call him Jack. Jack was not known for taking circuitous routes in his conversation. His speech was yea or nay according to the Gospel prescription.

One day I met Jack on the steps of the church. I felt good and tried to make some light conversation with him. He greeted my efforts with all the joviality of a Gromyko.

Then Jack said, "Fader, I have gift for you." *What an unexpected pleasant surprise*, I thought. He offered me a sack. "Thank you very much," I said. Reaching in the sack, I pulled out a book. The title was *How to Preach a Sermon*. Score one for fallen egos.

Somewhat later in my career, God saw to it that I was at McGuinness High School and Bishop Reed named me principal. High school principals, with a yen for survival, cannot stroll around laughing and joking all the day long.

As in athletics a game face was needed—corners of lips drawn down, the most level gaze one could manage, a frown half-formed in the muscles above the eyes. Underneath this exterior ran streams of giggles struggling to surface (as when a mischievous imp played an over-serious teenage ballerina's accompanying record music at 45 rpms instead of the appropriate 33-1/3 during the school's talent show) and of dark fears that someday all 650 students would decide in unison to trample me to death.

I thought I was playing the General Patton role fairly well, until I chanced upon the breezy Mrs. Zip (names have been changed for protection of my health and bank account). We had been acquaintances for some time, and she had children enrolled at McGuinness. Mrs. Z informed me that a friend of hers, Tulip Landfill—also a patron of our high school, wanted to speak to me about a problem with her children's education but was frightened of me.

As I was forming a message that Mrs. Zip might transmit to the trembling Tulip, namely that I wasn't as tough as I might appear, I heard Mrs. Z's voice ring out, "Can you imagine that? She's afraid of you! Ha! Ha! Ha!"

Thus came confirmation in weakness.

On another occasion I was assisting at Christ the King Church during Holy Week. For whatever reasons—foremost of which must have been the failure of someone to scout my larynx—I was designated by local authority to sing the "Exultet," the joy-filled paschal proclamation of the church, at the Easter Vigil.

I pled for a reprieve but was rebuffed with the world's most benign pastoral smile. I appealed my case to the church's music director, a really fine musician and composer by the name of Hal Tomkins. He assured me that he already had heard the "Exultet" mutilated beyond recognition and there was no way I could match that level of vocal ineptitude.

Came the moment of truth. Easter candle lit. A fog of incense smoke floating. I suck in a mighty reservoir of the stuff from which notes are formed and begin. The first three words ("Rejoice, heavenly powers!") weren't bad, and only seven pages of notes to go.

The remainder of my performance was like a train running along side a meandering stream. My voice was the train, and the notes were the curvy creek. At times we were within hailing distance of one another; sometimes we even crossed paths; never were we together. As cold panic choked my persona, the train pulled all stops for a mad dash to the finish—damn the notes, full speed ahead. All the while I was halfway listening for the splintering of glass as Tomkins hurled his body through the nearest window.

Afterward I asked Hal Tompkins if he had ever heard an "Exultet" sung so badly. He had not recovered enough to be capable of forming the word *no*. Humiliation can be humbling.

So life goes in the vineyard of the Lord. Not just for me. All priests, as well as other mortals, occasionally sip from the bitter waters of contempt and failure (as the Oklahoma cleric who not long ago received a clear, loud, well-pronounced "Boo!" during his sermon).

Therefore, it was no surprise to receive the communiqué that rests at my left hand as this is being written. Printed across the 1984 the *Sooner Catholic* Support Campaign letter in the bold strokes of a black felt tip pen is: "We throw the paper in the trash—no one knows why it comes here."

In the best traditions of affirmation, let me respond: "You print well, especially the why with the thick black underlining. We hope that our newspaper adds some weight to your used paper collection. We appreciate your use of our business reply envelope to express your feelings. Next year, if you would be so kind, please include your name and address."

Moving: It Shakes You up, Causes Tired Blood

April 1984

April 2, 1984, 8:30 p.m. We played taps on our flugelhorn, posed for photos, and left the *Sooner Catholic* offices forever. I walked away with several members of the St. Gregory's College board of directors stuck to my right shoe.

Let me explain. Last Monday was our staff's final working day in SC's first-floor location at the Center for Christian Renewal. By midday Tuesday we had packed and moved a half of a building east and one storey up to our new location. Even as we lugged our possessions away, we could hear the *smash, smash, smash* of a destruction-construction crew chewing a path toward our abandoned site. It reminded one of the Fall of Saigon.

(About those St. Gregory's board people. They were attached to my person in the form of a small piece of waxed newspaper copy that had been sliced away to make an article fit on page three of the April 8 issue. Those board members strode step by step with me to People's restaurant and home again where they were discovered during a time-out of the Georgetown-Houston game.)

Moving. It shakes you up, disorients by changing all your well-known piles of junk, and causes tired blood.

Here are three personal observations of the *Sooner Catholic*'s long walk into the Promised Land.

The move stirred up the embers of a permanent addiction of mine—wallowing in old photographs. And I didn't have that much opportunity to see the old pictures (Joan O'Neill, the tour guide of our exodus, had wisely sent the great body of historic photos on ahead of me).

However, one of the movers accidentally overturned a box, and photos spilled across the floor. I took one look and was hooked. As a matter of fact, I have a few of them on my desk right now. Would you like to see them?

This is a young Father Raymond Harkin leaning on a rail inside the Coliseum at Rome. And this is a rare shot of Bishop Kelley celebrating Mass in the former chapel of the "Big House" on North Hudson Avenue. Notice the electric fan placed in the middle of the floor. And this is Joe Skibb and Msgr. Don Kanaly— he's the one wearing the overalls—and Msgr. Harkin holding a string of twelve trout. It must be Colorado. And this is….

Well, I said I was addicted.

Like a mass murderer who thought his victims were buried too skillfully to be found only to have unearthed shocking stacks of unanswered mail and telephone queries, as well as unattended manuscripts. The move became literally a guilt trip.

What do you do with a 1979 letter asking for all the known data of the history of St. Quixote's Parish? Or a 1978 epistle demanding an explanation of Pope Paul VI's stance on Vatican-Israeli relations? Or a 1981 telephone memo requesting that photos of Msgr. Tannenbaum be forwarded to his birthplace of Farout, Nebraska, for the celebration that year of the parish centenary there? Or a poem submitted by Mrs. Murgatroyde?

You're correct. The only practical thing to do with all the above is to pitch them. And I did. Nevertheless, I anticipate nightmares of hordes of unrequited writers and callers pursuing me down the hallways of the Center.

If anyone reading this piece happens to be among the unanswered, you have every right to look away in disgust should our paths cross in the future, but I pray that a forgiving charity may win out.

The move provided absolute conclusive proof of my mammalian identification: pack rat.

Among the clutter around me as I write is a huge box labeled "Side of DFM's Desk," and another with the magic marker notation "Interview Notebooks of DFM and Other Debris," and still another with "Side of DFM's Desk."

These containers yield such gold as a copy of the April 22, 1977, issue of *The Florida Catholic* (wonder why I saved that; there must be some good reason), a pamphlet titled "Church Communication of the Seventies" (as Walter Mondale says it's not new ideas, which are important but true ideas), a packet of a 1951-1962 survey of the graduates of McGuinness High School (it's interesting that almost four out of five of them married Catholics—I'll have to look into that), and an April 1988 interview that reveals that the University of Oklahoma bought a secondhand Van de Graff accelerator in 1980 from the University of Kansas (little known facts can make one the life of trivia contests).

So here I am in my new digs on a quiet Sunday afternoon. Outside the branches of a lovely pine tree are moving lightly in the breeze. There are woods all along the far side of the driveway. Beyond the trees one sees the upper traces of the Northwest Expressway—Texaco and Taco Bueno signs and on the horizon the United Founders Tower and the Baptist Medical Center.

Awhile ago an executive jet lifted silently off the Wiley Post runway, rose in a clean line above the big cottonwood tree outside, and mightily swooshed over the west end of my government surplus desk. You know, once I get over the shock of the move, I may grow fond of this place.

In the meantime I should tell you the information contained in an "Immediate Release" discovered behind my desk's left-hand drawers. Senior citizens will receive free gate admission at Springlake Fun Park. But they'll have to hurry to get there by May 30, 1979.

If You Think the Little You Have Is Safe, Don't Bank on It

May 1984

When I was a little boy, my parents gave me a savings bank shaped like a green book. They taught me to drop my pennies in the slot at the top of the green book.

Now and again my mother would usher me and my green book savings bank into the National Bank of Tulsa. There the green book would be opened by a solemn clerk and out would tumble my treasure. The clerk would see to the stamping of numbers in my savings account book.

Then we would return home happy in the knowledge that my pennies were not only protected as securely as the crown jewels in the Tower of London but that my pennies also were begetting new pennies. It was the beginning of my experience with the great American banking system.

Time passed. Graduations occurred. Wars were fought. I was ordained a priest. My concept of banking remained as innocent as a butterfly in the garden of Eden.

Now, however, I moved a step closer to the guardians of our money by counting the Sunday collection with Msgr. Bart Murtaugh at St. Francis of Assisi Church. We would sit at the dining room table, open collection envelopes, sort the bills and package the coins. On Monday mornings I would often drive downtown and deposit the money at the First National Bank. I began to feel a certain kinship to those in the banking industry.

After several years of practice stuffing quarters into paper cylinders at the rectory, the first seeds of doubt about banking were dropped into the folds of my brain. I read a statement by one Walter Harrison who labeled the First National "the oldest and the coldest." That was our bank!

Father Ramon Carlin, a Socratic gadfly if there ever was one, lectured me on the thesis that "banks are the cathedrals of today." In the age of faith, cathedrals were the largest buildings and the centerpiece of cities, he said. In our age of secularism, banks had taken the cathedrals' place—right down to the marble walls. By golly, said observant I, the First National building is a bit more imposing than Our Lady's Cathedral.

More time passed. One fine day a banker friend of mine pointed out that the bank where I was doing my personal business (an institution that shall remain anonymous) was extracting from my trove everything except the two gold caps on my teeth and my shoelaces. The alleged fleecing had to do with a car loan. This disturbing revelation led me into the embrace of, guess whom, the Penn Square Bank.

At first things went swimmingly at Penn Square, but a new crew seemed to come aboard in the executive offices and my fortunes fell. As a matter of fact in February 1980, I described in this column how I managed to pay 18 percent interest in order to own a Ford Maverick with 82,415 miles on the odometer.

If all their customers had paid as painfully as this lowly sinner, Penn Square Bank would have sunk into the mud of Belle Isle Lake from the weight of the cash on hand. But they handed out their real dough to guys in Lincoln Continentals instead of Mavericks, and the whole ship went down in mid-ocean so fast that we proletariat customers were left standing in line anxious to learn if our greenbacks were on the list of survivors.

Shaken by the demise of Penn Square, I appeared at the door of Banco Jesse James (a pseudonym to protect my hide) to beg admittance, safety, and security and such. They took me in.

My dealings with Banco Jesse James has been enlightening. I realize now it is a progressive bank, progressively tightening the screws on my wallet.

Less than six months after beginning commerce with me, BJJ sent this note: "The government's deregulation of banking and the shifting of large deposit accounts to the higher interest rate is creating some unwelcome changes in banking."

I burst into tears at the thought of the government forcing poor old helpless BJJ and their ilk to deregulate. *A communist scheme,* I thought, *cleverly sneaked past the bankers' usually vigilant lobby.*

My tears evaporated, however, when I got to the end of the message. The bottom line read that monthly service charges were going up for the non-wealthy. Hey, that's me you're handing the "unwelcome changes," I hollered.

In fourteen months' time, Banco Jesse James sent two more notes, and service charges for folks with less than a $100 minimum balance in their checking accounts jumped successively from $8 to $10 to $12 a month. If Rip Van Winkle were around, he could wake up to find that his checking account had disappeared altogether like the morning mist on the North Canadian.

I'm still with BJJ, but if the tellers actually begin to wear masks and carry guns, I'm going the coffee can and shovel route. My backyard has no service charges.

Afterthought: Getting toward the end of this effort, I recalled that my niece's husband is the vice president of a local bank. Perhaps my next service charge will be no more invitations to dinner. I pray charity will win out.

The Nurse in Room 122 Said, "He's Ready to Go Home"

June 1984

Late on a Sunday afternoon, a quiet but ultimate event was running its course in room 122 at Mercy Health Center. Msgr. James Rooney was dying.

He inhaled rapidly great gulps of air aided by the plastic oxygen mask fitted over his mouth and nose. Blood suctioned from his throat ran in dark lines through plastic tubes into a bag attached to the back of the bed.

There was no agony. No sip of consciousness. The bed covers were neatly turned back. The scene was understated, and that in keeping with the modest style of the principal actor's life.

Mercifully his doctor had decided not to plug Msgr. Rooney's disintegrating body into futile technological contraptions.

It so happened that when I arrived in room 122, no one else was present with Oklahoma's stricken senior priest. I was touched by the irony that this good man, who had scattered the seed of God's goodness to so many thousands in a half century of pastoral work, was, in the end, by himself.

(My impression of aloneness was belied by the facts that Archbishop Salatka shortly thereafter entered the room to pray for monsignor; that Father John O'Brien, Sister Hugoline and the other nuns from the Center for Christian Renewal came to petition God id the church's prayers for the dying, and that George Platt, a man led in his journey of faith by Msgr. Rooney, made his way to the bedside to hold his mentor's hand.)

I prayed a few stumbling, teary words. Then I resorted to the breviary. A few minutes later a nurse appeared. She checked the patient's blood pressure. She took a cloth and wiped the old saint's forehead. Asked about his condition, the nurse replied, "He's ready to go home."

Before Msgr. Rooney's retirement in 1967, I had not known him well.

We were on opposite sides of the diocese. Although I was aware of his reputation as a pastor's pastor, I saw him only at diocesan gatherings.

My memory is of a man who stood up to speak for freedom in the church but responsible freedom, freedom with order.

From 1970 onward, my office and Msgr. Rooney's residence were in the same building.

I often sat next to him in the dining room. The breadth of his knowledge became more evident to me during those casual chats at the table. He had well-formed opinions on a wide variety of subjects, from professional football (the Steeler's "Old Baldy" Bradshaw was his favorite and the Cowboy's Tom Landry his equivalent of Darth Vader) to historical issues to church politics to theological questions.

I recall once when Msgr. Rooney debated another retired priest about the merits or demerits of the killing of Montezuma by the conquistadors in 1520. Monsignor considered the slaying an act of perfidy. He responded by asking if the infant sacrifice as practiced by the Aztecs to the attack on Montezuma. Seeing no end to the argument, Msgr. Rooney concluded his participation in it by saying quietly, "Poor old Monty! He never had a chance."

At times the monsignor would feel in the mood to recite poetry. Reaching hundreds of miles and many decades back to his native Prince Edward Island, he would launch into a flawless lengthy rendition of Oliver Goldsmith's "The Deserted Village," or "The Boree Log," or the like. To persons of less disciplined memories, me for one, it was always a dazzling performance.

When he came to the table after watching a genuine hell-for-leather football game—say the Steelers-Cowboys Super Bowl clash—Msgr. Rooney would be shining from the pleasure of it. "I never saw the like," he would say. "Greatest game I ever saw!"

But reading was his real passion in life during retirement. He zipped through several weekly news magazines, the daily newspapers, and shelves of books. The anteroom of paradise for him was an afternoon can of beer and a salty issue of the *National Catholic Reporter*. Of the latter, Msgr. Rooney would say with a great smile, "It keeps the bishops on their toes."

Perhaps the favorite image I have of him was his afternoon walk. Ball cap on his head, he would go ambling by our window, elegantly working his walking stick. Somehow his jaunty style communicated the idea that all would be well at the end of the road.

In Msgr. Rooney's last years, God prepared him for the big leap yonder by allowing numerous badgering trials. He lost his hearing completely. He suffered several strokes. He broke his hip. Now and again, he would lose his balance or faint and take a terrific fall. But through it all he kept a generally optimistic outlook, worked away at his reading and praying, and anticipated with eagerness, I feel certain, his eternal embrace by a loving God.

When his final breath was exhaled, Nurse Mary Lester and Mercy Sister Modesta Weyel were the privileged witnesses. "He was a very lovable old man," Sister Modesta said. Amen to that.

Something Insidious Is Happening Right under Your Feet

June 1984

As you are reading this column, something insidious is happening; something more certain and more awful than taxes is progressing on schedule; something more apt to enslave than communism is at work all around you right now. The grass is growing.

Respecting life in all its forms one might assume a benign attitude toward something so prolific and so freshly green as grass, if the great modem moral principle were not so clear and burdensome: grass must be cut.

Some of us, featuring ourselves to be free people with a "live and let live" approach to life, might choose to let the grass alone to extend its blades ever upward in its insistent drive to touch the sky. But, alas, less broadminded neighbors would invoke the police powers of the state. So again we would be forced to face the grim reality: grass must be cut.

My mind runs back through the decades to my early grass-cutting times. This was the era between the invention of the wheel and the discovery of power mowers. It was the terribly difficult Dark Ages of the Push Mower.

Sweating behind a push mower in those days could induce distortions of judgment and hallucinations. How had the side yard of our modest home become a half-mile long? What caused the grass at the Monahan's to grow at the rate of one inch an hour? Why had the fire hydrant on the corner assumed the form of an ice-cold bottle of soda pop?

And why was I, a mere runty youth, pitted alone against this snarling, vicious, chigger-crawling grass in our yard, while the Hellinghausen boys across the street could split the job several ways? It was enough to make me ponder the ultimate realities of human existence, like why wasn't I born to a family in Antarctica?

There is a defamatory tale that surfaces in our family circle from time to time that has to do with my grass-cutting ability.

My grandmother Monahan and my aunt Agnes lived together. Their yard also was afflicted with an epidemic of growing grass. I was volunteered to save the family name from disgrace.

Now it is true that occasionally I broke away from my attacks on the Bermuda to step inside the house for a chilled Coke. (After all Grandma, having the wisdom of her years and, being a woman of compassion, realized the importance of not muzzling or overstraining the working ox.) And there is an element of veracity to the claim that the Coke quaffing was now and again followed by forty winks on the cool kitchen floor. And I must admit that I did slash a hole in the screen part of the screened porch while trimming the hedge. But to say that I played on the sympathy of my grandmother or that I was lazy or incompetent.

When higher technology began to attach engines and gears and riding seats to mowers, I retired from the grass-cutting industry.

Now I see and hear things related to the mowing of grass from a different angle. After many seasons of keen observations, I have developed Monahan's First Rule of Institutional Grass Cutting: "Grass cutters at institutions hide in the shade for hours, days, even weeks, until a meeting is in progress featuring the human voice, before they slam their 500-horsepower Gargantuan Grass Guzzler into gear and proceed to mow slowly a ten-foot by fifteen-foot space directly outside the windows of the room housing the aforesaid meeting."

The results almost invariably are something like this: the world's preeminent authority is addressing you with a message so vital that it will be a practical impossibility to exist outside the lecture room without absorbing his every word.

The pre-eminent authority begins, "What I have to say is of utmost importance. I can summarize it very succinctly. In today's world...R-R-R-R-R-R-R...which if it happens will inevitably lead to...R-R-R-R-R-R-R...What can the ordinary person do? He or she can...R-R-R-R-R-R-R... If you only recall one item from my remarks today, let it be R-R-R-R-R-R. Thank you."

Once more grass has reared its ugly chlorophyll head.

Today if persons, motivated perhaps by a certain vanity, wish to speak of their latest possession, they are apt to describe it as "state of the art." If the same types desire to place themselves relative to others in particular endeavors, they may well say that they are "on the cutting edge."

Those of us in the know—all of us young, handsome yuppies—realize that such phrasing springs from the human race's subconscious preoccupation with grass and its cutting.

So it is with pleasure that I can report a visitation not too long ago to the home of a psychiatrist. This good man has succeeded in situating his comfortable residence in a setting of concrete and rocks and gardens—no grass. Now that is truly state of the art that is getting free forever from the cutting edge. May his kind prosper.

Even in a Golfing Eden, Beware of the Snakes

August 1984

It's the same old human story. Even in Eden there is a snake.

If there ever was a paradise for the common non-country-club hacker, the University of New Mexico South Golf Course is it.

Them on a recently past August 9 afternoon, Father Jim McGlinchey and I came across a four-foot rattlesnake busily sliding its way toward the seventh fairway where we were playing. Jim made bogey. I took a double bogey. The rattler did not turn in a score.

Bogies, double bogies, triple bogies, quadruple bogies (even one septuple bogey), a scattering of pars and a solitary birdie were the results of six consecutive days of quiet but fierce combat on the course overlooking Interstate 25 a few miles south of downtown Albuquerque.

The course easily won the fight, but like marathoner Gabriela Andersen-Schiess, we staggered and stumbled 108 holes to the finish. Never picked up in disgust without completing a hole. Never assigned a gratuitous score. Stamina not skill was our thing.

The University of New Mexico course is eighteen emerald swatches set on a desert hillside. The fairways are lush and finely manicured. The greens are rolling and very fast. From the back tees the course measures an extraordinary 7,253 yards—longer than any layout on the regular PGA tour.

For guys who can't hit the ball straight (*mea culpa, mea culpa, mea maxima culpa*), the first bit of rough covers half of the ball, a few feet farther astray and the little round object is completely out of sight. A yard or so more removed from the fairway begins the frightening combination of rocks, sagebrush, rocks, desert flowers, rocks, burrows of various varmints, and rocks where a jackhammer would be of more service than a seven iron.

While a player pauses to strap his psyche together again after scoring an eight and/or to allow his lungs to catch up with his feet (there is a rise of what seems to be hundreds of feet from the seventeenth tee to the eighteenth green, as an example of the course's upness and downness), he can gaze at the valley of the Rio Grande, including most of the city of Albuquerque, or absorb the scrubbed clean blue sky, or watch the continual air show of planes swooping lowly across the course onto the runways jointly used by Kirtland Air Force Base and the Albuquerque International Airport.

Summary: The University course dazzles and soothes' as it prepares to slit your golfing throat.

This New Mexico gem, unlike its class and cash restricted country club cousins, is marked with the essential democratic spirit of the true public golf course. If you go there with less than a foursome, you can count on joining or being joined by others.

Over our six-day stay, we became four-hour friends of brothers Theron and Butch, young Danny, Gerald and Brian—a father and son combo—a husband and wife team of Cortez and Joyce, and Jim, a part Choctaw who attended Bacone College in 1931-32.

Theron, Danny, and Brian were of that ever growing breed of slender, tall, elastic youngsters who take enormous full whistling swings and blast the ball ungodly distances. Danny, a high school senior, said he plays thirty-six holes a day. Jim, the only fellow we were around who was older than we, featured a no-nonsense arthritic punch swing. He putted the same way with devastatingly bad consequences. It was encouraging. One's golfing misery spreads happiness to others.

At this point, you are leaning forward in your chair, racing to the end of this column to learn who prevailed in the annual titanic McGlinchey-Monahan struggle for golf supremacy.

Well, I ain't gonna tell ya.

Suffice it to say that the two of us took a combined and exact 1,159 strokes for an average of 5.4 a hole. I will admit to the booby prize of a twelve on the par five first hole beginning the second round of play. That tended to put a crimp in the day's score.

Supreme highlight of the 1984 tournament: a Sunday night Irish whiskey toast at Ogilvie's to John Treacy of Ireland for his silver medal marathon run in the Olympics. The golf went toastless.

How Long Did Nannie Doss Cook in Your Kitchen?

December 1984

First the men carrying the canoe tried the impossible of moving the canoe through the revolving door into the lobby of Tulsa's Mayo Hotel.

Not succeeding in that venture, the gentlemen from the local sporting goods company went back to their truck. They reappeared with wrenches and screw drivers and began to take apart the revolving door.

That action had not proceeded far until an assistant manager of the hotel was at their side.

"What are you doing?" the assistant manager asked.

"We're taking the door down so that we can put the canoe in the lobby," the sporting goods people replied.

"Why, in heaven's name, would you want to do that?"

"Because the manager from the Mayo called our company and said he wanted a canoe from us as a part of a sports equipment exhibition in the lobby."

"He did? Well, I'll have to check on that."

Seated in an easy chair in the lobby, newspaper in hand but attention fixed on the scene at the door, was a man with a quirky smile on his face. In fact, he had been the "hotel manager" who had telephoned the sporting goods outfit about the canoe. He did it for the sheer delight of watching the resultant confusion. The man was my father.

Frank P. Monahan was a super-salesman hooked on practical jokes. Whether it was a matter of genes or education in the coal country of southeast Kansas or the effects of too much sugar in his blood, I never knew. What I did know was that given spare time, the urge would come upon him to play a practical joke. With his powers of persuasion, they were lulus.

Some of his tricks were so elaborate they would require 10,000 words to begin to describe. Others were sheer simplicity. Many involved the use (or misuse) of the telephone. Truth was not always the keystone of the jokes.

I recall one time, when I was a small boy, traveling with my father on a sales trip from Tulsa to Oklahoma City. Being Great Depression times, there was a lull in the sales action.

My father spotted a storefront operation advertising "disappearing clotheslines." It was apparently too great an opportunity to miss. We wheeled to a stop in front of the store.

Shortly I was listening to an amazing tale. My father told the owner and, I think, the inventor of the disappearing clotheslines that he was a developer. On the drawing board, he said, were plans for a mammoth housing development.

Would it be possible for the man to furnish, say 1,000 units of the disappearing clothesline for the new development? The man was saying "Yes, certainly, yes, yes" before my father could complete his fabrication.

The scene ended with one uplifted clothesline manufacturer-distributor, one confused boy and one salesman savoring a triumph of sorts.

Frank Monahan's telephone pitches were masterpieces of imagination if not charity. Some examples:

- On a Sunday afternoon, he represented himself to a woman as a Southwestern Bell engineer preparing to conduct experiments on her telephone. Specifically the lines were going to be "blown out." His instructions were for her to wrap her telephone in a heavy bath towel to prevent possible damages. As I recall, the woman did as she was told, and there followed a hilarious conversation with the woman attempting to hear and be heard through the towel. Oh my.

- A woman by the name of Nannie Doss was arrested in Tulsa and charged with the murder, by rat poison, of something more than a dozen husbands. With this lurid story on the front of every newspaper, my father called the Hollywood Supper Club and asked for the manager. He told the manager that he was with the district attorney's office and that he was trying to verify exactly how long Nannie Doss had worked as a cook at the supper club. The manager, no doubt with visions of what might happen if such a story reached the news media, told the truth and denied that Nannie had ever worked there. My father continued to press. "We know she worked at your place. We're just not sure of the dates." Me oh my.

- In more innocent days, city golf tournaments published names, dates, and times of matches in the local newspapers. Also printed were the contestants' telephone numbers in case some change had to be made in the schedule. My father promptly telephoned a player we will call Bill Brown. He told Bill that he was his opponent and because of other commitments he wanted to change the schedule of their match. Instead of teeing off at 10:00 a.m., could Bill be out at the first tee by 5:00 a.m.? My father said he planned to pitch a tent by the first tee, which he invited Bill to share with him so that they could begin play with the first glimmer of light. Oh my, oh my, oh my.

My father was never known to have taken the cure for his practical joke addiction. He has been dead for twenty years now, surely long enough for managers of Mayo Hotels, owners of disappearing clotheslines companies, women with towels around telephones, heads of supper clubs, sleepy golf contestants, and a cast of hundreds of others to have been afforded justice.

If, however, Frank Monahan is still seated in a back corner of purgatory with a telephone in his hands, I would advise the Lord not to accept any collect calls.

Plodding into New Year in My Wolverine Work Shoes

December 1984

God willing, I will go plodding into the New Year wearing my black Wolverine work shoes. They ain't pretty, but they're practical.

Let me tell you how a middle-aged priest came to wear genuine black Wolverine work shoes.

The tale begins in the sore-footed past. I had developed corns on the balls of my feet, and walking was rapidly becoming limping. In the course of a yearly physical examination, my doctor advised me to see a foot specialist.

So I made an appointment. On the given day, I appeared at the foot specialist's clinic. I was ushered into a cubicle and told to remove my shoes and stockings.

As I waited in my chilly bare feet, I could hear the voice of Dr. Slicer (a pseudonym to protect that good physician and myself) declaiming and questioning about other tender tootsies in nearby patients' spaces.

Dr. Slicer burst into my cubicle, grabbed hold of my right foot, squeezed the right little toe, and hollered, "That little pinkie will have to come off!"

(You see both my little toes overlap onto the next toe—always have and always will, an exact duplication of my mother's foot structure. The little toes had never caused me a moment's trouble.)

I was shaken by the foot specialist's pronouncement. Nevertheless, I launched into an explanation of why I had come to him – corns, doctor, corns, not my little toes.

Dr. Slicer studied the undersides of my feet. Then he explained that as some people grow older their feet begin to draw up, placing additional pressure on the balls of the feet, and hence the corns.

He said he would take care of the situation by cutting through a tendon or two in each foot, thus allowing the foot to flatten out and reducing the pressure points where the corns had formed. He named the price.

I hobbled out the door certain that I would resist the severance of my little toes, not so sure about the operation for the corns.

A short time later I was on the street in Edmond when, on impulse, I stepped into a shoe store.

It's hard to recall exactly how it all happened, but when I left the store I was wearing a pair of genuine black Wolverine work shoes.

Three things were certain about the shoes. They were economical. They weighed a ton. They looked like something my grandfather would have worn and probably did.

The rubber soles were "oil resisting" and a full one-half inch thick. The heels were solid one and one-quarter inch rubberized pedestals.

I was reminded of Tyrus Raymond Cobb, the legendary baseball player, who wore weights on his feet before he came to bat so that his feet would feel like feathers while running the bases. It seemed I might sail to the ceiling like a helium-filled balloon when I removed my clodhoppers at night.

A small miracle took place right under my feet. The longer I wore the Wolverines, the less bothersome were the corns. Finally, the painful rascals disappeared altogether into the corny netherworld.

My genuine black Wolverine work shoes and I have been together for some six years now. They have joined the footwear of Egyptian President Hosni Mubarak under a table at Cairo's Oruba Palace, stood beside the sixteenth green at Torrey Pines as Jack Nicklaus angled in a sidehill putt, strolled the hallways of the British Museum, been the underpinning for hundreds of celebrations of Mass, and tramped across miles of Oklahoma's red earth—with nary a corn.

I get comments about the Wolverines from two types of people. Sharp-eyed, fashion-conscious, and honest women will occasionally make gentle suggestions: "Those shoes look awful."

On the other hand, practical-minded men are more apt to inquire about the history and rationale and source of supply of the ponderous black shoes. After each of my explanations they say, "Hmmm."

In any event, my intentions are not hidden. I will stick with my genuine black Wolverine work shoes until death do us part. After all, I am probably the only one of the 50,000-plus priests listed in The Official Catholic Directory to have the honor.

CHAPTER 9

1985

Why He Gets Cold Feet Just Thinking about It

January 1985

If you are reading these words, it means you have survived at least most of January. Congratulations. But then there remains brittle cold February. Good luck.

The gist of this column is to warn innocent people away from a winter fate worse than an electrical power outage: camping in cold weather. I realize that citizens of sound mind would not give a second thought to camping out during subfreezing nights, but there may be those as loony as I once was.

Surprisingly my story begins not in January or February but in March. It was Holy Week more than two decades ago when I conceived the idea of a spring trip to Colorado. It was more or less springtime here. Who would guess conditions might be different in Colorado? (Notice the ignorance of elementary geography and the crooked logic that are two marks of the cold weather camper.)

At that time I was a member of the faculty of McGuinness High School. I invited three senior students—John, Dan, and Bill—to make the Colorado adventure with me during the Easter holidays.

We arrived in Pueblo just after the sun had set. We were determined to camp out our first evening in the state. Groceries were purchased. Directions were asked. Away we went into the night.

Twenty-five miles west of Pueblo, the road began to rise into the San Isabel National Forest. We were in the front range of the Colorado Mountains.

Our car lights picked out snow on the ground on either side of the road. Then it was covering the road as we inched upward. There were no lights save those on our car. We began to feel a sense of isolation. Nobody out here but us Okies.

We spotted a parking area for a camp ground. If you're going to camp out, you might as well use the parking area assigned for such purposes. We rolled to a stop.

Once the motor was turned off, you didn't have to listen hard to hear a deafening silence.

Thank God someone had remembered to bring a flashlight. Like astronauts leaving the safety of their space capsule for a free flight in space, we edged away into the woods—all of twenty-five yards.

The first order of business was to build a fire. We scratched around our site searching in the snow for fallen tree limbs. I forget who the fire maker was, but he was nothing if not persevering. The fire refused to ignite.

We stuffed newspapers into the tepee of twigs and lit them. There would be a brief flare up, and then nothing. This process was repeated and repeated. I began to have visions of a warm bed in Pueblo.

When hope and newspapers had almost run out, I'll be darned if the fire didn't catch. God apparently decided that if you're dumb enough to be here, you might as well make a night of it.

The fire's light revealed four persons shin-deep in snow under a starry sky. It was a scene from that immortal movie *One Million B.C.* The difference was that the cavemen in that production knew a heck of a lot more than we what to do next.

We ate. Not bear meat but Vienna sausages. Not Indian fry bread but Graham crackers. Not steaming plates of beans but Mars bars. It was great, if you could let your taste buds pleasure overcome the ache of your freezing feet.

The tale gets more embarrassing.

We had no tent in which to sleep. We had army cots and sleeping bags. Period.

Our technique was simple. Rig up the cots, slap them down in the snow, and throw our sleeping bags on the cots. It was cool, man, cool.

We ringed the fire with our cots, but as Brother Cold bored his way into our bodies, we began to jockey for positions closer to the fire. I have the distinct recollection of maneuvering my cot so that the end with my head was practically in the fire. Great gobs of smoke infiltrated my sleeping bag. At least that smelled warm.

Came dawn. We hobbled about on numb feet, stretched knotted bodies, clapped hands to restore circulation, and congratulated ourselves that we had made it. It was an experience to remember, in case I was ever tempted to try it again.

The next night the camping trip convened in two comfortable resort cabins.

Murdered Priest Left Memories Wrapped in Laughter

March 1985

Remember the priest who was murdered several weeks ago in Wisconsin? His name was Father John Daniel Rossiter. The report of his death was a special shocker to me. We had been classmates for four years in the seminary. John and I were good friends.

John was one of the thousands of World War II GIs who later entered seminaries. Although he was very serious about the priesthood, and preparations for same, he had a wild streak and a generous sense of humor, which made him a joy to be around.

As a young man, John was on the handsome side, not pretty handsome but in a peculiar masculine sense. He had devilment in his eyes. And his hair had a Medusa-like appearance, twisting black ringlets running off in all directions.

The Latin language was not one of John's strong points. Since the seminary textbooks, in those days, were mostly written in Latin, John had a problem. He solved it by becoming one of the world's most prolific publishers of English renditions of Latin.

He organized a group that divided up the chore of translating the Latin texts into English for the benefit of all. John's job was to coordinate the venture. Hence when one saw John Rossiter in a darkened corridor at St. John's Seminary in Little Rock, he usually had a fistful of translations that he was moving from one team member to another. Somehow he painted this activity with a cloak-and-dagger quality mixed with explosions of laughter.

One of my favorite remembrances of John was as a basketball player. He was singularly inept at the sport. If Latin wasn't his thing, neither were matters of hand and eye coordination. On a basketball court, he was a fury of elbows and feet and fingers—all parts apparently working independently of the others.

John played in the seminary's B league, but his spirit was on a championship level. With students and seminary faculty in attendance, he would grab the basketball, awkwardly unleash it in the general direction of the basket, and yell mightily, "Get in there, you son-of-a-bitch!" It never did.

One Sunday morning a fourth theology student, a deacon, from John's diocese gave the sermon at the students' Mass. We seminarians in attendance were formally dressed in cassocks and surplices. John and I were sitting next to each other.

The deacon's sermon dripped with sugary piety. The deacon hadn't proceeded far into his masterpiece when John began to giggle. Each line of the sweet stuff from the deacon brought an additional guffaw from John. In a move to hold down the noise, John stuffed an entire handkerchief into his mouth. Muffled bursts of out-of-control laughter continued. Tears ran down John's face.

John got down on his hands and knees. The deacon plowed ahead on his predetermined course. By this time many in the congregation were infected with John's strangled laughter, which could still be heard floating up from our pew. I swear the pew was vibrating with mirth. Finally, John bolted from the chapel with muffled hee-hee-hees trailing in his wake.

John told his share of war stories. One concerned a time in the Philippines when he was guarding a radar installation in a remote mountainous area. There was a report of Japanese paratroopers being dropped in the general vicinity.

Although the armed forces radio stated that the situation was under control, John, on duty at night in the jungle while it was raining, had no such illusions. His partner didn't help him.

As the two of them hunkered in the darkness with the rain splashing off their ponchos, the partner said he had heard the Japanese had such keen hearing that they could tell the difference between rain striking leaves and that landing on ponchos. Just the right words to soothe a shaky nervous system.

John would end the story with a colorful expletive or two and a roar of laughter at the incongruity of it all.

As Divine Providence wrote the script death didn't come for him in a steamy, remote jungle. Father John Rossiter was shot from behind while praying in church after having celebrated a morning Mass. It was the senseless work of a madman. But in terms of ways of dying, it was not a bad time. One imagines that John could appreciate that.

Twisting Down the Hog Back Road to Easter

April 1985

Memories of an Easter Sunday, a decade or so back.

This dawning Easter morning finds me twisting north on Oklahoma County Road #1. The Hog Back Road, the locals call it. The two-lane highway is a tame rollercoaster ride across the hills of this thinly populated area. Routine and weather can make the trip as lively as an Over-80 square dance. Today it is Resurrection glorious.

Spring green is beginning to catch hold this early April. The gnarled blackjack oaks—curmudgeons of the tree family—are loathe to admit any season's passing; but the locusts and the cottonwoods and the webby underbrush are converting, and, best of all, the redbuds are blossomed.

For some fifty weeks of the year, redbuds practice the extremes of modesty. Ordinarily they are nothing more to experience than dumpy women in Sears polyesters walking on crowded streets of a great city. But fitted by God with a magic inner clock, the redbuds annually celebrate Jesus coming forth from the tomb with millions of explosions of magenta.

Today the redbuds are singing a chorus of alleluias to me from the woods on both sides of the road. They are a delightful menace to safe driving.

My destination is the town of Luther, more specifically the mission Church of St. Theresa. Mass is, as always, scheduled for 7:30 a.m.

Luther is not a City with Pride or a Proud Town nor encumbered by any other of those anti-Gospel Chamber of Commerce slogans. Luther is a humble place, populated by 1,159 citizens who haven't made it big, the kind of crossroads at which you would expect to meet the poor man of Nazareth.

My Ford Maverick brakes to a stop in front of St. Theresa's. The church is a white-frame job, four windows to a side, absolute seating capacity of forty. The only aisle is so narrow that coffins won't fit. (All Luther Catholics upon exiting from the here and now have their lives and deaths celebrated in a Mass of Christian Burial at Jones, some eight miles away.)

As I unlock the door and enter, the familiar musty odor is not so offensive as reassuring. I light the gas stove to knock the chill out of the air.

The church has no sacristy. A steel cabinet in the sanctuary serves the purpose. I open it, remove the Mass utensils, and place them on the altar. I flip ribbons to set the sacramentary and the lectionary for their paschal runs.

Next, I don the limp alb, which has been hanging on a clothes hanger hooked to the top edge of the wooden housing of the Blessed Virgin Mary's statue.

Wearing a white stole, I duck into the confessional, a homemade contraption of screen and curtains nestled in a corner of the sanctuary. Two sinners present themselves for shriving. The business of mercy is conducted truly pianissimo, a few of the early arrivers being all of six feet away.

As I finish vesting, I note that the whole gang is here and a tad shinier than usual. Tiny Holly Loman is draped over the kneeler in the first row; Stanley Kubiak's burnished farmer's face fronted by his out of kilter reading glasses juts up from the second row; and so on the ranks of these homey saints, all in the exact spots they always occupy.

We sing "Praise to the Lord, the Almighty, the King of creation." No organ accompaniment (the organist died several years ago), not much vocal talent, and always the same hymn at the beginning—ordinary time, Advent, Lent, and Easter—but a prayerful try nonetheless.

"I take it you know what has been reported all over Judea about Jesus of Nazareth," Simon Peter says to us. The church in Luther takes comfort in "When Christ our life appears, then you shall appear with him in glory." Finally we sprint to the tomb with John and Peter, and we too believe.

Outside a rooster crows, not realizing he missed his cue on Friday.

We move to meet our risen Jesus in the Eucharist. The holy words draw us into the action of His death and resurrection. We mumble our faith "Christ has died. Christ is risen. Christ will come again."

Suddenly it's all done. Like a long watched pearly bud, which no one ever sees come open, Easter has bloomed.

While greeting M.C. Engle Sr. at the door, I recall that he bears a hidden secret—today he has shed his winter skin of long johns. No matter how much things look the same, they always change. That's Easter for you.

Is This Man's Hair Afflicted with Amnesia?

June 1985

Mirror, mirror, on the wall, Whose scalp is barest of them all?

For the moment, I'm still a few sprigs ahead of Tom Landry, Telly Savalas, and Joe Garagiola. But mirrors (especially the dratted multiple ones in motels) tell me that the thinning process has gone so far that my hair is on the endangered species list.

As with other unpleasant realities of life, one tends to deny what is happening when one's hair begins to say adios. Somehow the fact that the shower drain is consistently clogged with great batches of the stuff doesn't really register in the personal accounting office.

You can look straight ahead in a mirror and conclude that the hair situation isn't so bad after all.

However, from a neutral observer's angle that bald spot on the crown is not the size of a quarter but of a saucer. And the hair on top of the head is gapped like a picket fence rather than the glossy blanket you imagine it to be.

Others are involved in a conspiracy of denial. You and your barber manage to edge the part farther and farther to the side so that hair on the outer perimeter can be employed to cover the denuded top. In the end you find yourself with long strands of hair growing along a western slope and being pulled across the barren summit to anchor on the eastern uplands.

The balding man may seek the consolation of philosophy and religion.

There is a French proverb on our side: "Long hair, little sense." But then there's the Czech proverb: "A good man grows gray, but a rascal grows bald."

And Marcus Valerius Martialis, the Roman epigrammatist, contributed this downer: "There is nothing more contemptible than a bald man who pretends to have hair."

The Bible is kinder to us of the lost locks. Consider Kings 2:23 about Elisha the prophet: "While he was on the way, some small boys came out of the city and jeered at him. 'Go up, baldhead,' they shouted, 'go up, baldhead!'" For their bad manners the rowdy little tykes were set upon by two bears that dispatched forty-two of them. (Remember that the next time you are tempted to mock us skinheads.)

The Apostle Paul comes to our aid with "Does not nature itself teach you that it is dishonorable for a man to wear his hair long, while the long hair of a woman is her glory?" 1 Cor. 11:14

Then there is the Bill Cosby theory of amnesiac hair. Cosby says the hair is there all right and it is growing, but it has forgotten where to come out. So hair grows out of one's ears and nostrils and manages to thicken eyebrows, but it forgets to sprout on the top of one's head.

Leave us conclude this meditation with a properly somber tone. Making certain that you are alone would you please sing the following with me to the tune of "Taps."

> Bald is here.
> Gone the hair
> from the crown,
> from the top,
> byedie-bye.
> All is smooth.
> Be resigned.
> God is nigh.

When I Saw This Telephone Pole Pass Me...

June 1985

This composition is being written in room 216 of DeGrasse Hall at St. Gregory's College. It is Tuesday, June 4, the second day of Clergy Days—an annual gathering of Oklahoma priests and deacons. Clergy Days are designed to allow one to learn a little and talk a lot.

This year our guest speaker is Msgr. Fred McManus who is leading us on a guided tour of the liturgy from the Second Vatican Council to the present. In the daily schedule substantial blocks of time are set aside for casual chatting. It's a great place for telling and hearing stories of Oklahoma Catholic priests in the days of yore.

A sampling of the tales:

Father Mike McNamee was appointed pastor of Assumption Church in Duncan. It was the time of the Great Depression. Father McNamee arrived on the scene at Duncan to learn that his predecessor had left him a mighty stack of unpaid bills without the means to cover the debts.

Immediately Father McNamee became a magnet for all the bill collectors in Stephens County.

One day Father McNamee had to interrupt a conversation with his friend Father Leo Hardesty in order to tangle with another determined bill collector. The pastor and the bill collector were discussing matters in the office, removed only by a wall from Father Hardesty.

As the strained dialogue over money continued, Father Hardesty began to tinker with a .45-caliber handgun. The bill collector had reached a crescendo in his demand for payment, when the loud explosion of the .45 discharging came from next door.

"Just a firecracker," Father McNamee said. The bill collector stood up and without a word made for the front door. One could imagine the warning the collector was already forming in his mind as he scurried down the sidewalk. "Be careful when you go to that church. Those Catholics play rough!"

Father Bill Rath was a dynamic young priest with a finely tuned social conscience. In 1965, when the US civil rights movement was reaching the top of a long uphill walk and the nation's focus was on Martin Luther King and Selma, Alabama, Father Rath and four other Oklahoma priests piled in a car and drove to Selma. (One of the passengers thought he was on his way to play golf!)

At Selma the priests were caught up in the enthusiasm to march from Selma to Montgomery! The first and most uncertain goal was to get safely across the bridge at the edge of Selma. Two weeks earlier civil rights marchers had been turned back at the bridge by club wielding lawmen and tear gas.

There were many delays as the line of march was being formed. The Oklahoma priests had had only a couple of hours of sleep in the past twenty-four. Finally Father Rath said he was going to a nearby hospital, where mattresses had been spread on the basement floor, for a quick nap.

He fell sound asleep. Yes, the march, with his four partners, strode away to make national history and left him snoozing contentedly in the basement. Later he more or less swore the other Oklahoma priests to silence.

Father Andy Thomas, an overweight florid-faced man, was a gifted storyteller. (One of the local legends about Andy concerned a flight from Europe to the United States in which he was seated beside Mrs. Bob Hope. When the aircraft landed, she went to her famous husband and said, "I sat next to the funniest man I ever met.")

One day Andy was driving down a state highway when he collided with another car. Soon the Oklahoma Highway Patrol was on the scene.

Andy launched into a colorful account of what had happened from his perspective. The priest told the investigating trooper that he became disoriented by looking into the rear view mirror. Andy stated, "When I saw this telephone pole pass me…"

The trooper, who had been struggling to keep a straight face, at that explanation burst out laughing. No one recalls who got cited for what.

Summer Camp: A Time to Learn to Appreciate Home

June 1985

Summer camp is the season to be jolly for chiggers, ticks, manufacturers of suntan oils and, occasionally, for children.

Only yesterday I made an appearance at the Lake Murray site of the annual camp sponsored by the Office of Catholic Youth Ministry.

I want to report that all the best traditions of summer camping were being observed there: jugs of Kool-Aid were being swilled, wasps cruised menacingly at eye level in the handicrafts area, green stages of new friendships were sprouting, attacks of homesickness were being well hidden, and the stifling southern Oklahoma sun had everyone moving in low gear.

The experience had the effect on me of mental transportation to other camps in other days, camps in which I was a camper or a counselor.

The place: Camp Garland, Mayes County, 1939. It is a Sunday afternoon and the boys and leaders of Troop 34 (Christ the King Church, Tulsa) have arrived at their campsite.

We are issued two-man tents and given instructions on how to erect them. A period of struggle and perspiration follows. Fathers, who cannot stand the sight of their progeny's futile straining, step forward to help. They too learn a lesson in frustration. Finally the tents are assembled, complete with trenches around them to ward off the perils of flooding.

Night comes. Campers begin to learn the first lesson of camp life: henceforth living at home will be doubly appreciated. Our beds are "cots"—a piece of canvas stretched between two pieces of wood.

Theoretically the cots suspend one an inch or two above the ground. Practically, well….

One discovers that others of God's creatures inhabit the same space as one's person. Spindly long-legged spiders continue to make their appointed rounds. Stouthearted campers of Troop 34 are shown little respect. By the end of the week campers, without a second thought, casually brush the spiders off their bodies.

Camp Garland cameos:

- The cold clearness of Spring Creek, able to defeat any simmering summer sun, and the recollection of planting a big toe in the swimming instructor's eye during a drill on how to free oneself underwater from a panicky non-swimmer's desperation bear hug.
- Stepping on a large snake while walking along a woodsy path and the consequent rush of adrenaline that carried me far away.
- Evening softball games with the approaching darkness being greeted by mournful hoots of owls.
- Camp fire where we rookies were compelled to ever swifter repetition of the "secret" chant (Owha-tagoo-siam) until the message became clear to us.

The place: Camp Holy Cross, Canon City, Colorado, 1951.

There are several things this camp is not. It is not a rustic spot scrunched down amid blackjack oaks. It is not canvas tents and trips to primitive latrines. It is not established to care for the poor (one Texas lad arrives via the family airplane, lugging his own saddle).

I am twelve years removed from Camp Garland, a camp counselor now following my second year of theological studies. This summer I will learn not to hate horses exactly but to maintain a firm resolution never again to mount one willingly. I will learn that excitement is ascending the Pike's Peak switchbacks in a school bus. I will learn that I can do something involving heights that years later I can't even think of without feeling faint.

Camp Holy Cross maintains a mountain camp, the Abbot's Lodge, at about 9,000 feet on the side of Spring Mountain, one of the Sangre de Cristo peaks in southern Colorado. From the Abbot's Lodge one can hike up trails to the roof of the United States.

One day I find myself ascending a trail from the lodge accompanied by two small boys—a seed company's heir from Kansas City and an oil heir from Houston. They are about eleven years of age.

We huff and puff our way up through the aspens and the pines until we break out of the forest at the timberline. A little farther and we come to the moment of truth. Our choices are two. We can return the way we have just come, or we can continue on a circular route that will bring us down the other side of the mountain. The catch is to make the circular trip requires a considerable hike on a ledge around the face of a cliff with a long, long sheer drop off the ledge. It's called the Phantom Terrace.

We decide to try it. I place Kansas City in front of me and Houston (his name is Robert) behind. My instructions are definite. We will make the trek along the ledge in one steady march—no stops to rest, no clowning around.

We step onto the ledge. I look steadfastly at the trail in front or the wall to my right, fill my mind with Acts of Contrition, and walk.

Every fifteen seconds or so, I turn my head to check the youngster behind me. About halfway through the ordeal, I look back and there is no one there. The ledge undulates so that one cannot see the trail very far behind us.

I call out, "Robert!" No answer. "Robert!" Silence. As I'm about to conclude that Robert has tumbled into the abyss, he wobbles into view. Sure enough he had stopped to rest. We successfully reach the other side of the Phantom Terrace and return in triumph to the lodge. Strangely, the news media fails to mention our heroic feat.

Tired of the Heat? Try an Old-Fashioned Swimming Hole

July 1985

These days the sun dances a shimmering fandango across the sky. Thermometers are showing eighty at 7:00 a.m. The grass is tired of livin' and feared of dyin'. Tar in the seams of the streets mushes under one's feet. Walking between enclaves of refrigerated air a person is conscious of globules of perspiration coursing down his back.

It's deep heat time in Oklahoma. It's time to go swimming.

If you live in central Oklahoma, swimming is apt to be spelled White Water. That high-tech, splash-around certainly sounds like fun. Besides White Water there are pools and more pools. The common denominator of White Water and all the others is money.

Where I would take you in this column is to two old Oklahoma swimming holes—both free, both minus chlorine, both filtered only by God.

There is a patch of woodland on the south border of the town of Sulphur in Murray County, which once was called Platt National Park. Now it's known as the Chickasaw National Recreation Area.

Percolating through the sands and rocks at the east end of the recreation area are the waters of Antelope Springs and Buffalo Springs. Their marriage forms Travertine Creek. The creek is the main attraction of the Chickasaw National Recreation Area.

The National Park Service has constructed a series of low-water dams along Travertine Creek. The water is allowed to flow through the dams except in the summer. Then the dams are plugged and pools of blue-green water form behind them. Each pool is no deeper than about seven feet.

On the hottest August day a citizen hopping into the Travertine will rediscover the meaning of cold. It's shocking. But if one keeps moving, the sensation resolves into a pleasant chill.

One of the pools has been labeled Little Niagara. It features a waterfall of some six feet. People dive and jump (and fall) off it into the waters below. Others try to swim against the current to the base of the falls.

The recreation area is a family place. At this time of the year the campsites are bulging. Okies (and Texans) of all ages, shapes, colors, and sexes are there, and half of them are in the creek or along side it.

One hundred and fifty-six miles northeast of the Chickasaw National Recreation Area is Baron Fork Creek, more specifically that spot just a smidge east of the point where Oklahoma Route 51 passes over the creek.

The natural pool formed there is as clear as Mother Teresa's soul.

Don't be put off by the bottles, cans, and general assortment of trash on the bank above the creek. This is not an officially designated park so the junk does tend to accumulate. Closer to the water the rock ledges are clean and the creek is ordinarily free from debris.

There are few experiences more pleasant in midsummer than to float on one's back in that cool pool and to look up through the leaves of the big cottonwood (I think), which leans out to provide shade.

Let me caution: paradise is not always perfect. The Baron Fork is no good for swimming when rains bring the water level too high. And at the end of this past year's summer the pool had shrunk to unswimable size and depth.

At one time Oklahoma was home to a missionary priest from Germany who had what could be fairly described as an obsession with swimming. Father Bill Huffer was his name. He swam every day in the summer and, some folks say, most of the days in the other seasons of the year.

In our files of old photos, the *Sooner Catholic* has hundreds of pictures of rivers, creeks, ponds, lakes, and oceans with swimmers. Father Huffer was the photographer and occasionally the subject of those photos.

Did the grand old priest (he died at Enid in 1962 when he was eighty-four) ever swim in Travertine Creek or Baron Fork Creek? The odds are better than even that he did. When you get to heaven, check this story with Bill. He will tell you I understated the case for these Oklahoma swimming holes.

Route 66 and the Case of the Tired Truck

July 1985

The federal government made it official the other day. US Highway 66, the fabled concrete trail from Chicago to Los Angeles, is now a matter of memory. Old Route 66 has evaporated like dew on a July morning.

As many other Oklahomans, I have ridden US 66 from one end to the other—from Lake Michigan to the Kingdom of Smog beside the Pacific. There are recollections of those rides, lots of them. Those that are most memorable to me happened when I was a passenger rather than a driver. Of them all the one experience that ranks first in recall could be called the Case of the Tired Truck.

I was home in Tulsa during summer vacation in 1952. One July day Neal Towner called. "How about going to St. Louis," he said.

Neal described the trip. He would go to St. Louis in a truck he needed to drive there for his employer. We would stay at the seminary in St. Louis (a freebee), leave the truck at a glass plant to be loaded with bottles, take in a baseball doubleheader at Sportsman's Park, pick up the bottles, and go home. Leave on Friday, return on Sunday.

When Neal rolled the big semi-trailer to a stop in front of the Monahans' humble home, I was raring to go. Within the first hour of the journey, between sessions of reading gear shifting instructions to my partner, I discovered that Neal had never driven a semi-trailer until the very day we left.

Suffice it to say we arrived safely in St. Louis. We decided to cruise around the city a bit. The streets were a tight fit for our semi. Turning corners we would roll over curbs, block both lanes, and pray.

It seemed strange that we had seen no other trucks in the city. We noticed people staring at us. Only later did we learn that the Teamsters were on strike in St. Louis. Our ramblings through the city streets under those circumstances could have earned us tire tools embedded in our skulls as souvenirs.

On Sunday morning Neal steered the big truck across the Mississippi River to a huge glass plant at Alton, Illinois. The loading dock at the plant was long and crowded.

The fellow in charge of the loading dock yelled instructions to us to put our trailer "over there." "Over there" was one slot in a row of parked trucks, a slot that we calculated to be about an inch and a half wider than our trailer.

Neal fought the good fight. He backed the truck a little. He pulled forward. He put it in reverse again. He pulled forward. He sweated and he strained—back-ups and pull forwards to the power of 100. Having thoroughly learned the virtue of humility, he went in search of help.

A willing driver was found. Even he had problems parking in that narrow loading space. We buried the gentleman in thank yous.

Now we had it made, except we had not opened the rear doors on the truck. The doors had to fold back flat against the sides of the trailer for loading purposes. To open the doors Neal had to pull out of the parking slot.

Once more Neal went through the exercise of back-ups and pull outs. Once more the willing, but now aggravated, trucker was enlisted. Once more the trailer was parked.

While the trailer was being loaded with umpteen thousand bottles, Neal and I made for the ball park. We spent several hours there lolling in the comfort of an airless, sticky 100 degrees. Great stuff.

By late afternoon we had returned to the glass plant, hooked the trailer on to the tractor, locked the rear doors, and were ready to roll. We were in high spirits—nothing ahead but Route 66 and Oklahoma. We had suffered through misadventures, but they were all behind us.

As if on cue, the truck's engine began to play a different tune. *R-r-r-r-pop! R-r-r-r-r-pop! R-r-r-r-r-poppedy-pop!-pop!* We stopped to call Neal's boss in Tulsa. The boss proved to be clairvoyant. He assured us the truck was all right. His message: On to Tulsa!

We kept moving. *R-r-r-r-pop! R-r-r-r-r-pop! R-r-r-r-r-poppedy-pop! Pop!* on level ground, but now *R-o-o-o-o-w-boom!-boom!-baroom!-Baroom!-BAROOM!* on the upside of the Missouri hills.

Evening was slowly strangling the last light of the long summer's day, when the truck said: "This far and no farther!"

Consider our predicament. We were almost to the crest of a hill, stopped in the westbound lane of the two-lane Route 66, unable to back off the highway for fear we would overturn the truck, and in the company of frustrated, wild, ding-a-ling Sunday evening drivers.

Westbound cars were edging around us on the wrong side of the road. Eastbound traffic, suddenly meeting the westbound in their lane, were slamming on brakes, skidding across the shoulder and into the ditch.

I was dispatched with a flare and a red flag to slow down the eastbound traffic. What followed was a good two hours with a thrill a minute. At one point a carload of intoxicated soldiers was threatening Neal, who, in turn, was backed up by several beefy truckers ready to do battle with the army.

Finally, a wrecker arrived. Neal and I and the truck were hauled down the road to a motel. By midnight the semi-trailer was at rest. The semi-trailer's semi-hysterical occupants were semi-asleep. In their semi-dreams they heard *R-r-r-r-pop!-r-r-r-r-pop!-r-r-r-r-poppedy-pop! pop!*

Hitchhiking Is a Theological Problem for Me

September 1985

Hitchhiking is a theological problem for me.

Prudence and experience tell me that to pick up a hitchhiker is asking for trouble. Each time I read of a driver found minus his heartbeat because of violence perpetrated by a hitchhiker, I resolve—sort of—never again to open my car door for a gentleman of the open road.

Then the words of the Gospel start tapping on my conscience ("As often as you did it for one of my least brothers, you did it for me…as often as you neglected to do it to one of these least ones, you neglected to do it to me.") and I determine—kind of—to take the risk and to help those asking for aid with their thumbs.

The fact of the matter is that I have no clear personal decision about driving by or stopping and offering rides to those at the side of the road. My behavior in these cases is a matter of impulse. All of which more or less explains how I ended up with Junior in my Ford Escort yesterday afternoon.

I had concluded an interview in Clinton and was headed home when I caught sight of this older man reaching out for a ride. He was a Native American. He looked pitiful and a little desperate. I stared straight into his eyes and left him in the dust.

Gospel and common sense wrestled for control. I made a U-turn and went back to get the hitchhiker. The first few seconds told me he had been drinking. The next sixty seconds convinced me he was more than a little drunk—not staggering drunk but near to it. But by that time he and I were on our way to Oklahoma City.

The stereotype of the Native American is of one who is stoic and silent. But this man talked—rambled, questioned, emphasized (with fists pounding the dashboard), answered himself—in a nonstop slur. The best I could do was to catch about 10 percent of the flow.

He told me his name. He lived in Texas. He had relatives in Apache and in Oklahoma City. He refused to get specific about his tribal membership.

If I had trouble with his identity, Junior had more problems with mine. About two miles into our journey, he said, "Are you the police?" He was assured that I was not. He returned again and again, "Are you the police?" Finally he gave up on that one.

"I am a priest," I said. He smiled. "You priest?"

"Yes, I'm a priest."

Junior began talking about God and Jesus Christ. "You can't see God. Jesus Christ knows everything, knows all about us. You can't see God. "

As near as I could figure out, God and sex seemed to be Junior's two major lines of thought. He would weave a crazy quilt of indecipherable words then ask: "What would you do?"

I would look into Junior's seamy copper face—eyes bloodshot, straight, long hair hanging on both sides—and say, "I don't know. I can't understand you."

He would receive that remark with varying reactions: scowling disbelief, a wide grin, fist-pounding disagreement, or disgust at my failure to get the drift of what he was saying.

The longer we rode, the more uneasy I felt. My wild Irish imagination produced pictures of a knife or a gun suddenly produced by Junior.

Actually, all he pulled out of his pockets were a crushed Styrofoam cup, some pieces of cloth, and a penny. This was done as he searched for a mysterious $5 bill, which he was convinced I had given him.

At long last we reached a sign, at the bridge over the North Canadian, which read Oklahoma County. The realization that we were in Oklahoma City stirred new sources of energy in Junior.

He rolled down the window on his side, despite my protests that we had air-conditioning, and began waving and yelling good naturedly at every vehicle we passed. So that's the way we arrived in Oklahoma City late Saturday afternoon.

We left I-40 at the Walker Avenue exit, turned left, and scooted up the street to the bus station. I gave Junior all the change in my pocket—enough for telephone calls, I reasoned, not enough to buy more alcohol.

As I pulled away from the curb, I could see Junior standing with hands at his forehead shading his eyes from the sun.

The pendulum in my psyche had moved to "No more hitchhikers—maybe."

State University's Game Proves to Be Memorable Event

December 1985

Are we having fun, or are we having fun!

Here am I sloshing through the darkened campus of Oklahoma State University during a downpour at 5:30 p.m. on November 30. The trees are encased in wintry ice, but the thunder and lightning are of April. The rain is a swirling, slashing curtain. Water races curb deep in the streets. *Wouldn't it be ironic*, I think, *to be killed by lightning on November 30.*

It's the night of the OU-OSU football game.

Are we having fun, or are we having fun!

Having purchased my dinner of two hot dogs from a soggy vendor in front of St. John University Parish, I enter the church lobby to assess the damage from the deluge:

Feet dry. Good show by galoshes.

Front part of cap soaked.

Overcoat wet in lower part and on back.

Upper part of rain suit wet outside and in. Uh-oh.

Gloves damp.

I reassemble my equipment. Red stocking cap replaces English cap. Wool lined gloves substituted for lighter pair. Buckle up, button up, tie up. Ready for the first half.

Are we having fun, or are we having fun!

I lumber across the street, through the parking lot, and into the stadium. The rain has stopped, but the remains of the rain are transforming to ice. My ticket—Section K, Row 22, Seat 8—is torn in two by a shivering man at the gate. I rent a stadium seat and proceed to my allotted niche above the west end zone.

The field is covered with a light glaze of ice. A student leads us in prayer. The OSU band plays "The Star-Spangled Banner." I cannot work up enough courage to uncover my head out of respect for God and nation. I feel a little guilty.

The athletes come slip-sliding unto the field.

Oklahoma's white uniforms give the players the appearance of camouflaged ski troops. It may be a night for trip plays, illusions in shades of white. But when you are as huge as Keith Jackson or Tony Casillas…well, mountains are clearly visible even when the prairie is covered with snow.

About ten minutes into the game, quarter-sized drops of rain begin to splatter us. Not too bad. But a few minutes later, when we are momentarily distracted from the weather by the game, the rain turns to sleet.

As though some hand were turning a nozzle slowly to open, the sleet gradually intensifies. At some points the press box across the way recedes into a ghostly veil of sleet. The exit ramp immediately to my right covers with grainy ice. Thunder and lightning add to the surrealistic feel of the scene.

The wind changes abruptly, and now the ice pellets are driving straight into our faces. The tiny rascals sting. I cover my face with my gloved hands and peep through a small opening to follow the action on the field. Aching fingers and toes are saved by halftime.

Are we having fun, or are we having fun!

I crunch through the ice to the lobby of St. John's.

The church hospitably opens its doors to dozens of frozen football pilgrims. Ah, blessed warmth. After only several minutes of centralized heat, it's time to return to centralized cold.

Are we having fun, or are we having fun!

The second half sees an improvement, of sorts, in the weather. There is no more precipitation. We settle in to pure unfettered gelidity—flag-straightening gale from the northwest, mercury plummeting in the thermometer, minus zero wind chill penetrating into ears, noses, hands, and feet.

These conditions promote lots of muffled hand clapping, foot stomping, and steamy hollering. A skidding two-yard run merits ten claps. A tune by the Oklahoma State Band—standing seven seats and an aisle to my right—makes for good foot stomping time.

As the hurt of the cold grows, my mind wanders to cowboys. How did they handle nights like these? Did they sit tall in their saddles, humming a few bars from "Red River Valley"? I'm glad I was not to that work called.

Sitting next to me are D.W. and Paula Smith Hearn. We arrived on a bus from Our Lady's Cathedral with thirty or so others (thanks to the organizational efforts and generosity of Sam Kearney and George Grace). "Did you ever read *One Day in the Life of Ivan Denisovich* by Solzhenitsyn?" I ask Paula as the OSU quarterback fires another wild pass across the tundra. "No," she says. I explain that in the story prisoners in a Siberian labor camp were lined up outside each morning. One of them would climb a pole and announce the temperature reading from the thermometer at the top. If it was more than forty below zero, the prisoners did not have to march out to work. "See this isn't so bad!" Somehow my own anecdote fails to warm me. I doubt it had much effect on Paula.

With consciousness centering more and more on the temperature, I decide to check conditions in the press box. Through my binoculars I observe the scribes at work in sweaters and suit coats. Very comfortable. Below the working press area, I spot a larger enclosed section. I'm startled to discover rows and rows of folks lounging in unconcern about frostbite and numbness. These are the elite cowboys, certainly distant relatives of those who saddle up in good times and in foul. I feel like the third-world gazing at North America—jealous.

In the fourth quarter the folks in our area—not many now—
become clock-watchers, frequently craning our necks to read how
many blessed seconds have ticked away. To counteract the official
clock's march to the final whistle, ESPN begins calling more TV
time-outs. We mutter.

At last it's done. The Hearns realize their blanket, on which
they had been sitting, is frozen to the seat. There is no solution
but to rip it free. Next spring a visitor to the west end zone will
find on seats nine and ten in Row 22, Section K, a rather beautiful
pattern of red plaid. Unique is the word for it, but isn't that an apt
description of this whole memorable event.

Are we having fun, or are we having fun!

CHAPTER 10

1986

Confession of a Banana Caramel Addict

June 1986

It's a shameful thing to admit, but as I begin this column I am in the very act of eating a Beich's Banana Caramel. This candy—a luscious, gooey, yellow square—ordinarily about a half an inch thick, will be the death of me yet.

While others wrestle with addictions to tobacco, alcohol, and jogging, I'm hooked on Beich's (say Bikes) Banana Caramels. Only twenty minutes ago, while elbowing for position with a ten-year-old boy at the candy display in the nearby 7-Eleven, I had a moment of panic when I couldn't spot the Banana Caramels in their usual place. But, at last, there they were in a jar on the top shelf. *Ah, blessed relief!* I bought eight of the delicious yellow devils at four cents each.

Why eight? The truth is I could consume 108 in one sitting. Earlier I had chomped my way upward to twelve, fifteen or twenty at a time. Now a limit of eight has been self-imposed. (I've written fifteen lines, and I'm already working on number four of this go-around.)

There is something nostalgic about Beich's Banana Caramels. I get a feeling of having lived through gluttonous binges of Banana Caramels before. Even their wrappers look old-fashioned. (The yellow waxed paper with the plain brown paint has a logo of a smiling banana, wearing a bow tie, slipping on a banana peel or riding a skateboard or swinging on a playground swing—take your pick of interpretations.) But I'm not certain these things date from an earlier period of my life.

My imagination tells me that Beich's Banana Caramels were sold at Mr. Taylor's candy store, a half block from Marquette School on East 15th Street in Tulsa during the 1930s. Memory certifies Mr. Taylor, lightly jingling coins in his pocket as grade schoolers' hungry eyes devoured sweet confections lined in orderly fashion behind the glass of the counter, parted with two cinnamon squares for a penny and handed out bubble gum and baseball cards for an appropriate coin of the realm. But Beich's Banana Caramels? I think so, but I can't be certain. It could be that some 1980's whiz kid of a huckster decided old guys would purchase glued sawdust if it appeared to be an item connected to an idealized childhood and so developed the stuff in the hokey yellow wrappers.

Beich's Banana Caramels are manufactured by the Paul F. Beich Co. in Bloomington, Illinois 61701. The Paul F. Beich Co. may consist of two elderly men, who inherited a secret candy formula from a Dutch uncle, laboriously cranking out sheets of yellow taffy-like substance, hand-cutting them into Banana Caramel squares. Annual production 10,000 units. Sold only in Oklahoma.

Or the company may have 2,000 uniformed employees and a white-smocked research department working relentlessly to produce an ever more perfect Banana Caramel. Beich tankers, bearing liquid tons of the makings of Banana Caramels, may at this moment be moving through the Suez Canal and discharging at Singapore and Lagos. Who knows, Beich's Banana Caramels may be sold in Peking and Paris as well as at Love's Country Store in Watonga.

Nearing the end of this piece, I find eight Banana Caramel wrappers on my writing table. It reminds me of my car, which is habitually littered with the bright yellow wrappers. On windy days they are prone to rise and fly erratically about the car like dazed butterflies.

Dear readers, please don't be too shocked if one of these days my body is discovered on a roadside and the police report tells it like it is: "Male, Caucasian subject ODed on substance from yellow wrappers."

Flagged Out at Northwest Expressway and Rockwell

June 1986

Memorial Day is a week from the Monday of this writing. Flag Day will arrive on June 14. Out here on the Northwest Expressway we are over-prepared for both events.

There is a spot on the median of the Northwest Expressway, a little west of Rockwell Avenue, where one can stand and see nine American flags flying at the same time. A very tall pole with a flying eagle emblem on the top is prepared to receive a tenth flag any day now.

It seems a bit much.

I'm not an opponent of display of the flag. Quite the opposite. I hold my hat over my heart and join in croaking the Star Spangled Banner as the American flag is raised before football games at Owen Field. I am moved by the photos and the sculpture on the west bank of the Potomac of the US Marines struggling to raise the flag on Iwo Jima in March 1945 at a cost of the blood of more than 20,000 of their fellows. I get a thrill out of watching the Stars and Stripes raised over American winners at the Olympics. I'm all for private citizens—from Nichols Hills to Mulligan Flats—showing the flag on the Fourth of July and other special days. I like to see the flag in front of post offices and other government buildings and schools. I appreciate the flag flying over American embassies in Dublin, Paris, Cairo, etc.

What bothers me is the meanness of spirit of those who use the flag for commercial purposes or to create an atmosphere wherein citizens or groups are pressured to wave the flag lest they be judged suspect regarding their patriotism.

The latter situation happened at the time of World War I. Americans with Germanic roots were forced into extraordinary demonstrations of patriotism to prove their loyalty. Predominantly German-American communities were wrapping themselves in the flag in attempts to demonstrate their Americanism even as their sons, brothers, and husbands were suffering and dying in Europe. Kiel, Oklahoma, became officially Loyal, Oklahoma. In the same era when the German language was banned as a subject in Texas schools, Governor "Ma" Ferguson reportedly defended the prejudice by saying, "If English was good enough for Jesus Christ, it's good enough for Texans."

A few years ago many peasants in Guatemala carried their nation's flag as they strode along the roads and flew the flag from their small huts. This was done not out of a burst of patriotic fervor but rather to assure the authorities the peasants were not on the side of the guerrillas. Carry a flag and walk somewhat safely. Don't carry a flag and you might disappear.

Cheyenne Chief Black Kettle was given a medal to wear on his chest by Abraham Lincoln and an American flag to fly above his teepee by the commissioner of Indian affairs. The old chief was told that as long as the flag flew over his camp, American troops would not attack. Col. George Custer and his cavalry charged Black Kettle's camp, flag and all, on Nov. 27, 1868, and in the morning fog massacred Black Kettle, the chief's wife and 101 other Cheyenne. Fifty-three women and children were captured. Eleven of the dead were warriors. Custer's orders had read "to kill or hang all warriors, and bring back all women and children."

Meanwhile back at the intersection of Northwest Expressway and Rockwell, flags fly bravely in the sweet late spring air in front of Tenneco, Brixton Square, Taco Bueno, Continental Federal Savings, Kentucky Fried Chicken, McCartney's Food/Drugs, Crystal's Pizza and Spaghetti, Expressway Bank, and Pioneer

Pies. A few yards farther west, the pole is ready for the American flag to be hoisted in the air to mark the opening of a Hyundai automobile agency. The Korean car is expected to be a big seller under the red, white, and blue.

The code of etiquette for the US flag, as spelled out by Congress in 1942 and 1976, stipulates: "The flag should never be used for advertising purposes."

Please don't think I'm so crass as to suggest the flags flap in the breeze for advertising purposes. For all I know the owners of the various commercial institutions send in double their taxes to help reduce the federal deficit.

But I, for one, must confess that I am flagged out. It would boost my patriotism quotient (and lower my cynicism count) if the flags were kept packed away until really big events came along, as say, Memorial Day and Flag Day.

A Limp Salute to the Texas Sesquicentennial

July 1986

Early morning stupor. Red traffic light on the Northwest Expressway. Slowly, slowly I become conscious of staring at the license plate of the pickup ahead of me. The plate reads Texas Sesquicentennial.

A ragged line of memories begins a disorderly march through my brain. Other drivers are endangered.

Msgr. Raymond Harkin's dictum: "Three things in life which are overrated—adultery, home cooking, and Texas."

- Mark Russell's funny on a recent TV show: Q. What is the difference between a Texas oilman and a pigeon? A pigeon can still make a deposit on a Mercedes.
- The enthusiasm with which the *Dallas Times Herald* greeted Oklahoma's seventy-fifth anniversary as a state in 1982. The *Times Herald*'s headline: "Oklahoma struggles with backward image."
- Sam Houston. There was a man for you. The father of Texas. A rootin' tootin', gun-slingin' progenitor of Texas, he was. If old Sam had lived in the age of cinema and television, John Wayne would have been known only by those to whom he delivered milk. Sam was six-foot-six, as intelligent as he was big. With only 800 troops, he defeated Santa Anna at the decisive Battle of San Jacinto. Yep, Sam Houston was the true prototype of a Texan.

But wait! Sam was born in Virginia. He became a lawyer in Tennessee, and the voters there elected him to two terms in the US House of Representatives. Later he served as governor of Tennessee, resigning that post under mysterious circumstances. He moved to Indian Territory and lived with the Cherokee Nation. The grave of Talihina, Sam's Cherokee wife, can be found in the middle of the Fort Gibson National Cemetery near Muskogee.

Only in 1833 did the great man venture into Texas. Following Texas's independence from Mexico, Sam was picked to be first president of the Lone Star Republic. Five years later he was reelected. From 1846 to 1859, buckskin-clad Sam Houston again strode the corridors of the US Capitol, this time as a senator from Texas. He closed his political life as governor of Texas, 1859-1861 or, more correctly, as the deposed governor of Texas who refused to agree to secession from the Union. Still, rumor has it, the Texans named a city after him.

I recall taking a tour through the Houston home in Huntsville. Our matronly Texas guide described Sam Houston's overthrow as governor because of his loyalty to the United States of America and said "Tha-a-a-t wuz his lowest momint." A male voice from the crowd was heard: "Or his highest." The gentleman did not receive a ticket to the annual ball of the Daughters of the Confederacy.

Sesquicentennial? Heaven help me. I must confess I attended the Texas Centennial. My father took me. We traveled south with his friends, Herb and Merle, and their sons.

The adult members of the party saluted the ties of Texas to the Confederacy with frequent toasts of that favorite beverage of the Old South—bourbon and water. I imagine a red-faced Merle bellowing, "Go easy on the water!"

The only particularly vivid memory I have of the Texas Centennial is a trek through Robert E. Ripley's Believe It or Not exhibition.

Among other wonders my dad and I saw were a fellow with a hole in his back, about six inches above his belt line (it didn't look gross, just peculiar), who could smoke a cigarette and blow the smoke out of his uncommon aperture, a rugged character who lay down on a bed of nails with railroad ties then crossed on his chest and four men standing on the ties, one to each end; and a gent (perhaps the inventor of Murine) who lifted two large buckets filled with sand, which had been attached by hooks to his lower eyelids, by simply standing up.

If the above description has made you queasy, remember it was the era of the Great Depression and people did strange things for the privilege of eating.

Let it be known, in this year of the Texas Sesquicentennial, that this column does not support the suggestion, made by growing numbers of Americans, for a discount sale of Texas to Mexico.

The consequences of the sale would be nasty. Imagine the US Border Patrol chasing rascals like J.R. Ewing, Willie Nelson, and Ross Perot as they waded the Red River seeking economic opportunity in Oklahoma. Do those Texans think fast-food jobs grow on trees?

Sweetie Pie Is Seventy-Five and Still on His Pedestal

August 1986

Last week Chick Finn stepped gracefully past the seventy-fifth anniversary of his birth. The event isn't so important—the man will be playing racquetball in the year 2036—but it provides an occasion to say nice things about a nice guy (Ramon Carlin didn't call him "Sweetie Pie" for no reason at all).

In an age of priestly angst, torturous ambivalence, and crises of identity, Chick (AKA Msgr. C. E. Finn) has proved to be the most secure and serene Roman Catholic clergyman this side of Pope John Paul II. He likes the job. He likes the people associated with it; he probably likes the drunks who telephone rectories in the middle of the night.

Nearby emergency warning sirens, howling the news of an approaching tornado, have been known to cause Chick to toss (once) and turn (once) before returning to a deep slumber. Shaken rudely awake and told, "The Russkies have fired their missiles," Chick would hurry to the phone to see if he could get an earlier starting time for his racquetball game.

He was my boyhood hero. And not only mine. From 1937 when he first arrived on the scene at Christ the King Church until he departed for an assignment at Elk City in 1944, Father Finn was the model of priest for hundreds of Tulsa youngsters.

We placed him on a pedestal. And darned if he hasn't stayed there. While others were falling, jumping, and doing half gainers off their pedestals, Father Finn was busy admiring the world from a better vantage point.

In the classroom we traveled with him through the maze of tunnels of a Roman catacomb. As altar boys, after serving Mass, we swam with him at Crystal City Park (the Riviera of West Tulsa). As high school athletes, we perfumed the rectory by way of our curious football locker room in the basement and set back Jewish-Catholic relationships by our philistine behavior in the synagogue where we practiced basketball—both physical arrangements made by Father Finn in that wonderfully simple but practical way he has of solving problems.

He took us on visits to his family's farm near El Reno. When he moved to Elk City, we followed by railroad and by thumb.

Did Father Finn influence our gang? One day a Benedictine Sister asked a group of us why we didn't smoke. We hemmed thisaway and hawed thataway and we concentrated fiercely on the tops of our shoes, but the best and only answer we could fashion was, "Because Father Finn doesn't." Holy smokes!

In the past third of a century, my time with Chick Finn has been generally "off" days from clerical duties.

In later years, his home at Madalene Church has been open to receive this wayfarer whenever the trail has led to Tulsa.

We have been associates on numerous vacations (or "trips" as he prefers to term anything short of two weeks).

If there is an ocean available, Chick will be the distant figure doing the Canadian County crawl along the line of the horizon, while his companions stand thigh deep in the surf imagining seaweed to be a giant octopus and nothing at all to be a great white shark.

But it's golf images of Chick which crowd my mental VCR. Golf is not really his game, but he plays it with a lovely blend of effort and equanimity.

I possess a photograph of Chick standing in a sand trap. The trap is about the size of the beach at Padre Island, only this one happens to be part of the property of the exclusive Royal St. George's links in Kent, England. He hasn't got a prayer, but do you think he's flustered? Hogan couldn't have been more calm. And Chick enjoyed it more.

Padre Ramon Carlin neatly packaged Chick Finn in these words: "Whenever we have a new project in the diocese, Sweetie Pie always asks two or three of the dumbest questions you have ever heard. Then he goes home and does the best job of anybody." Amen.

Like a Bulldozer Running Full Throttle into Mound of Lard

October 1986

There was only one explanation for the accident. The light was good. The hand was steady. The equipment in tip-top shape. The procedure had been practiced thousands of times.

Then came a distinct feeling of blade cutting through flesh, not scraping the surface, nicking here and there, but slicing thickly as if a bulldozer was run full throttle into a mound of lard. So happened in mid-September the all-time gash in my shaving career.

I'm certain even such renowned practitioners with the knife as Dr. Denton Cooley and Dr. Nazih Zuhdi occasionally make teeny mistakes. However, my cut was the Chernobyl of shaving disasters, an inch-long slash on the underside of my chin.

As I pondered the why of this incident and surveyed the damage in the mirror, the terrible truth seeped into my consciousness. The trouble wasn't with the cutter but with the cuttee. This man staring at me in the mirror has a well-developed set of jowls. As the prophet Nathan said to another David: "You are the man!"

Jowls is not a pretty word. Makes one think of a hog, doesn't it?

If a jowly one looks for a bit of solace in the dictionary, I'm afraid he will find the opposite.

For example, Webster's New Collegiate Dictionary defines "jowl" as "usually slack flesh (as a dewlap, wattle or the pendulous part of a double chin) associated with lower jaw or throat."

If old slack flesh turns to an unabridged Webster (as this sinner did), he is greeted thusly with the definition of "jowl": "a marked fullness and looseness of the flesh about the lower cheek and jaw usually associated with aging." (Okay, Noah, you don't have to rub it in!)

Masochism leads me further and I check out the synonyms:

> – "dewlap: a hanging fold of skin under the neck especially of a bovine animal – see COW illustration";

> – "wattle: a fleshy dependent process usually about the head or neck (as of a bird)."

Webster can be really ugly when he puts his mind to it. I grab the cover of the big dictionary and throw it open to see the great lexicographer's portrait. Sure enough, the lower jaw line is as straight and trim as the edge of a ruler. No "slack flesh," no "marked fullness and looseness." Suspicions rise as to the accuracy of this likeness.

By now I am intensely in to jowls. I find a book with the official White House portraits of the American presidents.

Yes, yes, yes. George Washington, John Adams, Thomas Jefferson, James Madison, and James Monroe—all men with observable jowls.

At this point, some public relations man undoubtedly warned the presidents future generations would be watching for jowls. So John Quincy Adams covered up with sideburns and high collar. Andrew Jackson wore a higher collar plus a voluminous cravat. Martin Van Buren went with sideburns and high collar, but it was futile. The "slack flesh" refused to be contained.

Then there were the bearded presidents—Lincoln, Grant, Hayes, Garfield, Benjamin Harrison. What jowls there might have been were totally buried by the brush.

In the modern era, Richard Nixon was famous for his solemn shaking of jowls. Indeed he helped keep mimics in business.

Of all the presidents, the undisputed jowliest was William Howard Taft. The jowls poured down his chin and around his neck like cascades of melted butter that had hardened into place.

The above is history. But what do psychology, theology, and the arts have to enlighten us about jowls?

Psychologically there are three possible reactions to jowls:

A) Depression
B) To hell with 'em
C) To the plastic surgeon with them

Option C is, of course, reserved for the rich.

Theologically it is the common consensus of Dominicans that jowls, like sweat of the brow, are one of the dire consequences of original sin. (Wasn't Thomas Aquinas kept humble by a fully developed set?)

Jesuit theologians, on the other hand, are inclined to blame the blubbery mess upon prolonged tarrying with the seven capital sins. (Perhaps this explains why Jesuits habitually elect superior generals who appear to be in need of a solid meal.)

Among the poets, the first quote I found on the subject was Robert Browning's:

> His cheek hath laps
> like a fresh-singed swine.

I did not read farther.

With flesh slacking, dewlap hanging, and wattle flapping, as I stomp into old age, I say: To hell with 'em.

The Four Worst Spoken Words in the English Language

October 1986

There is a tribe in America whose mark of identification is a fierce passion for the game and/or the team.

Which game? Which team? The answers are our game (angling, baseball, basketball, badminton, curling, diving, dominoes, equitation, football, golf, hurling, etc., etc., etc., through the alphabet) and our team (Chicago Bears, Boston Celtics, Oklahoma City 89ers, Central State Broncos, Hooker Horny Toads, John Carroll Eagles, Mother McGee's DayCare Micromidgets, or whatever).

By its enemies the tribe is referred to as Philistines. In their self-description, members of the tribe call themselves sportsmen (or sportswomen or sportspersons). A compromise term is sportsophiliacs. I confess I am an irremediable sportsophiliac.

To a sportsophiliac the four worst spoken words in the English language are: "It's just a game."

Example: On the afternoon of September 27, a respectable sportsophiliac in these parts could have been expected to have sat and paced and fretted while the Oklahoma Sooners were clashing with the Miami football team in. After Miami's victory, an Oklahoma sportsophiliac—distraught, angry, feeling the full pull of gravity—slouches into the next room only to be met by his wife. She is beaming with the joy of life but exaggerates woe as she sees the stricken appearance of her spouse. "What's wrong with my baby?" she coos. "Was it that old football game? Remember, it's just a game."

Example: Homer Hogan had played the great game of golf for thirty years. He had placed himself under the tutelage of the best golf instructors. He had read all the how-to-play books. He had practiced as much as his work schedule would allow. And he had never scored lower than eighty-five. But on this day, all the years of Homer's effort suddenly come together for the payoff.

He is long and straight off the tee.

His irons are struck crisply and his shots rain down on the greens one after the other. Leaving the seventeenth green, Homer is only three over par. He can afford to make a double bogey on the final hole and still finish in the seventies. On the eighteenth tee, pride struggles with vanity and sheer elation for the leading emotion. Homer pictures himself playing for the club championship. He is certain now he is Ben's cousin. However, he pops his drive seventy-five yards forward and thirty yards to the right. He hits behind his second shot and moves the ball only twenty yards. Panic sets in. He scores a nine on the par four hole. He walks away in despair, head down. Dr. Lance Boyles, Homer's extroverted playing partner, places an arm around Homer's shoulders. "C'mon, Homer, laugh it off! It's just a game."

It's just a game. Of such stuff are made aggravated assaults, homicides, kicks in the shin, and terrible ten-minute glares. It's just a game. Meek men have been known to turn instantly into raging Rambos. It's just a game. Timid librarians have attempted to drive slender fists through metal doors. It's just a game. Benevolent bishops have been heard to utter "Darn!"

To the ears of the sportsophiliac, "It's just a game" means:

- My, aren't you childish,
- What you have given your totally concentrated being to the past several hours is worthless,
- You poor barbaric boob, your values are all backward and you are, practically speaking, a mental zero.

- Why can't you be more coolly civilized as, for example, I am.

Knocked off balance by "It's just a game," we sportsophiliacs, competitive to the end, are apt to respond with logical profundities:

- If someone entered the Louvre and punched holes through the Mona Lisa's eyes, would you say "It's just a painting"?
- If some nut went into the National Archives Building and tore apart the original copy of the Declaration of Independence, I suppose you would say "It's just a piece of old paper"?
- If someone set fire to the Sunday collection at church, do you think the pastor would say, "It's just money"?

Those kinds of statements are too polite to represent the sportsophiliac's real feelings when someone says sweetly, "It's just a game."

The honest emotions of an offended sportsophiliac can be learned by anyone able to see the images of the mind of the distraught one. In the sportsophiliac's mind, Charon, the mythical lower world boatman, can be seen slowly rowing his skiff across the misty River Cocytus toward the shore of the damned. Charon's lone passenger looks amazingly like the last person to say to you "It's just a game."

As the tiny vessel makes its way surely toward the far bank, the groans and moans of the damned can be heard distinctly above the lap of the water. Cerberus, the three-headed guard dog of the lower world, begins to bark ferociously. The passenger, realizing what is happening, argues with Charon that she has been a good person, kindly disposed to all and a giver of old clothes to the Junior League thrift shop. Gloomy Charon doesn't answer but rows steadily toward the looming shore.

In the last fifty yards, the shrieks and howls of the damned are overpowering, the sulfurous odor would make a three-days-dead catfish nauseated. The passenger's terror rises with each dip of the oars. As the skiff touches the land, wrinkled Charon turns to his trembling charge, and, cackling hideously, says, "It's just a game."

Your Choice:
A Brooding Lincoln or
a Muddy Grant

November 1986

Drivers maneuvering their vehicles along the Northwest Expressway these days see an old duck wearing a short-billed cap behind the wheel of a 1981 Ford Escort, license YZ-54. What they don't realize is Chuck Yeager flies again.

That isn't an Escort at all but the X-1, experimental rocket airplane. And the figure in the cockpit is Yeager, jaunty hero of 10,000 air adventures.

Even now Yeager's hand reaches toward the switch that will fire the rockets and take the X-1 and him bursting through the sound barrier. But darn! There's the stoplight at MacArthur. While waiting for the light to go green, Yeager notices Texaco unleaded is selling for 67.9.

This month I'm Chuck Yeager. Next month I may be Barry Switzer, tensely pacing the sideline as Oklahoma and Nebraska slug it out or Vladimir Horowitz, magically stroking the piano keys in concert at the Kennedy Center.

The reason I'm Yeager now is *Yeager* the book. Good books can cause this metamorphosis in me. So can films or magazine articles or a good piece in a newspaper.

I interview youngsters for the *Sooner Catholic*. I often ask them who their heroes are. Most frequently they reply: "I don't have a hero." That's hard for me to understand. I think I've got hundreds of heroes, and I'll be happy to loan you a few. Would you like to be Gen. Patton crossing the Rhine on a pontoon bridge as shells burst overhead or Jesse Orosco coolly nicking the comers of the plate with his pitches in the last game of the World Series?

My weakness for heroes may explain why I saw the movie *The Secret Life of Walter Mitty* six times. In this classic, written by James Thurber, Mitty daydreams of being an unsinkable sailing ship's captain, an incredibly deft surgeon, a dashing RAF ace, and a cunning Mississippi riverboat gambler.

If you're too mature to soar with your dreams, forget about being an authentic hero worshiper.

When you have mastered your roles well, you can switch from one character to another as the situation requires. Otherwise you may be a humble Francis of Assisi strolling quietly into a gunfight at the OK corral. It won't work.

Some examples of heroes to fit the occasion:

If you are a guest at the lodge on the east side of Glacier National Park and you are by yourself and the sun is setting and laughter can be heard in the background and you're gazing at the darkening waters of St. Mary Lake from the balcony of the lodge, it's a great time and place to be Humphrey Bogart. You are Bogie, drink in hand, surveying the scene with that tough but sad look in your eyes. The chilled air finds paths to your skin, and you pull your collar up around your neck. A particularly moving memory floats across your consciousness, and your right cheek twitches. Your eyes narrow as you take a long drag off your cigarette. (One problem: You will have to holler loudly to let the piano player hear "Play it again, Sam." Sam is three floors below.)

If you are playing golf at Lake Hefner Golf Course, you might want to be different personae as the scenes change.

- Having somehow crisply struck a 3-iron and landed on the green at the long number two hole (the third time you have accomplished that feat in 316 rounds there), you want to stride purposefully up the fairway a la Arnold

Palmer, tossing a lighthearted comment to your caddy (if
you had a caddy) and, of course, hiking your pants.

- Facing a perfectly flat three-foot putt on the eighth
green, with ten cents riding on the outcome, you become
Fuzzy Zoeller, pursing your lips in a silent whistle as you
nonchalantly approach the ball. As the ball falls in the
cup, you wink confidentially at a rake in the trap.

- Walking to your ball from the eighteenth tee with the
whole match to be settled on this final hole, you are the
dreaded Texas Hawk, Ben Hogan. You make 117 precise
calculations about the next stroke as you limp along—
direction of wind, degree of humidity, positions of the
planets, etc. Tight-lipped you pull out your deadly five
iron, and you wonder: Did Hogan ever play his second
shot on the eighteenth from the tenth fairway?

If you are the chairman of the annual parish picnic and the
whole project begins to come apart at the seams—the butcher,
who is the pastor's nephew, has delivered 100 dozen second-class
wieners at a deluxe price; and the evening news' weatherman has
changed his prediction from mild and sunny to a forty-degree
drop in yesterday's high with either sleet and/or high winds; and
the president of the altar society is telephoning you ten times
a day to argue about the color of the paper napkins; and your
friends are avoiding you because they think you will want to put
them to work; and the treasurer for the picnic has disappeared
with the $2,000 collected for the event as well as his neighbor's
wife—you might want to consider Abraham Lincoln or US
Grant. You could be a brooding Lincoln after Chancellors-ville
or a mud-spattered Grant outside of Vicksburg. (My personal
opinion is Grant would go better at a picnic.)

Stepping Warily into Faith, Hope, and Hollywood

November 1986

Reality. Southwest Airlines Flight 757 skims a smooth ocean of air 30,000 feet above the Mojave Desert in the evening of November 3.

I am observing life from seat 4D. Across the aisle in 4B, a young mother holds a baby in her lap. Baby is expressing herself, i.e. wailing. A perfect pitch is reached, and baby's slightly older sister in seat 4A launches into a counterwail. We have a wail duet in the fourth row.

A middle-aged gent in 4C looks neither left nor right. He stoically partakes of his pacifier, a can of lite beer.

The caterwauling momentarily distracts me from studying Blondie Red Nails in 3C. She wears a bright red sweat shirt but not as bright as her stiletto-like fingernails. She has recently completed a retouch project on her face. Working out of a small kit, she performed a precise lube and dab job. With a mirror the size of a quarter, she surveyed her physiognomy for signs of uncamouflaged erosion. She is no kid. A second chin is beginning its inevitable fall toward the floor.

Now the Mormon Tabernacle Choir of Wails causes her to take a quick look over her left shoulder. Her glance conveys annoyance. I feel for the mother. I'm angry with Blondie Red Nails.

I, a celibate with neither chick nor child, muse on the condition of American society. What a strange outfit! Children have become foreigners here. We want to cruise comfortably in the night isolated from the sounds of life. Would that fifty babies crying were on board! I imagine a slogan: "Save the Wails."

But what's this? Blondie Red Nails is smiling and waving to the children. The volume of the crying turns down, then off. Blondie is destroying my image of her. When I look again, she is reading a thin book: *The Seven Cardinal Sins*.

As Flight 757 whistles across the spangles of light that is Los Angeles, I'm left with the ashes of rash judgment gritty on my conscience.

Step into the future. I'm in LA to attend a convention. It is the annual gathering of The National Catholic Association for Communicators, also known as UNDA-USA.

To be frank I anticipate feeling as at home as Brian Bosworth in Austin. Here I am short, shy, and shriveled at an extravaganza whose theme is Faith, Hope, and Hollywood. In a land of transponders and microcomputers, glamour and Gucci, where people network instead of talk, I walk in my Wolverine Work Shoes, clutching my trusty BIC pen. I step warily out of my league and out of my era.

Future shock strikes early, on the elevators at the Marina Beach Hotel. Having had the faith to check into this palace of pizzazz, I now have the hope of getting to my room. But a ghost of Hollywood appears as I surely recreate an old Buster Keaton role in *The Elevator*.

My room number is 8313. But I can't push the button for the eighth floor. That is, I press and press and press all around the numeral eight on the panel of the elevator, but the door doesn't close. I get off the elevator #1 and board elevator #2. Same problem. No light on the panel, no ascension.

Logic goes to work. I think: *the seventh floor is closer to the eighth than the lobby is*. I push the button for seven, and away I go. The seventh floor is nice, but there is no ladder to the eighth. I try elevator #3. No luck for eight. I return to the lobby. In the lobby,

I go back to elevator #2. I push 8. Nothing. I stare at it. Another man enters the elevator.

"How do you get to the eighth floor?"

"You have to insert this plastic card, which is your room key, into this slot by eight."

"Oh, sure. Heh-heh-heh."

Comes the dawn. Time for the good old shower. There is no warning a degree in hydraulics is needed to operate the shower. There are two handles. One has a succession of circles around its base each circle slightly larger than the one before. The other handle has some blue circles and some red circles.

Calmly I choose to apply reason to the process of the shower: I grab both handles and begin to twist and turn them. Eventually a burst of ice water explodes on my skin.

Now there is only one course to follow, blind panic. I twist the handles. I push, I pull. I'm jumping around saying "Oh! Oh! Oh!" when suddenly the water becomes warm. It's all Yankee know-how. We Americans breathe it in with our culture.

Retreat into the present. Somehow I get to the opening luncheon of the fifteenth Annual Assembly of UNDA. For $18 we are served a salad, which is topped by stuff that one guesses was the packing used in the crate carrying a large valve delivered to the hotel's maintenance department.

Our speaker is a handsome curly-haired young man. He carries his suit well. He is suspected of being a fugitive from a nighttime soap opera. I follow his speech, as he reads it, right up to the point where he says "that is the EP-i-tome" (rhymes with home).

In the panel presentation, after the luncheon, we take off on the wings of "Forecasting the Future." The concepts soar toward the ozone, until a stout woman rises to comment. One hundred and fifty people are firmly seated around her, as she says, "We all know that or we wouldn't be standing in this room."

I have been wrong. Rash judgment again. These are my kind of people.

CHAPTER 11

1987

A Seven-Course Feast of Laughs for a Condemned Man

March 1987

I met Danny Kaye for the first time on a warm summer evening in 1945. The place was the Ambassador Theater on Grand Avenue in St. Louis. He was on the screen. I was in the audience.

The movie was "Wonder Man."

Danny Kaye played the role of identical twins. One was a comedian linked to the Mob; the other an introverted academic who wrote simultaneously with both hands.

Inevitably there was mistaken identity. The bookworm was taken against his will and thrust upon the stage of a nightclub. So I was introduced to Danny Kaye as the terrified scholar reciting "Under the spreading chestnut tree, the village smithy stands" to a crowd of hoods and molls.

The occasion is glued to my memory, because on the next day I walked into Glennon Preparatory Seminary to begin eight years of preliminaries leading to ordination. In a sense, "Wonder Man" was the proverbial last meal for the condemned man. And it was a seven-course feast of laughs. (Eventually I saw it five times, by actual count.)

In the latter half of the 1940s and through the 1950s Danny Kaye appeared in about one film a year. (Altogether he made 17 or 18.) I watched for those gems with the avidity of Columbus's lookout squinting across the water for the first sight of "India."

There was a personal problem for me viewing his movies. I laughed so hard it became painful. Not only would tears run down my face, but my sides would ache. Finally I would have to turn my eyes away from the screen lest I succumb of hilarity. (How would The Daily Oklahoman have reported my death in that event: "Coroner says priest victim of acute risible spasms" or "Inquest reveals clergyman's death was a laugh"?)

Danny Kaye died this past Tuesday. Ne was 74, a nimble spirit whose body grew old.

I was shocked when a well-educated young woman who works at the Pastoral Center said, "Who was Danny Kaye?" That quote was a Lenten meditation in itself. But the answer to the question has to be two-sided: Danny Kaye was a comic genius and a genial man of self-sacrificing goodwill.

In his latter role, he became identified with the United Nations Children's Fund. He crisscrossed the United States, once zooming his· act on behalf of children to 65 American cities in five days while piloting his own jet, and toured the world for UNICEF. He raised enough cash over three decades to keep millions of Third World youngsters alive and healthy.

Some readers may recall TV news shots of Danny Kaye, in a remote non-English-speaking area of Africa, convulsing the villagers with his rubbery face, graceful hands and feet, and rapid-fire gibberish.

Although he could read music no better than a crow, he became famous as a zany guest conductor of symphony orchestras. All for the sake of others – musicians' pension funds and local symphonies mired in debts (including Oklahoma City's).

His was a beautiful American story: Born David Daniel Kaminski, the son of a Jewish tailor in Brooklyn, he courted and married Sylvia Fine (to whom he stayed wed for his remaining 47 years), and burst upon the Broadway scene in 1941 by sprinting melodically through the song "Tchaikovsky" in which he clearly articulated the names of 57 Russian composers in 38 seconds.

Sylvia Fine was Danny Kaye's partner not only in marriage but also in entertainment. She wrote many of his songs and skits.

His movies were plain cotton strings of plot from which were suspended four to six dazzling jewels of comedy. His fans might not remember the titles of the shows but might have near perfect recall of a single excerpt. Some of my favorites:

- Kaye's character is pursued by two ruthless groups determined to kill him. He finds himself seated under a table on either side of which two would-be assassins are discussing the situation. Each places a hand on one of Kaye's knees instead of their own. Kaye immediately places his hands on their knees and then attempts to copy their hand movements on his knees – one scratching, the other patting etc., etc.
- Kaye is forced into knightly combat in "Court Jester", but before the contest a toast must be drunk. A witch whispers to him that one of the goblets contains deadly contents. First she says something like, "The chalice from the palace has the brew that is true. The vessel with the pestle has the potion that is poison." A moment later the witch says, "There's been a change. The brew that is true is in the flagon with the dragon. The potion with the poison is in the chalice from the palace." Kaye's wild-eyed stagger toward the cups, while tying those rhymes into unbelievable knots, is an event to see and hear.
- The opera scene of "Wonder Man" in which Kaye is suddenly carried into a mixture of muscular baritones, a Himalayan-sized soprano, a frantic prompter, and, yes, the bad guys intent on killing him.
- Any segment of "The Secret Life of Walter Mitty."' – the ship's captain, the surgeon, the riverboat gambler, the RAF fighter pilot – leaves an onlooker limp from guffawing. About that film, *The Christian Science Monitor* stated, "Few audiences have laughed as hard as those who

watched Kaye as the meek and drably decent Everyman grappling with the barbarisms of daily life and dreaming of gallant alternatives." Few? Speaking for myself, I say "None."

Danny Kaye was a Wonder Man.

Being an Account of an Exodus to the Promised Land

April 1987

Easter was late in 1946, April 21 to be exact. To a young seminarian in St. Louis the period from the end of the Christmas holidays to Easter had seemed merely several centuries.

In keeping with the odd liturgical calendar of that era, when the Easter vigil somehow had slid back to Holy Saturday morning, the freedom starved inmates of St. Louis Preparatory Seminary were not sprung until the Alleluia rites had been duly observed.

It was a sweet, sunlit 8 a.m. into which Charlie Skeehan and I ran. We plunged down the hill east of the seminary building, crossed the railroad tracks and descended further to the highway. We were going home to Oklahoma. Alleluia! Alleluia!! *Alleluia*!!!

The highway was U.S. 66, two good lanes – one in each direction – from Chicago to Los Angeles. America had taken to the road that spring morning.

The Second World War had ended eight months earlier. Gasoline was available again. Civilian cars were rolling once more off Detroit assembly lines.

On Route 66 these new flivvers were being pulled west by a fleet of trucks without cabs. The goggled drivers simply sat there in the open, washed by the wind and vulnerable to every airborne insect, as they barreled their vehicles down the concrete path.

Charlie and I set about our task of hitchhiking. Several details of the drama remain clear to me. One is that we had 14 rides between St. Louis and Tulsa over a period of more than 20 hours. Another recollection is standing for quite a stretch at the identification marker of Cuba, Mo., and singing our theme song: Alleluia! Alleluia!! *Alleluia*!!! Then there was a ride in the back of an open truck, and one, in a car with folks on their way to a wedding reception, and a downhearted trudge in the dark through the outskirts of Springfield, Mo., and a mysterious midnight stop outside a seedy motel near Joplin when our host driver disappeared amid shouting and coarse laughing (which did not seem to be identical with the biblical cries of joy in the tents of the just).

Our greatest adventure began in Rolla. We had been strolling along the shoulder of the highway, trying to get to the other side of the town, when a 1930s vintage Ford came sliding to a stop.

We were more naive than Tom Sawyer on Wall Street. We hopped into the back of the car as soon as the door opened. By the time the door slammed shut, Charlie and I knew we were in trouble.

The driver and his front-seat buddy were more completely lubricated than the automobile. With all due respect, they were roaring drunk – a pint or two beyond control, a few swigs away from paralysis. They were sharing a bottle filled with a green substance – hair oil, cough medicine, or an unusual batch of bourbon.

We left Rolla faster than Apollo 9 left Florida. Unfortunately old U.S. 66 west of Rolla was an extraordinary series of curves. We skidded safely around those curves at terrifying speeds – in clouds of dirt on the shoulders, crossing center lines to the horror of oncoming drivers – thanks to the skill of the driver and the work of a cloud of guardian angels.

On the passenger's side of the car, the door was not firmly shut. When the driver discovered this, he raced the Ford as hard as he could, then slammed on the brakes. The door flew open, and the passenger came close to leaving us. Both of them howled with laughter as though this were on film and not in real life. We repeated this thrilling scene a half a dozen times.

To compound problems, please recall that in this American spring following the four-year winter of war, two out of three citizens were either traveling to California or returning from there, all on a two-lane road. When our driver hit the brakes, automobiles and trucks scattered in all directions trying to avoid collisions. We left a trail of foul language and shaking fists.

Meanwhile, in the back seat, Skeehan and Monahan were not inactive. No, sir, we were reciting Acts of Contritions with intense fervor and lightning-like speed.

The ordeal ended when the Ford popped its fan belt. Voices quavering, we excused ourselves from the steaming car despite the message from the driver "If yoush wait chust a few minutesh, we're gonna railroad outta here."

The exodus across the Missouri desert concluded at first light on Sunday morning as Charlie and I walked away from our final ride on East 11th Street in Tulsa. It was a joyful day in the promised land. Alleluia! Alleluia!! *Alleluia*!!!

Pre-Match Prophecy: May the Worst Player Win!

July 1987

The last we heard of our golfing heroes they were slogging through a cold October rain at the Shangri-La Blue Course at Grand Lake.

On that occasion, J. McGlinchey (the left-handed Lee Trevino) scored a narrow victory over his sodden but undaunted opponent, D. Monahan. (For weeks after the October match D. Monahan rubbed his right elbow with his left hand and winced frequently to indicate the handicap under which he labored in the sporting contest. No one paid attention to the rubbing, but the wincing did bring one suggestion "about treatment for the tic in your face.")

About 5:00 p.m. on June 24, J. McGlinchey and D. Monahan could be seen moving ever so slowly along the eighteenth fairway at Fire Lake south of Shawnee. The temperature touched ninety-five, and the relative humidity was not far behind. No wind.

Spectators on the clubhouse porch, observing the twosome, were placing wagers on the likelihood of the golfers being physically able to complete their round. The odds were even on the slender player in the white hat, white shorts and white sneakers. The odds leaped from 25-1, to 50-1, to 100-1 over the probability of the poor creature in the straw hat making it. He limped badly and his forward motion was of the zigzag variety.

B. Hogan, B. Nelson and S. Snead, the golfing immortals, are seventy-five this Year of the Lord 1987. J. McGlinchey and D. Monahan, the mortals, have reached sixty.

The fact that this was an anniversary contest put J. McGlinchey and D. Monahan on the alert for the real possibility of troubling crowds gathering to follow their biannual clash.

The two Titans of the Tee slipped away to a different course in their attempt to avoid an emotionally overcharged gallery. They were successful. Nary a spectator showed, unless one counts squirrels, turtles, one long-billed bird and a guy watering the third green.

Highlights and lowlights:

- J. McGlinchey's long chip shot on the par three eighth hole which, like a heat-seeking missile, rolled unerringly toward the cup and dropped for a deuce.
- D. Monahan's putt from the fringe on the par three eleventh, a bit too fast, but it hit the middle of the hole and stayed put for a birdie.
- The scores of six, seven and eight on the first three holes (all par fours) to start the second round, by D. Monahan. Being an astute gatherer of trivia, the player in question calculated this progression carried through nine holes would bring a neat fourteen on the ninth and a tidy first nine total of ninety.

The sexagenarian opponents played at opposites in their Fire Lake encounter.

D. Monahan's short game got worser as it got shorter. If the immemorial duffer's rule (one need not putt those "within the leather") did not apply, the man would have needed a personal computer to total each hole's score. From three feet away he could and did miss the entire cup by six inches, repeatedly.

If D. Monahan pulled out his pitching wedge, J. McGlinchey vacated a 180-degree arc in front of him. D. Monahan shanked right, pulled left, or went straight forward with the wedge, but, in the latter case, either rolling along the ground or as a line drive. It was as though he were a trick shot artist who first learned the

278

DAVID MONAHAN

comic part of his act and got frozen there. J. McGlinchey admits he had to look away at times lest he become nauseous.

On the other hand, J. McGlinchey's long game was a sad sight to behold. One often beheld it by arching one's neck far back to follow the extraordinary upward flight of his tee shots which fell back to earth some eighty yards from the point of club striking ball. These zoomers were alternated with Screaming Mimi hooks.

Somehow J. McGlinchey had arrived for the match without his venerable driver, Old Smoker. In place of Old Smoker, he had substituted a new metal three wood. (If a metal three wood sounds contradictory such are the surprises found in the great puzzles of golf, astronomy and the like.) On the second day of play, at the first tee, an onlooker remarked about the peculiar shaft of the metal club. In golf as in war the shiniest technological toy does not always deliver the greatest bang for the buck.

D. Monahan won the match play event six and five. It was his first victory over the wily J. McGlinchey in four years.

The victor reminded the press that his triumph perfectly fitted his pre-match statement: "May the worst player win!"

On a Tired Evening, Twenty Years of Rock 'n' Roll

December 1987

Last week I was stumbling tired. We had had serious mechanical problems with our typesetting equipment. The completed pasted up copy of our newspaper due at the printer's at noon arrived there at 5:30 p.m.

At last, I wandered into my room and flipped the on button of the television set. Suddenly I found myself in the middle of Rolling Stone's "20 Years of Rock 'n' Roll."

"They say they know me," said a sour Bob Dylan. "They don't know me."

I agree with Bob; I don't know him. And I certainly don't know that larger matter of rock 'n' roll, which has been so much of Mr. Dylan's life. As I watched the various exponents of this modern art form come within millimeters of swallowing microphones whole, I lolled in my chair and prayed, "Lord, help me understand!"

Strangely enough, I have had more experience with rock 'n' roll than one might suspect of a sixty-year-old celibate bachelor. God's providence ("Lord, I believe; help my unbelief!") placed me in its beating way. I was a high school principal precisely in the time period when rock was born and started pounding along its path toward a maturity of sorts. When Madonna was being baptized and punker Sid Vicious was still a sweet cooing infant, I was already a trembling veteran of too many rock dances.

Once someone at McGuinness High School had the creative idea of holding a school dance at a motel on Interstate 35.

(Creative in this context probably meant it was less expensive.)
The room for the dance was too small for the event and the rock
band could have remained in Yukon and have been heard clearly
where we were.

In the course of the dance, I was in the hall outside the music
area and happened to place my hand against the wall. Vibrations,
man, vibrations! In the next thirty minutes, I checked other parts
of the motel for vibrations. The whole joint was vibrating. One
could imagine some guy who had been driving on I-35 all day
from San Antonio and was worn out. He checks into this motel,
falls into bed and has his nerves twisted into the tightest coils
ever by the vibrations. At 11:30p.m., the vibrations stop and the
uncoiling process starts only to be interrupted by a 6:00 a.m.
wake up call.

As old artillerymen who have had one too many explosions
next to their eardrums, so former chaperones at rock 'n' roll dances
walk through the remainder of their lives with hands permanently
cupped behind their ears and saying "What? What?" to every
comment or query.

The noise was so overwhelming at those rock dances I was
convinced that you could say anything to anybody there – shout
it into their ear – with the perfect confidence that nothing would
be heard. I feel certain perceptive students have yelled at me
during such dances, "You are the dumbest jackass ever to set foot
on this property," and I have smiled and nodded in agreement.

I recall an idealistic young nun's worried look when she met
Andy, a disheveled, wet-with-perspiration ninth grader, in the
hall during a school-sponsored rock dance. This once innocent
child screamed at the Sister, "Isn't this great! I feel wild!"

Rock 'n' roll pursued me after I left McGuinness. Once I was
helping two young adults prepare for a wedding scheduled to be
celebrated at a regular Sunday liturgy. The groom was a devotee—
no, a wild fanatic—of the rock group Led Zeppelin. He was not
a Catholic.

The Led Zeppelinite sat patiently through instructions and discussions and paperwork required for a wedding in the Catholic Church. Finally, he had but one request: as an entrance hymn for the wedding Mass could we play "Desperation" by Led Zeppelin? Request denied.

So I stared at "20 Years of Rock 'n' Roll." It was a national review of the passing columns of rockers: Elvis Presley, John Lennon with purple granny glasses, The Grateful Dead, Dylan, Grace Slick, Mick Jagger and Tina Turner, Cyndi Lauper, Neil Young, Marvin Gaye, The Jefferson Airplane, Prince, Kenny Rogers, Talking Heads, Fleetwood Mac, Blondie, Alice Cooper, Michael Jackson, Moody Blues and onward into the night.

There was a lot of talk about rebellion and expression thereof. One weary fellow with a band around his head and a face eroded by time and decibels spoke of rock as the spring of eternal youth. An odd spokesman for that point of view.

In the conversation, there was a grasping for an elusive something that…that couldn't be quite nailed down with words.

Somehow I was reminded of Ken Kesey, as described in Tom Wolfe's "The Electric Kool Aid Acid Test." Kesey was concerned with "lags" in life, that is, for example, the little gap between "the time your senses receive something and you are able to react." He wanted to close that gap, make a "breakthrough" so he could actually live in the present.

Kesey's yearning for a "breakthrough," his huge desire to make life something more than it is, is that what the rockers are finally all about? A chase of God?

One fat, bald, bearded rock musician concluded: "The damage has been done. The world is going to have to live with it." At least until some sound as yet unknown takes its place; and Madonna is interviewed at the nursing home pining for the "sweet old music"; and Bob Dylan is the conservative nominee to the Supreme Court.

CHAPTER 12

1988

You Are Responsible for the Life in Your Aquarium

January 1988

On Sundays and major Church celebrations Catholic priests pray a canticle from the Book of Daniel: "You dolphins and all water creatures, bless the Lord."

I don't have a dolphin yet, but a water creature, yes. Exactly six paces from where I scribble this, there swims today a filmy blue water creature.

When Brother Fish was splashed in my lap, so to speak, on the eve of Christmas Eve; I was, as Elvis used to say, all shook up. The smiling givers were Judith and Gene O'Brien.

My condition was akin to a man who left home in the morning unaware of new life in the offing only to return home in the evening to discover his wife has borne a son. Well, almost akin.

Somewhere deep inside my being, the thought burbled: Your life never again will be the same. You are the parent of a fish.

The blue note which accompanied the blue finny one said Brother Fish was "glorifying God by breathing with gills and being fluidly handsome."

As any new parent, I stared through the translucent plastic walls into the watery nursery. My fish obviously was a beauty, truly "fluidly handsome." In fact, very probably the most handsome darn fish in this city.

He is long and slender, but only about the size of a minnow. His fins trail after him in a silky revelation of light blues.

Brother Fish travels under the label of a Betta or Siamese Fighting Fish. I can see myself now being sucked into an argument with an eight-year-old altar server: "My Siamese Fighting Fish is tougher than your Siamese Fighting Fish!" Can't he see it is so?

On Christmas Day, I read the instructions about the care of tropical fish and the maintenance of an aquarium. I studied a two-page, legal-sized, single-spaced typewritten copy.

At the very bottom of the sheet, typed totally in capital letters, was this sentence: *"you are responsible -for the life in your aquarium."*

No fanfare. No emotion. Just the cold crushing declarative sentence: *"you are responsible for the life in your aquarium."* Holy cow! One day you are breezing along without a care and the next: *"you are responsible for the life in your aquarium."*

I imagined such responsibility only tapped the shoulders of airline pilots and brain surgeons. But here I am going eye to eye with Brother Fish, and he is saying, "OK, buddy! It's all up to you."

Then I read the actual instructions.

"Every three months change the air diffusers or air stones in the lift tubes of the under gravel filter system."

Huh?

"Use of an aquarium water buffer product is often necessary to prevent pH levels from dropping below neutral."

How's that again?

"Connect the air lift tubes with the elbows and diffusers in place to the plate…you should see water flowing from the elbows."

I pulled up the sleeves of my sweater, but I'm sorry to report there was no sign of water flowing from my elbows.

The only thing I am certain of in the instructions is the misspelling of the word relieve in the last paragraph on page one.

However, the O'Brien's foresaw this very' problem: my inability to grapple with earthly matters. Their practical friendly advice: "Get your staff to help you."

My pitiful appearance this Monday morning after Christmas- anxiety lines grooved in brow, dark circles under, eyes, twitching muscles at corner of mouth has called forth an outpouring of compassion from Joan O'Neill. Brother Fish and I may swimmingly make our ways to 1988.

P.S. At the bottom of the second page of instructions it reads again: *"you are responsible for the life in your aquarium."* Then there is added solemnly: *be prepared.*

In 1945, There Were 144,000 Bald-Headed Women

January 1988

A record breaker! I'm looking out my office window at a Siberian scene. A fellow from Resurrection Cemetery riding a big yellow scraper is gouging a path through the snow in front of the archbishop's house. Drifts are three and four feet deep around the corners of the Pastoral Center. Weathermen say it is the greatest single snowstorm in Oklahoma City's history.

We Americans love records and breaking them. The fastest, the highest, the tallest, the heaviest, the lowest—just so it's the mostest. On the day of the 1987 stock market crash, even as we watched in horror, there was some weird part of us whispering, "I hope it sets a record!"

Coming of age in a sports-oriented family, I began early on to assemble a mental warehouse full of facts—Ty Cobb's .367 lifetime batting average, Babe Ruth's 714 home runs, Tulsa's population 142,157, and so on. My high school English teacher thought I was pleasant enough but despaired when she discovered my desk drawer stuffed with scraps of paper detailing football players' weights and basketball players' heights (I'm still checking to see if the OU offensive line of this past season was the heaviest of all time).

In the seminary I made the mistake of announcing a little-known fact of 1945: "There are 144,000 bald-headed women in the United States." I was labeled "Odd Facts."

Peculiarly enough I was in the process of becoming a priest in a diocese which already boasted a master of trivia of the same title, Father John C. "Odd Facts" McGinty. And, stranger than fiction, we ended up seated next to one another at table for several years. There the odd facts evolved into odder facts and, at times, nearly reached the zenith of oddest facts.

Known therefore to be a person with pronounced difficulties in operating pencil sharpeners but always able to recall the background of the invention of the Popsicle' it is only to be expected that others would kindly build on my strength by presenting me with-gifts of "Amazing Facts."

"Amazing Facts: the Indispensable Collection of True Life Facts and Feats" by one Richard B. (for Brimful?) Manchester was handed to me as a Christmas present by a colleague who regularly is buried in heaps of odd facts gushing out of my mouth. I have not yet concluded whether "Amazing Facts" was her choice because of a pixie-like Irish sense of humor or a get-even rage because of time forever lost in the retelling of the 1962 Oklahoma-Notre Dame game in which the Sooners started a 178-pound tackle (can you imagine?).

In any event, "Amazing Facts" on its dust jacket holds out hopes of learning – the tallest house of cards ever built, the record distance for bed pushing and the vegetable which sells for the highest price per pound.

So, you want to know about snow! Alright. Your ordinary snowflake takes eight to ten minutes to strike the ground from a height of 1,000 feet. A little known but amazing fact.

How about some data on extinct animals? For example, the glyptodon was a humongous mammal which lumbered about South America more than a million years ago. Later it migrated north as far as what is now the southern United States.

(If you are camping out at the Chickasaw National Recreation Area next summer and the animal nosing into your tent looks a bit like an armadillo but is as big as a Mayflower moving van, you may have been discovered by a scientific rarity.)

Which brings us to eyeglasses. Did you know the earliest surviving portrait of a person wearing spectacles is of Cardinal Ugone? It was painted by Tommaso da Modena in 1352. The funny part about this is that Cardinal Ugone died in 1250 before the first appearance of eyeglasses. Another amazing fact.

Then there is the ever-gnawing worm which gives the publication of newspapers (and their editors) some interesting perspective. It's not literally a worm but the acids produced by alum-rosin compounds used to coat pulpwood paper. The acids eat away at the paper. Thus the pages of all newspapers as well as most books published new will be yellow and brittle within a half of a century. Approximately one of every three books of the 18 million in the Library of Congress is already too fragile to be handled. Dust to dust.

The research of George Washington Carver made peanuts a widely grown crop, but a nameless St. Louis physician of 1890 came up with peanut butter. About half of the four-billion pound U.S. peanut crop is now made into peanut butter. (Which reminds me that peanuts are called goobers and Goober Crawford, second baseman of the Tulsa Oilers 50 years ago, was my Aunt Agnes's unfavorite player. And who was the right fielder on Goober's team? We all remember Stan "Pappy" Schino, don't we?)

Snowflakes, glyptodons, Cardinal Ugone, paper and Goober Crawford. As Casey Stengel was wont to say, "Amazin'! Simply amazin'."

For the answers to the tantalizers in paragraph four turn this newspaper upside down and read the amazing facts.

A) Either Carter Cummins (51 stories in a tower of 2,206 cards, 9 1/2 feet high) or Joe E. Whitlam (73 stories, 13 feet 10 inches high) is the house of cards winner. Joe's feat is disputed because he bent some cards.

B) Twelve young Pennsylvanians pushed a hospital bed
   1,776 miles in 1975. (The kind of patriotism that makes
   you want to emigrate.)
C) Asparagus.

"Today Nothing Will Upset Me," Said the Principal to Himself

July 1988

A story is told about an archbishop of Canterbury of the Victorian era who had a passion for smoking. At certain times of the year the archbishop was required to lodge at Buckingham Palace in order to take part in official ceremonies.

The astute churchman was aware of the queen's extreme dislike of smoking. What could he do? The poor fellow was tense with cravings for nicotine, but mightily fearful of attracting the lightning of her majesty's wrath.

What he did was place a pillow in the fireplace, he on his back with his head on the pillow, light up his beloved stogie, and blow the smoke up the chimney.

Now I'm not certain of the archbishop's background, but there is good reason to believe he must have been, at some time, a school principal.

Why say that? Unknown to the general populace school principals are among the more cunning and resourceful of the human species. They must combine the outer blandness of a dirt wall at parent/teacher meetings with a linebacker's instinct for the jugular of fourteen year olds in a school hall. Ethically they must steal along the rim of darkness without abandoning the light. The ideal principal's constitution includes a visage of hawk-like ferocity, the nerves of A.J. Foyt, a plastic-coated gastrointestinal system impervious to acids and guaranteed for a millennium, and a bullhorn of a larynx.

May I hasten to say I write, of course, not of present perfect principals with purified principles, but of that unseemly lot which peopled the profession say from 1958 to 1971, a period when one DFM trod the corridors of McGuinness High School.

The following are true word pictures of those pragmatic principals at work. Some names have been changed.

How to Handle Parent-School Differences

The Oklahoma City Symphony Orchestra under the deft direction of Guy Fraser Harrison filled the McGuinness auditorium with beautiful music. On the other side of the building an angry Horatio Murgatroyde burst through the front door.

His son had called to inform Horatio that Father Monahan had suspended him from school. Why? Because, said the son, he had spoken back to a teacher. (To be more to the point he had called a woman faculty member a SOB—all letters included.)

God's eternal providence dictated that the first person the enraged Murgatroyde saw was Monahan.

"What do you mean having my son call me in the middle of my busy day for some damn silly reason?" yelled Murgatroyde.

"I didn't ask your son to call you. I just suspended him," Monahan screamed back.

The parties in the matter were now only feet apart. "Now take Toby home."

"I will not take him home. He belongs right here in this school," Murgatroyde bellowed.

"He's suspended, he has got to go home!" Monahan hollered.

"You little pip-squeak!" Murgatroyde shouted.

"If you don't get out of here, I'm going to call the police," responded Monahan, demonstrating his real interest in fair play.

Meanwhile the school's office manager, having observed the purplish faces and finger waving of the two combatants and being a woman of common sense, had sent a message to the auditorium for stout male faculty members to report to the main hall. She was certain blows and blood were imminent. But the belligerent forces disengaged.

And the orchestra played on.

How to Solve Unexpected Situations

Joe Shy was principal of a public high school close by McGuinness. He had an aptitude for becoming enmeshed in peculiar situations.

One day a report of nefarious activities in the second-floor girl's restroom came to Mr. Shy's office. The evidence, said the report, could be found now in the restroom.

Being ever circumspect, the principal asked the school nurse to accompany him to the restroom. They searched the place. The twosome started to leave but the exit door was stuck and the entrance door could only be opened from the outside.

Suddenly Mr. Shy realized a break between classes was due in a few minutes. Young women would come swinging through the entrance door. They would find Mr. Shy alone with the school nurse in the girl's restroom.

Mr. Shy, perhaps having witnessed too many episodes of "Mission Impossible," decided on bold action.

He would climb through the window, edge along the ledge, and step into the classroom next door.

Out he went. But a class was still in session in the classroom. Again boldness. He got on his hands and knees and began to crawl along the ledge below the line of sight from inside to the next classroom.

As God would have it, a youngster came strolling along the sidewalk below, spotted the familiar man in the gray suit and tie crawling along the ledge, waved and called out, "Hello, Mr. Shy." This despite Shy's frantic motions to keep quiet.

The attempt to shush the boy below caused the principal to raise up just a bit. It was enough.

"Look, it's Mr. Shy outside the window," rang a voice within. It was not a good day for a man with a Shy name and nature.

How to Keep Cool under Fire

The McGuinness High School principal talked to himself as he walked to the school. "Today," said he, "nothing is going to upset me. I am going to keep calm about every situation. I refuse to become disturbed or excited."

He entered the front door. A student stood inside.

"Father Monahan," said the student, "there is a fire in the auditorium."

"There is a fire in the auditorium," repeated the principal in a flat voice. "Let us go and look at it."

The two walked deliberately down the hall. Serenity in the face of alarm.

"Where is the fire in the auditorium," asked the cool principal.

"Backstage," replied the informant.

"Very well, we will look backstage," said the principal with the iron nerves.

The principal produced a key and unlocked the door to the backstage area. He stepped inside and saw flames leaping, fully six feet high out of an oil drum.

"There's a fire in the auditorium!" hollered the principal. "Get Mr. Zvonek! Get Mr. Genzer! Get a fire extinguisher! Oh, my Lord!!"

Thus another pacific day began at McGuinness High School.

A Thousand Soft Drinks Wore Bicuspids to Nubs

July 1988

The Founder and president emeritus of The Crooked Tooth League of America sat rigidly comfortable in the dentist's chair. A charming dental hygienist picked, scraped and washed away the residue of six months' coffee, tea, gin, wine, gumdrops, licorice, Beich's banana caramels and Oklahoma City water from the Founder's appropriately crooked teeth.

The Founder was in a melancholy state. As the hygienist peered into a mouth with more gold than South Africa, the Founder's thoughts drifted to the sorry state of his incisors, canines, bicuspids and molars. The bicuspids were worn to nubs by the downpour of a thousand thousand Dr. Peppers. The nubby bicuspids reminded the Founder of the Arbuckle Mountains, once high as the Rockies, they say, and now....And the canines! Long of tooth, did you say! That morning's glance in the mirror reminded the Founder that his canines, fully bared, would make a Doberman pinscher envious. The advancing disintegration of death is already in my mouth, the Founder brooded.

A photo on the wall caught the Founder's eye. A beautiful woman with dazzling even teeth. And the words: "Do you like your smile?"

"Ha!" said the Founder to himself. "Just what I might have expected in a dentist's office, a sneak attack by the orthodontists." To soothe his mind, the Founder imagined the Crooked Tooth League's hero of the '80s—Ronald Reagan.

As quickly as the image of Reagan's ragged Depression dentition blossomed in the Founder's mind, so it was followed by mental photos of the choppers of G. Bush and M. Dukakis. No League members they. The one with teeth arranged as a salute to WASP tidiness; the other with cool ivories symmetrically in place as though a reflection of the Doric columns of the Parthenon. The next four years, thought the Founder, will be a vexing period indeed for The Crooked Tooth League of America.

So I proceeded into my semiannual visit to the dentist. For thirty-five years, my teeth have been, so to speak, in the dexterous hands of the Drs. Lucas—Lawrence first, then Jerry. Battling against near impossible odds they have somehow kept all my original teeth in my mouth rather than at the local landfill.

This fact of all teeth present and accounted for—even four wisdom teeth—seemed to fascinate the charming hygienist. Very few people ("your age" she might have added, but delicately did not) have all their wisdom teeth, she said. Then, perhaps lost in a kind of anatomical reverie about wisdom teeth, she said, "You probably still have yours because you have a big mouth."

The charming hygienist continued, explaining why wisdom teeth seldom survive. Over the ages smaller jaws have evolved, she said. Big-mouthed, unevolved Cro-Magnon man, he of the thimble-sized brain, sat dumbly in the chair ever so slowly trying to connect the words of the charming hygienist.

My childhood dentist, Dr. Wadlin, never, in his wildest dreams, imagined I would reach three score plus one years with all my teeth intact.

When I arrived at his downtown Tulsa office, Dr. Wadlin would gaze into the big Monahan mouth and say sadly, "David, David." Doc Wadlin was a bald-headed guy with a small mustache. He was not noted as a great smiler. And when all the lines in his face ran sharply downhill and he gave me the "David, David" treatment, I felt like the dirty-mouthed, crooked-toothed fellow I was.

Then the drilling would commence. I mean Tulsa was known as the Oil Capital of the World, but more drilling activity went on in my mouth than in the surrounding five counties. Even at that time I must have been Cro-Magnon man, a creature with underdeveloped nerve endings, there was all that drilling, not much evidence of Novocain, and yet I can't recall excruciating pain.

But Doc Wadlin didn't throw me out in the street as an unrepentant candy eater. He kept me in the chair, grimly drilling away hour after hour, fighting the good fight. In the end, Doc defeated the Mars Bars.

Now we live in the era of painless dentistry. We drift effortlessly through the gentle attentions of a charming hygienist until we float into the keen focus of our benign dentist.

If a tiny cloud of decay shadows the X-ray, the benign dentist removes it with a superfast drill. No pain. No sweat.

Yes, modern dentistry is painless dentistry, but also sickening dentistry. Just as it seems you have beaten the rap, the charming hygienist hands you a small cup of colorless Sicky-Sweet. Swish half of it for one minute, she says, then the other half.

While I am sloshing Sicky-Sweet around my teeth I try desperately to distract myself. I concentrate on the Jackie Cooper sign on the building across the street. Two minutes are up. Once more I have survived Sicky-Sweet with my breakfast still in its assigned after-breakfast place.

Whatever Happened to Characters in the Priesthood?

November 1988

Nowadays when grizzled priests happen to sit down together for idle chatter—say after a communal penance rite or following a round of golf—one of them is apt to bemoan the demise of colorful characters in the priesthood. "Too bad, too bad," the others will agree.

Then veteran Oklahoma priests will reach back into the bag of their collective memory and pull out remembrances of—

- Father Bill Huffer, the free-spirited missionary from Germany, who swam in creeks, rivers and ponds, summer and winter (there is an extant photo of Bill, in his bathing suit, calmly standing on the frozen surface of an Oklahoma creek), and who, in his eighties, owned a three-wheeled car which he once mistakenly drove down the sidewalk bordering downtown Sheridan Avenue believing he was in the street;
- And Father Edward Van Waesberghe, who wrote his sacramental records on the walls of the sacristy at Immaculate Conception Church in Pawhuska, and who succeeded in converting personal dishevelment into high style;
- And Father Ramon Carlin, the diocesan gadfly, who led all-night dialogic "sessions" on any one of a thousand

topics, and who ranked as one of the all-time great evaders of his long-running and needed diets (once he, who had no problems with the bottle, conceived the unique notion that the surefire way to avoid alcoholism was to follow each drink with a candy bar).

Alas, eccentric clerics are a thing of the past, think we senior priests. That is, we thought that before reading the NC News Service wire copy of November 8. Therein we were introduced to the Iron Priest and a bishop with the world's bulkiest memoirs.

The Iron Priest is Father Joe Whitehead. In the news story, the Iron Priest rushed from a 7:00 p.m. Mass of Christian Burial to the National Guard Armory for an 8:30 professional wrestling match with the Super Destroyer.

(Father Whitehead is associate pastor at St. Matthew's Church in Jacksonville, Fla., the scene of this tale.)

The Super Destroyer was already rampaging about the ring, whanging the ropes in rage, while Father Whitehead was calmly changing from his meek parish priest image into his underwear costume as the indestructible Iron Priest. What allegedly agitated the Super Destroyer was a loss the previous week, on the "Florida Championship Wrestling" TV show, no less, to the Iron Priest. The Iron Priest had sunk his hulking opponent with one shot to the superstructure from his Iron Elbow.

To the crowd's chant of "We want priest! We want priest" the Iron Ecclesiastic bounded down the aisle for the rematch. Wearing a shirt reading "Mt. 25:31-46," he vaulted into the ring. (The Super Destroyer's T-shirt message was less obscure: "Priests are sissies.")

Twenty minutes after the opening bell and the ensuing grunts, thuds, growls, and smashes (a half dozen of them being users of the dreaded Iron Elbow), the tussle ended with the Iron Priest being sailed over the top rope and out of the ring, as though he were the Frisbee Priest, by the Super Destroyer. Ah, but justice prevailed when the referee disqualified the evil S.D.

The second NC News story had to do with this retired Catholic bishop, who shall remain nameless.

The bishop has been busy about his memoirs. How busy can be gauged by the report that his "Reflections – Memoirs" presently run 20,000 pages.

The good bishop did not jot them down overnight. He didn't rashly run to his desk one day this year and declare, "By golly, it's time I got to those memoirs!"

As a matter of fact, the bishop plunged into this memoir business almost before he had any. By his own account, he first put pen to paper when he was seventeen years old in 1933. After that they just growed, so to speak. And there could have been more, but his parents moved once and misplaced an entire box of the things.

Reflections on the "Reflections-Memoirs":

- What the bishop has done just might be the greatest literature since Shakespeare. And then again…
- His efforts will prove a boon to those who try to entice others to keep journals.
- The 20,000 pages will no doubt add weight to the prestigious Vatican Archives (to which he has arranged their passage).
- The Guinness Book of Records will want to check this one.
- The bishop has to be a true blue colorful character.

Final note: The autobiographical bishop has announced to a somewhat waiting world, he has begun work on part two of " Reflections—Memoirs."

Even here in beloved Oklahoma we may not be totally bereft of colorful-character priests. We do have one who brews his own beer in the basement. And another who keeps his 1920s St. Louis Cardinals Knothole Gang card in a safety deposit box. And the odd little man who writes weird commentaries with a BIC pen on long sheets of yellow paper.

Now to get to the day's work "Reflections—Memoirs, Part I."

CHAPTER 13

1989

You May Yet Be Able to Save Your Nose

February 1989

Dear common cold symptoms pain-bearers, I too know what it is to suffer. Yes, because this winter has been either too warm or too chill, I have been stricken with a pernicious common cold.

It happened without warning in January. A homeless virus hitched a ride into my system and yelled, "Tag, you're it." I was.

This was no creative virus, just the same old one, two, three: sore throat, sneezing and runny nose, and coughing.

The chief victim was my nose.

My efficient mucus factory went on an around-the-clock schedule in order to keep things flowing out the old proboscis. Blowing my nose became my second most important business. The first was feeling sorry for my pitiful little self.

Companies, battalions and even regiments of Kleenex were rushed to the front. The Kleenex fought the good fight. They also quickly transformed my nose into a fiery red glob of soreness. Persons with weak stomachs averted their eyes when passing me in shopping malls. Women of tender hearts wept openly at the sight. Rumors floated from the Vatican that my nose might be declared a martyr.

At this point, Florence Nightingale, AKA Sister Martha Mary McGaw, took action. She handed me a box of Puffs. "Here, use these; you may yet be able to save your nose," she said, at least in effect.

Being wretchedly proud of heart as well as a loyal user of Kleenex since Franklin Delano Roosevelt's second term, I scorned the new tissues. But blow by blow and sneeze by sneeze, I underwent a conversion of heart.

Perhaps it was the fact that Puffs are, as the advertising on the side of the box says, "so comforting, so comfortable." Or maybe enticed by the realization that Puffs are "softly scented" and "specifically designed to complement any decor," I embraced Puffs as the only created thing between me and a permanently corrugated nose.

My nose has had a rough life. Only a few days after birth, an unseemly event happened which very probably caused my nose ever after to score low in self-esteem.

It seems murmurings had been passed between senior members of our extended family that Evelyn's baby had, let's be frank, an oversized schnozzola.

Uncle Wells Montgomery strode through the corridors of the maternity ward to see for himself. (It should be noted that Uncle Wells, who drilled for oil in Borneo and drove an electric car, was ruggedly independent regarding proclamation of the truth.) My gentle mother proudly cradled tiny me in her arms. Uncle Wells leaned forward for a close-up. Said he, "Hell, Evelyn. I don't think his nose is so damn big."

The murmurings were out of the bottle. The maternity ward nurses had a weeping mother in their care. My nose glowed with shame.

After that humiliating start and no doubt tugged hither rather than yon by psychosomatic influences, my nose has been accident prone.

In high school football the beak became more of one. My football career unfolded after the soft helmet era but before the invention of the face mask. I specifically recall a devastating collision between my nose and the person of an Oilton High School defensive end. My nose grandly swelled, but not in pride. The end result is a certain off-centered interior to my snout.

As any teen-ager, I had the possibility of the most dreaded of all diseases—acne. My nose proved a fertile field for that "disorder of the skin caused by inflammation of the skin glands and hair follicles." I got acne, and I've still got it. It beats leprosy, but not by much.

Then there was the great sunburn. The giant blister where my nose should have been resembled a sickly orange party favor hanging between my eyes. That noble experiment in not wearing a hat has led directly to the dermatologist's firm application of dry ice to precancerous spots on the old olfactory organ.

Despite all, my nose continues to lead my way through life, like the prow of a stately ship cleaving its way through uncharted seas (or, perhaps more accurately, like the battered bow of a creaky ferry churning on its modest everyday course between two undistinguished points).

Epilogue: for those of you who have to know, Procter & Gamble reminds us on the box: "If you have questions or comments about Puffs, please call us toll-free. In the continental US, call 1-800-543-0480. (Ohio residents call 1-800-582-0490)."

I wonder who calls those numbers, if anyone. Who answers the telephone? And what do they say to each other? Can you become User of the Month?

When the German Sisters Spoke, People Listened

March 1989

Hospitals are okay by me. I was born in one. St. John's in Tulsa was my hospital of choice. The big event happened on a cold (or mild) day (or night) of March 6, 1927. My birth at St. John's was a signal for Charles Lindbergh to fly across the Atlantic, Babe Ruth to swat sixty home runs and President Calvin Coolidge to utter his immortal declamation: "I do not choose to run."

The entrance of little me into the antiseptic world of hospitaldom followed almost exactly fifteen months after my grandfather Connolly's dramatic death while speaking on behalf of the same St. John's Hospital.

According to the newspaper clippings, David Connolly was speaking at a victory dinner in celebration of a successful fund drive to complete St. John's. (It seems the people of Tulsa had been trying to raise the necessary dollars for the hospital since 1916.) At the high pitch of his talk, and he apparently was something of a true Irish orator, grandpa gasped, grabbed the table and slid to the floor.

Moments later he was pronounced dead.

For decades there stood in the basement of the hospital a statue of St. Monica dedicated to David Francis Connolly. As progress progressed St. Monica and her glass eyes disappeared.

From the second floor bathroom window of our house, one could see St. John's Hospital to the east. And scrawny me was indoctrinated about the struggle to build the hospital and the role my grandfather played in its becoming.

St. John's was an accepted part of my life much as Christ the King Church and Marquette School and Woodward Park and the Plaza Theater.

Being a flesh-and-blood type of creature, I was periodically hauled over to St. John's for repairs. My tonsils were snipped there. A ripped up left leg, aggravated by a severe reaction to a tetanus shot, put me in there for a stay. Dr. Paul Grosshart manipulated a dislocated arm back into its proper shoulder socket in one of the operating rooms. Fancy stitching was done over my left eye in the emergency room after a wayward elbow landed in it. Quite ordinary kid's stuff.

In those days, if you were a Catholic in Tulsa, St. John's was your place to be when you hurt.

The atmosphere at St. John's was firmly set by the Sisters of the Sorrowful Mother. Theirs was a Germanic spirit: hard work, order, hard work, compassion, hard work, family, hard work, piety and more hard work.

There were no cutesy names in the group. Their names marched with authority—Sisters Humilitas Heinrich, Leonina Zirkelbach, Kunigundis Weingartner and Gerharda Ott, as examples. When they spoke, people listened. Doctors, nurses, pastors, bishops, police chiefs, bank presidents and formerly thought-to-be tough guys kept their mouths closed and listened.

I picked up early that one respected the Sisters and walked softly in their presence. Once I witnessed a withering semipublic face-to-face blast of an eminent doctor by one of the Sisters. Her complaint: the doctor was keeping a hopelessly ill patient alive by pumping fresh blood into him each day. Her charge: the physician was profiting from this practice and the patient's family was being financially ruined. They spoke their piece – raw, rough truth.

The only person I knew who regularly swapped shots across the bow with the Sisters at St. John's was the profane Dr.

Grosshart. He good-humoredly referred to Sister Domitilla as Sister Damn-it-to-hell. She loved him. They all did.

You see Dr. Grosshart being a surgeon knew the secret about the Sisters of the Sorrowful Mother. If one cut through the tough crust of their being, one discovered they were filled with sweet charity.

Major and minor events in my adult life have brought me back repeatedly to the corridors of St. John's Hospital.

The day the Japanese government threw in the white towel to end the Second World War, I came through the confetti and wild joy of downtown Tulsa to St. John's. My sister, Helen, that day gave birth to her first child. Of course, the hospital nursery hadn't seen such a beautiful baby as Robert George Perrine Jr. since that other wee fellow in 1927.

Some years later there was a hasty post-midnight ride down the Turner Turnpike to St. John's. My mother was dying in a room on the fifth floor. We stood red-eyed around her bed as she told lies about our goodness, straightforwardly called on Jesus for help and stepped painfully through the door of death.

My father was a sometimes notorious impatient at St. John's. Once after veering away, at the last moment, from the outstretched hand of Brother Death (and during the crisis acting about as obnoxiously as one could), he decided it was time to make amends. Turning on his considerable salesman's charm, Frank Monahan said to an exhausted nurse, "Was I the worst patient you ever had?" Her answer: "Yes."

Our family continues to be served by and to serve St. John's Hospital. Helen has volunteered thousands of hours there. Aunt Agnes ran the mail from room to room for years. (She was fascinated by Oral Roberts somewhat secret stays as a patient at St. John's. She never saw the renowned healer while he was in the process of being healed. She handed his mail to the guard at the door.)

The place has changed. In fact, none of the original building is standing. The bricks my grandfather wore himself out to buy are long gone. Yet everyone agrees it's the same hospital. In that sense, it's very human, something like the church.

Crucial acts of life take place there—birth, suffering, healing and death. Christian hands and hearts still offer help. May its kind live a long life.

Presenting the 1989 Restaurant Lighting Rating

April 1989

Some folks are said to live to eat. My case is a teence different. I eat to read.

This oddity can be explained thusly. First, I am hopelessly addicted to reading. Second, I am an old single man who eats alone most of the time. (I just perceived with a certain fright that the last statement is liable to unleash the tender mercies of good Christians who may want to rush me to their dinner tables lest I perish from lack of conversation. May such holy ones resist this impulse to invite! Repeat: stand firm against any desire to upgrade my dining habits.) Third, my evening meal is one of the few occasions when I have time to do recreational reading.

So when the sun drops kerplunk in the west, Monahan can be seen, book in hand, entering one of the numerous beaneries along Oklahoma City's famed Northwest Stop-and-go-way.

The entrance is where the trouble starts. Restaurants pretentious enough to employ hostesses or hosts seem to hire mostly those with one-track minds. These young men and women, moving languidly under the weight of a pound or so of hair gel, are unanimously but wrongly under the impression that each customer's main motivation in approaching their lintel is the intake of food.

"Smoking or non-smoking?" they say.

My response: "I prefer nonsmoking, but my main concern is to sit under a good light so I can read."

"This way," they say. (If Newsboy Moriarity, the saintly bookie of the past, were working this route, he would place the odds on the latter part of my response having been really heard at 999 to 1.)

I walk humbly behind the official bearer of the menu. Usually our safari will pass by decent lighting here and there until we arrive at some distant table twenty-two feet from the last fifty-watt bulb. On these occasions I have been known to mutter sarcasms, building a tidy sum of confessable matter.

The fault is not all with the gelled ones or their blasé managers, but may well be shared by the designers of restaurants who have lusted too much after "ambience," "effect," "atmosphere," or "environment." "Ambience, shambience," grumble we curmudgeons. "Just give us some light!"

Realizing there may be one or two other bachelor reading types in these parts, I hereby present the 1989 Restaurant Lighting Ratings for selected joints along the Northwest Stop-and-go-way.

> *** Wyatt Cafeteria. Monahan's acquaintances may be startled to find Wyatt on the list at all, much less at the top, since he has scarcely ever had a kind word to utter about the food served there. The food may be iffy, but the lighting is spectacular. The entire place is as bright as the playing court of the NCAA basketball finals. In fact, it is so well lit the serious reader has to be careful how he lines up his head and his book. Shadows can cause slight problems. Sunglasses, however, are not needed.

> ** Tippins. One must be assertive enough to insist on a table with good light. I've groused enough about dimness that the hosts and hostesses have taken the course of least resistance. ("Give the old duck a seat with a light or you'll have to hear his line: 'I would rather read than eat.'")

> ** Pizza Grandioza. If your nerves can stand kids playing video games and you're not upset about the lettuce being now and then on the wilted side, it's a pleasant democratic place to read and chomp. At Pizza Grandioza

free enterprise is honored in the search for the bright lights. Personally I like the long table just west of the salad bar.

** Queen Ann Cafeteria. The average age of the clientele at Queen Ann is (a well-kept secret). But I believe I have seen a few Keep Cool with Coolidge bumper stickers. People leave each other alone there. There are enough pockets of light to take care of the few of us who tote books. My favorite spot is a table for one opposite the end of the serving line.

* The Florida Cafe. Carlos Gonzalez serves the best food but furnishes the worst lighting of any outfit on my list. I must admit his Shrimp Diane lures my taste buds through the door on Fridays even though I must grope for a table in the dark. Nevertheless I manfully squint away at the printed page as I shovel the scrumptious victuals into my mouth.

Sometime in the near future you may catch my TV commercial for OG&E.

The scene: I'm seated in a dusky candlelit cafe. A comely waitress places a cold can and a mug before me.

The audio: "That certainly looks like a nice cold Bud Lite. *But I didn't ask for a Bud Lite! I asked for a light!*"

Golf at Its Nadir at Mc&M International Competition

April 1989

As the sweet-souled Father Martin Reid once said, while standing knee-deep in coarse vegetation and staring down at the visible dimples of his golf ball, "It's a humbling game!"

Humbling as in lashing a tee shot with all that is in you only to find, after the ball rolls to a stop, it is forty yards closer to you than it would have been five years ago. Humbling as in gouging out a score of ten on a 300-yard par 4 immediately after swelling with pride over a par three on the previous hole. Humbling as in surveying a short pitch shot fifty yards from the green at 10:07 a.m. and studying an identical situation from the other side of the same green at 10:10 a.m. and one stroke later.

It's a humbling game.

And humbling it was even for those two ancient stalwarts J. McGlinchey and D. Monahan as they struggled through their annual Spring International Competition, April 3, 4, and 5.

In the end they bathed jointly but proudly in a veritable pool of golfing humiliation. It was golf at its nadir as the two perennial combatants clashed at three exclusive venues: the Grapevine Municipal Golf Course, just north of D-FW Regional Airport; Cedar Crest Golf Course in Dallas; and Falconhead Resort and Country Club near fashionable Bourneville, Oklahoma.

Because the Mc&M International was scheduled during the week of the Master's, neither the media coverage nor uncontrollable galleries were major problems this time around.

J. McGlinchey arrived for the battle having substituted a handcrafted metal driver for his traditional termite riddled wooden club. There is little doubt that this decision was made after a winter's quiet contemplation of the matter. The clever left-hander must have surmised that this new metallic weapon would create panic in his opponent. It did.

For his part, however, D. Monahan had squeezed two additional instruments into his tattered plastic bag—a scarred two-wood and a previously retired and rusted two-iron. (The two-wood proved to be an object of wonder to a youngster at Grapevine who claimed never to have seen one before.)

Gunfire at Grapevine

The starter at Grapevine teamed the grizzled Oklahoma linksters with Chris, an electronics student from North Texas State University with a rubber band swing, and Connor, a ruddy man with a quick pragmatic slash at the ball. (Golf on public courses is a democratic affair.)

The sun shone. The winds blew. The birds chirped. The jets into DFW glided overhead.

J. McGlinchey first pulled out the fearsome handcrafted metal driver at the fourth hole. The scorecard reveals a par beside his name.

On the watery number eight, D. Monahan, imagining himself to be Mr. Severiano Ballesteros, attempted a faded four-wood into the green. What he got was a ruler straight shot and a solid splash eighty yards to the left of the green.

At the end of the front nine, J. McGlinchey was three up.

But an odd thing happened on the back side. After an outlandish quadruple bogey on the thirteenth, D. Monahan suddenly parred 14 and 15, then birdied the sixteenth. It was enough to make one wonder.

At the end of the day, D. Monahan led one up.

With the Ghosts at Cedar Crest

Cedar Crest's opening hole sweeps downward in a 60S-yard arc to a small green. D. Monahan floundered to an eight. J. McGlinchey managed a seven. It set the gray tone for the day.

The antagonists pushed and pulled ineptly for some three and one-half hours. In the end D. Monahan stood shakily one up for the eighteen and two up for thirty-six holes.

Shot of the day: J. McGlinchey's whistling two-iron which traveled up a slight rise more than 200 yards to the 16th green. Alas, he three putted for a bogey.

Cedar Crest, now a public course but in its day the pride of the Dallas rich, was the site of the 1927 PGA Championship. Walter Hagen won it. Both McGlinchey and Monahan reported sightings of Hagen's ghost. The Great One was holding his hands over his eyes.

Falconhead for the Birds

The above title is not meant as a slight at the golf course nor the retirement community which surrounds it. Nor does it refer to the score of one under par, none of which were achieved. The title does refer to the two old birds who flew in unannounced to flutter about the golf course.

J. McGlinchey and D. Monahan exchanged pleasantries with the handsome fellow behind the cash register (surprised him, as a matter of fact, with personal recollections of Waco Turner, the eccentric who built what is now labeled Falconhead). The twosome was dispatched to the tenth tee as "the members" were about to begin play on the front side.

Water is a fact of life at Falconhead. The liquid stuff lurks on ten of the eighteen holes. D. Monahan dunked one at the seventeenth (the eighth hole on the Mc&M round). But on perhaps the wettest of all the water holes, he ironically captured final victory in the Spring International.

This latter feat included a true "chicken" tee shot away from the water and to the right of the green with his quaint two-iron, a so-so approach to the green, and a long putt for a par 3.

In post-match interviews, the winning putt was described as "lucky" by J. McGlinchey. "Spectacular" was the adjective selected by the victor.

Confessor Gasped, *"Ego te Absolvo"*

June 1989

The other day a good woman told me that her daughter had come to me in a bygone era to make her first confession. The wee child had an attack of the heebie-jeebies as she opened the door to the sacristy in the church at Edmond where confessions were being heard, the mother said. According to mama's account, I correctly perceived the little one's distress and held her in my lap during the pouring forth of the tot's terrible offenses against God and humanity. (I say this was a bygone era because today priests who so much as lay a hand on a child's head in a confessional do so with the apprehension of being charged with unspeakable crimes.)

There is no doubt that the confession part of the Sacrament of Penance, especially the first time around, has been a nerve jangler as far back as one can see in the history of the church.

Priests around these parts only recently have concluded rounds of first confessions by children of the proper age and older baptized people being received into full membership in the Catholic Church. These priests witnessed wide-eyed fear, nervous giggles and absolute lapses of memory on the part of chicks and chickens alike. As of the last report all confessees survived.

Once upon a time master writer Frank O'Connor penned a miniature classic titled "First Confession." This seven-page gem details the travails of an Irish lad on the road to his first confession.

Jackie is convinced by the elderly Mrs. Ryan, the parish's morose delegate to prepare children for the sacrament, that there is no way he can possibly make a good confession. His sister Nora does her best to compound his suffering.

After a calamitous start in the confessional, Jackie blurts out all, even his plan to do away with his grandmother because she eats boiled potatoes with her fingers. He receives three Hail Marys as a penance and a jawbreaker to suck on as he wends his way home.

Upon learning the holy church's leniency to poor Jackie, a disgusted Nora concludes, I might just as well be a sinner like you."

As Jackie, each of us adult Catholics has a memory, albeit a dim one, of a first confession.

My own was made in the darkness of an old confessional set against the back wall on the north side of Christ the King Church in Tulsa. My little heart no doubt pounded mightily, but I emerged triumphant. As I recall, the worst part was waiting for the slide to open and the priest to come into view. That tense pause was akin to what the convicted must feel strapped in an electric chair while the executioner waits the signal to throw the switch.

After my confession, my mother quite directly asked me what I had said in the confessional. "I said I had disobeyed about 500 times." My gentle mother, who could have tabulated my violations of the Fourth Commandment much more accurately, said. "You said that, David! Oh, my goodness."

Some two decades later another kind of first confession took place for me. I had been ordained a priest by Bishop Eugene J. McGuinness on a Saturday. I had received my assignment as assistant pastor at St. Francis of Assisi Church in Oklahoma City and, as the others in my class, I was given a two-week vacation. The vacation was spent dubbing shots on a Tulsa golf course.

One vacation evening the telephone rang. It was the serious, super-zealous young man who was the assistant priest at my home parish of Christ the King. "Hey, Dave!" he said.

"How about hearing confessions during the 8:15 a.m. Mass tomorrow morning?"

Well…well…well, thought I.

"Well, what about it?" said he.

"OK, sure, I'll be there."

It wasn't that I didn't know that being a confessor was part of the job or that there hadn't been training in the seminary to be a confessor. It's just that I hadn't expected to be sent in as a relief pitcher before I got to the ball park.

The next morning young Father Monahan perhaps looked calm and businesslike as he strode down the side aisle to the confessional in the rear of the church, but inside the cassock he was all skyrocketing blood pressure, bubbling stomach acids and overworking sweat glands.

He managed to get through the middle door of the confessional and have a seat. Like lightning, confessional doors on either side of him opened and a head appeared in the window to his right. It was probably some scrupulous old saint or it might have been the local multiple murderer.

Whoever it was and whatever was said, the secrecy of the confessional never was more secure. The confessor was somewhere on the dial between extremely agitated and hysterical. He did gasp out, *"Ego te absolvo."*

First confessions are something else.

My Motto: Talk Softly but Carry a Big Magazine

July 1989

Take a hot summer afternoon, complicate it with a paralyzed air-conditioning system, and what do you have? Open windows, of course.

That was my situation on Sunday, July 2. I was struggling with an article on Judaism. The two windows that open in my office are about three feet by one foot. They don't let in much air but some. At least the open windows kept me from exploding like a kernel of popcorn in a sealed aluminum bag.

But along with the breeze a wasp glided into my airspace. My internal warning system flashed a message: Alert! Alert! Alert! Unfriendly hymenopterous in the vicinity. Words "King of Sting" printed on hymenopterous's abdomen. Man your battle station!

I grabbed the July 3, 1989, copy of *The New Yorker* magazine and took my hitting stance. The wasp continued to cruise near the windows, casing the joint. You have heard that dogs can tell when people are afraid of them. Well, so could this wasp. I believe he had a sneer on his teeny-weeny insect face as he buzzed my starboard side.

I'm not afraid of much, only about two or three thousand things and several million people. Included on this list are wasps.

I rolled up *The New Yorker*. The aggressor wasp had landed on a pane of the window. I stepped forward and swung a mighty swing. Whack! The wasp gyrated crazily but regained his equilibrium. I lost my equilibrium and gyrated crazily backward. The wasp flicked his buzzer up to maximum anger speed and gave every indication of being a highly agitated insect.

So the battle was joined. My motto was T. Rooseveltian: Talk softly but carry a big rolled up magazine. The rhythm of the contest went:

Whack! Whack! Whack! Bzzzz! Bzzzz! BZZZZ! Followed by a cowardly retreat of the Whacker.

After some thirty minutes and half a dozen whackings, the terrible winged beast lay mortally squashed on the windowsill. Taps were played. And the body of the valiant wasp was dumped out the window.

If you read the July 3,1989, copy of *The New Yorker* in our office, please excuse the rumpled condition of the cover and the scarred ad for Bombay Sapphire gin on the back.

Yes, it is the season when insects rise once more to challenge human society. Given the June monsoon, that there are swarms of the wee creatures should not be surprising.

Only two days after the contest with the wasp, I toddled forth to eat Fourth of July hot dogs with old friends. The hostess planned an outdoor feast. Having a great aversion to the stings of mosquitoes, she had installed the latest anti-mosquito technology just feet from the table. This consisted of smoldering punks, giving off a bit of smoke and a not too unpleasant odor.

There was but one flaw in her devices. Mosquitoes are impervious to all anti-mosquito schemes. Rumor has it that young mosquitoes in flight school are taught the truth: Nothing can stop you!

About two bites into the second hot dog, the lead mosquito sank its proboscis into the hostess's arm. A disorderly retreat took the diners indoors.

The week before, this old fellow made the trek to the Catholic Youth Ministry Summer Camp on the shores of Lake Murray. Summer camps are the places where insects go to get away from heat in the city. What Las Vegas is to the human species, places like Lake Murray are to the creepy, crawly kingdom.

I was not surprised to hear the following tale, Screams came from the girls' shower room. Sister Betty Paul, camp director, answered the alarm. Four or five girls managed to gasp, between screams, "There is a tarantula in the shower room!"

Sister Betty's unwritten code concerning tarantulas is: Don't kill them; they won't hurt you; move them out of the way.

The camp director stuck her head into the shower area. The shower was running full blast. In one corner was a cowering tarantula.

"Turn the shower off," said Sister Betty to a child wrapped in a towel. Anything but that, cried the camper. The other girls were equally adamant. Finally, the director plunged into the shower, got properly wet, turned the handle to Off, then used a broom to sweep the hairy spider out of the building.

Chalk up one for the environmentalists, those people who say: "I never met a wasp (mosquito, fly, tarantula or scorpion) I didn't like."

Meanwhile one D. Monahan of Oklahoma City has reported a near fatal assault by an unidentified flying insect.

It seems D. Monahan was seated in his room one evening in June when it was not raining. He heard the welcome music of the June bugs pinging against the floor-to-ceiling screen beside his chair. What a joy it proved to be to sit there and read while the chaos of the insect world was contained outside.

D. Monahan inhaled. There was the distinct feeling that a tiny fluttering thing had been sucked in with the air and down the old throat. He tried to cough it up. No luck. He drank water rapidly, unsure as to what purpose. The certainty: D. Monahan had swallowed whole an unidentified flying insect. A summertime event.

Here's to the 'squito and here's to the fly. This is your season
When strong men will cry.

So fasten the latches, keep out of the dell, pray to the good Lord to send them to—

Ouch! What was that bit my ankle?

Webster States Kook Is an Alternative Form of Cuckoo

July 1989

Her name was Lena. She wore a large flat hat with artificial fruit on top of the brim in the front. As I recall, she also wore a grim expression.

Lena was a presence in our parish church. She helped give the place a certain added identification. Parishioners might recall the striking mosaic of Christ the King behind the altar, the unusual stained-glass windows, the relic from the table at the Last Supper and Lena.

She might be found in the church at almost any time. Her position for Mass, in those days, was Gospel side, front.

One would hardly suspect that a soul as sober as Lena would call the pastor by his last name only and to his face. Msgr. D.C. Fletcher wore 'the mantle of benevolent familial authority. But when Lena accosted him, he was reduced to "Fletcher" not Father Fletcher or Msgr. Fletcher.

Assistant pastor Father John Walch modestly went about his duties with goodwill toward all. But Lena watched him with a suspicious eye. One fine day it apparently became clear to Lena why she was suspicious.

The telephone rang at the rectory. Msgr. Fletcher was wanted. "Fletcher," said Lena, "tell Walch to stop praying against Hugo. He's giving Hugo headaches."

Hugo was her brother who lived in St. Louis.

Almost needless to say, the plea from Lena to "Fletcher" to stop' the long distance zapping of Hugo was repeated and repeated and repeated.

Lena was, for want of a more felicitous term, a parish kook.

The Lord did not say, "Parish kooks you will always have with you," because He probably did not want to unduly discourage future pastors. But the fact of the matter is a high percentage of parishes have one or more parish kooks.

How does one define a parish kook? A parish kook is one who regularly manifests patently odd behavior in a church kind of way.

The behavior has to be decidedly different as in wearing a wool overcoat to daily Mass in August (contributing only lead slugs in one's collection envelopes does not qualify). And the behavior should have a certain consistency to it—one-shot adventures such as loud booing of a homily on peace fall short of the mark. Furthermore to be a valid Catholic kook the individual need be an actual member of a parish; someone whose credentials include name on the parish list and membership in a church organization or two; a person who is expected to show up and yet whose every appearance occasions a vast spray of acid in a pastor's gastrointestinal apparatus.

Webster states kook is an alternative form of cuckoo: one whose ideas or actions are eccentric, fantastic, or insane: a screwball.

It seems probable that neither Karl Rahner nor St. Thomas Aquinas concentrated on kookism as a pressing question. Yet might not it be that parish kooks often are striped with a wide slash of sanctity or that a kind of wild wisdom blooms among the peculiar weeds?

Some folks thought Ed had the makings of a kook, 1940s style. Ed claimed he had a vision. In the thrall of the vision, Ed promised he would receive Holy Communion every day for a month.

Ed's vow came with a problem attached. He went to work very early in the morning, so early in fact that the regular 6:30 Mass did not fit his schedule. He appealed to a priest he knew, a happy young fellow with an overload of health.

The result: the priest struggled manfully out of the sheets at 5 a.m. every day for a month so that Ed could keep his vow.

Poor Ed. Never again did he report a vision. No doubt this was a response to the young priest's fervent petitions. The guardian angel of kooks struck Ed's name from the certified list.

Parish kooks come not only in all sizes and sexes but also in all ages. Or perhaps the younger type should be called junior kooks or kooks-in-training.

In any event, Willie was such a case. Willie was only ten or so when all three priests serving in his parish had identified and labeled him a kook.

Willie had a wonderful knack of being omnipresent. If the pastor turned around suddenly he fell over Willie. If the pastor stretched out for a siesta, a mild explosion or the sound of the metallic buckle on the flagpole clanging loudly reminded him that Willie lived.

Willie especially attached himself to one of the assistant priests. He became Willie's confidant, one who could be trusted for sound advice in a busy boy's ever-changing life.

One Saturday afternoon, Father Black was in the confessional, listening, advising, encouraging, absolving. Willie decided it was time for a conference. He marched to the confessional and pulled on the handle to the confessor's compartment. Father Kerns, tending to his shriving, pulled back. Thus began a tug of war. Willie pulling mightily, proceeded to yell, "Black! Black! I know you're in there, Black!"

Thus we leave in mid-action this meditation on parish kooks. But even as we do, this writer somewhat anxiously recalls the repeated advice of many a sage: It takes one to know one.

What Has Jimmy Mastered That Creates the Urge to...?

October 1989

"Happy Jack" was the inevitable nickname pinned on the priest who served as spiritual director at one of the seminaries I attended. This particular priest's first name was John and his last could well have been Gloom.

Happy Jack had not been swept off his feet by tidal waves of Christian joy. He appeared to be confirmed in the notions that life consisted of an uphill march around the chasm of the fires of hell and that the path was devilishly slick with temptations. One fall and—dum-de-dum-dum! He was an authority on temptations, a kind of temptationologist. His regular prediction: Temptations are in blizzard conditions today, but expect worse.

Little did we suspect that Happy Jack would be a temptation for us.

He had warned us that men who bound themselves to celibacy and then proceeded to act otherwise were often afflicted with prostate troubles (a concept which held little scientific water, but neither he nor we were scientists).

The temptation Happy Jack unconsciously visited upon us struck the day he was carted off to the local Catholic hospital for a—you guessed it—a prostate operation. Hilarity erupted. Unseemly demonstrations of laughter rolled around the seminary's halls and "It couldn't happen to a nicer guy" statements were as common as gripes about the food.

Our behavior was, in short, a disturbing display of morose delectation.

Yes, dear readers, morose delectation.

Morose delectation is the apt term plucked from the dictionary by a moralist of yore to describe delight in evil, or, in our case, the unholy glee at poor Happy Jack's painful set-to with the knife wielder.

If Happy Jack were still with us, he would be proclaiming the bad news of near overwhelming temptations to morose delectation. And he would be right. He would be so "right he might even have cracked a tight-lipped smile at his own rightness.

Look at the present opportunities for morose delectation. On the national level there are the spectacular downfalls of Jim and Tammy, Leona Helmsley and the HUD Gang of Five (Hundred). Regionally there are the vexations of Jimmy Johnson and the Dallas Plowboys.

In this situation it's almost more than a body can do to keep from indecently wallowing in morose delectation.

If you're not convinced yet, consider some specifics.

Take the Bakkers. Jim was cursed with his TV face forever cast somewhere between a simper and a smirk. And Tammy stared at the world through a cave of cosmetics. For a long while only those who somehow liked them watched them.

Then a matter of adultery popped to the surface of their watering hole. And this was followed by wilder and yet wilder accounts of how the Bakkers and their henchmen diverted the river of contributions into their own pockets. (It reminded one of Lefty Gomez's statement about the manner in which he and his patron, Babe Ruth, freely dispensed US currency even during the Great Depression. "We didn't spend money," said Lefty. "We shot it out of guns. ")

Soon a school of comics' writers began circling the babbling Bakkers and ripping off daily chunks of their dignity for the entertainment of the public. It was funny but bloody. ("When Jim and Tammy moved from Malibu, all that was left behind was a small mascara slick. ") Morose delectation.

And then Leona H. As I recall, some of us hinterlanders first stumbled across the redoubtable Ms. Helmsley in the pages of *The New Yorker* magazine. In a single issue there was ad after ad picturing Leona welcoming the world to one of the family hotels. The advertising was hard to understand. One was tempted to think it was some kind of expensive joke.

Then came the indictments and the two-month trial this summer which rolled away the facade to reveal a poor Brooklyn girl turned rich and mean. "Only the little people pay taxes," she reportedly said. Her attorney resorted to the argument that Leona's employees so detested her that they set her up for the federal tax charges. She was convicted on thirty-three counts.

The common folks across the land cheered. Let the New York fat cat be put in her cage! Morose delectation.

Last November at 3407 E. 13th Street in Tulsa, Oklahoma, Aunt Agnes yelled, "He's getting red in the face! He's getting red in the face!"

He was Jimmy Johnson, then coach of the Miami University Hurricane football team. The occasion: what Mr. Jimmy perceived to be an incorrect call in the destruction derby called football between Notre Dame and Miami.

Aunt Agnes's call certainly was true. Mr. Jimmy's round mug shown tomato moving toward eggplant. His legion of haters loved it.

What technique has Mr. Jimmy mastered which creates the urge to boo in others? Is it the pouty visage? Or the lacquered hair? Or the fat boy's strut? Or the singular lack of grace ("We gave the national title to Notre Dame by going for the two-point conversion")? Or all of the above?

In any event, it's difficult for some of us sinners to watch the Dallas Cowboys play this year without taking inordinate glee at the success of their opponents. Morose delectation.

It is, indeed, a bad season for us afflicted with morose delectation. If only Happy Jack had been here to sound the alarm.

And to think that tomorrow some evil—perhaps athlete's foot or the heartbreak of psoriasis—might befall the likes of Donald Trump or Frank Lorenzo. Then where will we be?

As for me, I'm putting down this BIC pen and going in search of a local chapter of Morose Delectators Anonymous.

CHAPTER 14

1990

The Case of the Befuddled Burglar and Chaos Security

January 1990

On the Sunday after Thanksgiving Father Jerome Talloen was praying in the small upstairs chapel at the Archdiocesan Pastoral Center. He became aware that someone other than God was present.

The interloper was a tall thin man. He informed Father Talloen that he had come to burglarize the Center, that he had been in prison and that he wanted to become a priest.

Realizing that the Office of Seminarians and Vocations was not open on Sundays, Father Talloen decided to conduct his own preliminary interview.

"Are you a Catholic?"

The answer was vague, somewhere between "If I need to be a Catholic to become a priest I'll become one" and "If I am a Catholic but not practicing, I'll become fervent tomorrow."

The tall thin man left the chapel.

Shortly thereafter on the first floor, Father Talloen informed Father D. Monahan about the strange encounter. Father Talloen left the building hoping he could avoid for the remainder of the day any more tall thin men who wanted to become priests. Father D. Monahan returned full attention to the travails of the Chicago Bears.

Forty-five minutes pass.

The kickoff arched through the air as a tall thin man opened the door to Father D. Monahan's apartment and invited himself in.

"I want to become a priest," said the tall thin man.

"Are you a Catholic?" asked the shrewd TV viewer.

The answer was vague, somewhere between "If I need to be a Catholic to become a priest I'll become one" and "If I am a Catholic but not practicing I'll become fervent tomorrow."

The tall thin man presented a request. "Could you give me some gas money?" Gas money was provided. "Could you give me some more gas money?" More gas money was not provided. The tall thin man exited.

Forty-eight hours pass.

Folks at the Pastoral Center are chattering about a tall thin man and a buddy who were seen wandering about the place earlier in the day.

A late-on-the-scene Father D. Monahan is told that a tall thin man was seen leaving his living area. Furthermore, said the witness, the tall thin man backed out of D. Monahan's door waving to the inside with a "See you later, Father."

Father D. Monahan enters his room to see what might be missing. A number of coins lie on the floor as though scattered by the swoop of a hand over a heap of quarters, dimes and pennies on the shelf above. Everything else seems to be in place, muses D. Monahan. But how can that be, he reconsiders, since nothing in this room has a place?

He decides to sit down and reflect on the situation. Moving assorted papers, magazines and unfolded laundry to a second chair, he has a seat.

Ahead of D. Monahan is a scene of chaos or "heterogeneous agglomeration," as Webster puts it, or "a mess," as D. Monahan's late mother might say. The room is a nightmare to a Mr. or Ms. Neat, an anarchist's delight, and an everyday sight to sloppy old bachelors.

Take the low table in the center of the room. Besides the ordinary row of books between bookends, there are a stack of last year's Christmas cards atop an empty box, a red and white stuffed duck with "OU" on one wing, a 1944 edition of "Prayers and Devotions," a tape recorder, a basket, a wooden box and a stack of dusty magazines. Below the table are heaps of more magazines and yellowed newspapers and photographs. On the top of one stack is an April 16, 1988, *America* magazine and on the bottom a Jan. 3, 1986, issue of *The Christian Science Monitor.* An opened sack of photographs discloses scenes shot on a 1986 trip to Guatemala. Immediately to the side of the low table is a good-sized globe and a cardboard "Henry McKenna Sour Mash Straight Bourbon Whiskey" box filled with bric-a-brac.

The truth is, D. Monahan admits, multiply the low table area by ten and one has a somewhat accurate picture of the entire joint.

Then comes the sudden flash of intuition: The burglar didn't steal anything of real value because he couldn't figure out what to steal! It was a case of the befuddled burglar thwarted by Chaos Security. The poor fellow must have felt he had broken into the Cairo city dump. The tall thin man couldn't tell the treasure from the trifles and the trash!

The moral of this story: Mothers go easy on your wayward sons whose rooms are living garbage cans.

I Did a Forty-Six-Year Back-Flip and Landed in a Defensive Crouch

March 1990

On Sunday, Feb. 18, 1990, my spirit did a 46-year, 1,400-mile back-flip off the couch and out of Joe and Carole Dillon's living room in Vista, Calif. The mental trampoline for this feat was a big brown "Scrapbook" with an Indian head embossed on the cover.

I land on Feb. 27, 1944 in a defensive crouch on the east end of the Cascia Hall basketball court in Tulsa, Okla., USA. The packed record crowd of 850 Catholic bodies, all with mouths open and larynxes overworking, is intent on the action on the floor.

The clock is sweeping through the last minute of the game between the Cascia Hall Commandos and the valiant (my side) Marquette Meteors. The score is tied at 32 each. It is the third and final game of the season between the arch rivals. Cascia Hall has taken the first 17-14. We waltzed off with the second 18-8.

The outcome of this contest doesn't matter much. Our mothers have reminded us "It's just a game." But, if it wouldn't draw a technical foul, we might kill to win. And, I think, our pastor, Msgr. D.C. Fletcher, would cheerfully absolve us, given the foe.

Now the Commandos are moving the ball to our end of the court. My man is Bob Beuke. He dashes toward the free throw lane. Someone passes him the ball. Beuke leaves the floor, twisting his body as he turns to shoot. I stretch my left arm as high as I can, but the ball soars past my fingertips and…

338

Memories of high school basketball are commonplace among adult American males. The game is the same but the times, places, characters and circumstances are wildly different. Ours at Marquette High School in the World War II years came close to being unique.

We had no gymnasium to call home. We had no coach. We didn't belong to a regular conference. Gasoline was severely rationed so it was nigh impossible to travel out of town to play. Rubber products "had gone to war" so it was a task to find a good pair of basketball shoes or a basketball that was actually round or even a decent athletic supporter. After a furious game, Uncle Sam snatched one of our more warlike players to take part in the real world conflict. And one season in this period we fielded a mixed team together with Holy Family, another tiny Catholic high school and longtime rival in Tulsa.

Being a homeless team, we begged for practice sites. Boston Avenue Methodist Church took in the Marquette orphans on many days. (It may indicate an ungrateful soul, but my recollection is Boston Avenue's gym gave every evidence of being a building committee's bad idea that was then treated by the church administration with benign. neglect.) On some evenings, the Midcontinent Refinery gymnasium was opened for us. And the good Augustinians at Cascia Hall often allowed us into their venerable house of sweat on Saturday mornings. A year or two before, we had practiced in the gym of a Jewish synagogue; but correctly assessing us as the Philistines we were, the synagogue's officials politely but firmly suggested we break things elsewhere.

I'm holding a photo of the 1943-44 Marquette Meteors basketball team in my left hand. There are seven players on the squad. Front and center, holding a basketball with a white M on it, is a smiling Joe Dillon. He, a sophomore, was both captain and coach. To Joe's left is Hank Hellinghausen, a truly superior athlete, but in March 1944 still on the short side. To Joe's right is Jack Charon, a senior. In the back row is seen, left to right, D.

Monahan, a junior, Terry Barge and Jimmy Hayes, both seniors, and the exuberant Bill Matheny, a sophomore.

(In another version of this photo, the seven-boy squad is wearing its warm-ups. Unfortunately, we were one warm-up short. So Terry Barge appears in a pair of pajamas, not just any old pajamas, but those with elastic around the wrists and ankles, a game try at coordinating our costumes and an A+ act of humility for Terry.)

Because of the limits imposed by the war one might assume that the Marquette Meteors basketball schedule was limited the year of '43-'44. Quite the contrary. We played 36 games—20 wins and 16 losses.

We entered the Tulsa Church League, all games contested at Central High School's infamous dungeon court. Two nights a week we would arrive at Central via city bus, bicycles or my mother's elegant '39 gray Dodge to do battle with the likes of First Baptist, Bullette Presbyterian and Immanuel Baptist.

The teams in the Church League were not limited to high schoolers. I have a distinct memory of a portly minister who launched two-handed, underhanded shots from way out yonder, always with a hearty "Hi-ho!" as he let the ball fly.

The Scrapbook revealed that we Meteors finished second in the Church League, then were eliminated in the playoffs by First Baptist with their star, Kraus, the Magical Mouse (an apt nickname bestowed by Joe Dillon). Joe and I agree that one name in the First Baptist lineup was that of a Catholic lad who later entered the seminary.

In that playoff game, we used a zone defense which First Baptist disdained to attack. As a result First Baptist had a mere 3 points at half time and 7 at the end of three quarters. The final score: First Baptist 15 Marquette 13. Darn!

Besides the Church League games, we played the two other Catholic schools in Tulsa as well as smaller public schools near the city—basketball powers like Kiefer and Keystone. Kiefer was an intriguing place to play—no locker rooms, clothes changed in a classroom, and players required to keep constant awareness of two large red hot open flame stoves, one at each end of the court.

I watch in horrifying dismay as the ball passes through the rim, swishes the net and wipes us out 34-32. My man scores the winning basket. Ah, the bitterness of human existence.

In the Scrapbook next to the clipping of this game, Joe Dillon has written: "It was almost heartbreaking." Almost? Speak for yourself, Joe. After the crowd filed out custodians swept up little pieces of my Marquette heart and threw them in the nearest trash can.

I feel morally certain that upon arriving home at 2139 E. 20 with tears in my eyes, my gentle mother said, "It was just a game, David. Just a game."

Not Even a Twitch of Weak Will to Write Tomorrow

April 1990

The other night I suffered through a chase dream. Pursuing me hither and yon were creatures bent on clobbering my physical frame. At one point I was cowering under a bed; at another the scene was the basement of a service station; in still a third a big city provided the setting; and finally, the chase concluded inconclusively in a kind of elaborate shopping mall.

Some, having read this far, no doubt have psychological explanations based on Freud, Jung, Geraldo or like diviners of the psyche. But what about a theological interpretation? One that occurs to me is that the dream prefigures my purgatory of being hunted down by the angry shades of hundreds whose letters I have failed to answer.

Hell, they say, is paved with good intentions. What about those who have slipped below the surface of good intentions—a kind of state of paralysis, where incoming letters are set aside rather than tossed in the waste can, but there is not even a twitch of weak will that "I will write tomorrow"? Ah, me.

I receive a lot of letters. Most of them are gentle pats on the back, nostalgic recollections of good times past, short statements of appreciation for this or that, perhaps soft suggestions for changes or corrections.

From me there issues nary a written word. I am the postal Sphinx of the Northwest Expressway, non-committedly gazing into the distance, while the sands of unanswered mail pile about me.

This is not the way to win friends and influence people. Now and again a spunky soul, who has had enough of this inexcusable sloth, takes pen in hand and, in a manner of speaking, shoves it in my ear.

Just today a letter arrived. The opening sentence "Now is the time to write" alerted me to dangers ahead. It seems photos were sent. They were neither used nor returned. The last sentence "I'm trying awfully hard not to get too mad over this" is an apt illustration of why I am purgatory bound, if there is a merciful judgment.

(There will be a pause here at 9:02 p.m. on March 20 while I search the debris on my desk for said photos. After search missions and an all-points alert the photos are recovered unharmed at 11:55 a.m. on March 21. This interlude serves to remind me that a factor which interferes with current letter writing is the intermittent slabs of time used to repair the damages of past sins in the omitted epistle department.)

Thanks be to God, there are some letters that do not call for an answer. One arrived this past month from a good woman who had had a youngster at McGuinness High School while I was principal there more than two decades ago.

She was moving away from Oklahoma, she wrote. But before taking leave she apparently felt the urge to do something that needed doing, namely telling me what a rotten job I had done for her son at 801 N.W. 50.

According to her story, her son was a bit short for his age and as a result other lads made his life miserable with assorted and sordid meannesses. When his mother approached me about the situation, the mother wrote, I nonchalantly tossed it off as boys will be boys.

Despite this difficult period in adolescence, her son has risen from the dust of the common herd to make oodles of money per year. "No thanks to you," mama added.

We who suffer from those failures of will and performance in writing letters seek desperately for solace and rationalizations. Here are a few of mine.

The late Father Jim McNamee, himself probably no great shakes at drafting replies to incoming missives, was wont to say: "If you hold unto a letter long enough, it will answer itself." His was the philosophical stance.

Possibly influenced by his friend Father McNamee, Bishop Victor Reed had a reputation for being something of a one-man dead letter office.

And the Italian postal service has helped to salve many a properly sore conscience. Once during a postal strike in Italy, the postal people there stored incoming mail in warehouses. When the strike ended, so the tale goes, the warehouses were simply sealed shut and the mail was never delivered. Life went on.

In my own case, twenty years ago this April, a tornado hit my living quarters, shearing off the whole floor where I had been sleeping. The report is I emerged from the bathroom unscathed and wearing a silly grin as I realized a decade of unanswered mail had been ripped from my numb grasp by an act of God. Talk about special deliverance.

Nichols Hills Never Had It So Bad as That Holy Week

April 1990

The crime was committed in the mid-1960s. The grisly deed was premeditated, sort of. And it happened in full view and, more to the point, in hearing range of several hundred people. I did it. On the most sacred night of the year.

How It Came About

I was laboring in that vineyard of the Lord known as McGuinness High School at the time. Unassigned to a parish, I signed on with Christ the King Church for the duration of Holy Week. Nichols Hills never had it so bad, but that only proved to be true in the course of events. There were no roiling thunderheads to warn of the calamity that would follow.

Cast of Characters and Preliminaries

The pastor of Christ the King in those days was a roly-poly Father Charles Conley. Few people, probably none, rolled off God's production line who were easier for me to be around. Now that I think of it, he was my confessor at the time.

Father Conley was short. And he had one of those perfectly bald heads which reminded one of a knob of good hardwood polished to perfection.

The pastor had a sense of humor. When tickled he displayed a peculiar sounding chuckle—nyuck! nyuck! nyuck!—something akin to one of the Three Stooges' snort-laugh. (For the life of me I can't remember which of the Three Stooges did that.)

Organist and music director at Christ the King was Hal Tompkins, a temperate and talented fellow. Hal was not only an excellent organist but also a composer of note. He knew his way around church music. A man one could rely on.

On a Doomed Path

A day or two before Easter, Father Conley said to me, "Why don't you sing the Exultet at the Vigil?" Being as the Exultet is a kind of liturgical summit of the proclamation of the Good News of Jesus' resurrection by the whole Holy Roman Catholic Church, and being as I had been told in the fifth grade that "Your voice is too weak" to make the exalted fifth grade choir, and being as I had butchered my share of High Masses in the first decade of my priestly life, therefore I was not exactly transported by this question/request.

"Well, I don't know," said I, digging the toe of my right shoe into the carpet and hanging my head.

"Oh, go ahead and do it," Father Conley said. "It won't hurt. Nyuck! Nyuck! Nyuck!"

I kept my peace.

The next day, however, I said to Father Conley, "I don't think it would be a good idea for me to do the Exultet."

"Oh, don't worry," he said. "You'll do all right."

I tried another tactic. I went to see Hal Tompkins. "I don't think I should do the Exultet," I said.

His face creased in a kindly smile. "Don't worry, Father. I've heard some really bad renditions of the Exultet in my lifetime. Let me assure you, you can't be as bad as some of those. "

I began to practice the song. The practices were so pitiful even I could tell they were so pitiful. Some charitable soul loaned me a record of the Exultet. It didn't help.

As a condemned man, I appealed for relief to Judge Conley and Judge Tompkins. What I got were two buckets of warm encouragement but no stay of execution.

My hour approached with sickening speed.

The Evil Act

I staggered through the opening ceremonies of the Easter Vigil, all the while humming the tune of the Exultet I had heard on the record.

All at once the Easter candle was lit and processed in and placed in the big candleholder and I was incensing it and, Oh, my Lord! Here was I standing in front of this book with pages of impossible notes staring coldly at me.

I attempted a deep breath, got a shallow one, and leaped into the Easter candle flame, so to speak.

Here's the way it went (the proper route marked in the usual notation, but my path shown by the trail of the Os as in zeroes):

Re-joice, heav-en-ly pow-ers!

Sing, choirs of an-gels! Ex-ult, all cre-a-tion a-round God's throne!

Some five minutes or five hours later, I chugged flatly but perspiringly into The End. The congregation sat there, frozen in that famous Catholic stoicism, neither guffawing nor barfing. Father Conley was gentleman enough not to go nyuck! nyuck! nyuck! I was gentleman enough not to say "I told you so."

I couldn't see Hal Tompkins at the time but later I imagined his struggle to control twitching facial muscles while grasping the organ bench with white-knuckled desperation.

Epilogue

After the assembly had dispersed, I asked the music man, "Was that the worst you ever heard?"

"Yes.

Not long afterward, Hal Tompkins quietly resigned at Christ the King and took a position at the cathedral in Cincinnati.

'y Ballou Reporting from the North End of the Water Hole

April 1990

My father and I are humming down a two-lane western Kansas road in his black Ford coupe. He is driving. I am in charge of the radio. The period: the latter part of the 1940s.

Suddenly we are conscious of this dull voice on the radio matter-of-factly offering for sale a Home Brain Surgery Kit. Write to NBC, Radio City, New York, NY, to order the kit, says the voice. Then another voice, deeply solemn, announces that the first 100 persons ordering the kit will receive as an added bonus a pair of green linoleum spats.

It was my introduction to Bob and Ray.

Three weeks ago, a letter arrived at the *Sooner Catholic* from Father Paul Mollan. He is probably the Oklahoma City metropolitan area's leading authority on Bob and Ray.

In the envelope were two newspaper clippings, obituaries actually, from Chicago newspapers. The headlines read "Comic Ray Goulding at 68; was part of Bob and Ray team" and, more simply, "Ray Goulding, 68, of 'Bob and Ray.'"

Ray Goulding is described as "half of the Bob and Ray team that delighted radio and television audiences for more than four decades with low-key humor and gentle satire" and as "the heftier half of 'Bob and Ray,' radio's four-decade-long testament to mirth and gentle mayhem."

In each obituary there is a photo of Ray, looking slightly upward with a half smile on his lips. On Ray's left shoulder there appears in the photo a part of a hand. Bob's? In any event, this peculiar ambiguous photo would seem to fit the occasion perfectly. One might even imagine the picture inspiring a Bob and Ray skit about the "Annual Encouraging Hand on the Shoulder Award" made possible by a grant from "The Whippet Motor Car Co., observing the forty-fifth anniversary of its disappearance."

The April 9 issue of *Time* magazine allotted only 12 lines to wave good-bye to Ray, "zany radio and TV comedian and costar, with Bob Elliott, of the beloved 'Bob and Ray' show."

"Beloved" is a proper adjective to describe their audience's long-term summation of the product ground out as the world passed between the imaginations of these two New Englanders. And note that the word "gentle" is used in both Chicago newspapers' obituaries, an unusual phenomenon in the "City of the Big Shoulders," one would think.

For years, Bob and Ray were heard several times a weekend on the NBC Monitor program. They would perform several short skits in which the two played all the parts, male and female, young and old. For Americans who liked the twosome's style, the skits' characters – even the mention of their names—jiggled the beginnings of a laugh.

For examples, there were the radio broadcasting team of Wally Ballou ("winner of twenty-one awards in diction") and Artie Schemmerhorn; Natalie Attired (whose specialty was to "say a song" that is, read the lyrics of current popular hits, in a deadly but precise voice) and her drummer, Eddie; sportscaster Biff Burns; cooking expert Mary McGoon; and writer 0. Leo Leahy.

The pair couldn't resist, thank God, shooting marshmallow spoofs at then-celebrated soap operas. So one heard the travails of "Mary Backstage, Noble Wife" rather than "Mary Noble, Backstage Wife," and "Mr. Trace, Keener than Most Persons" evolved from "Mr. Keen, Tracer of Lost Persons." "Jack

Armstrong" became "Jack Headstrong" and "One Man's Family" was reincarnated as "One Feller's Family."

The Wally Ballou character was a universal favorite. He came on the air as though an engineer habitually failed to get Ballou's sound up fast enough. "'y Ballou here," he would say.

Wally Ballou and Artie Schemmerhorn brought a chuckling nation such intriguing events as a taffy pull over Niagara Falls, with Ballou broadcasting from the Canadian side and Schemmerhorn from the American.

One of my favorites was a "report" from an African water hole. It went something like this:

"'y Ballou reporting from this world famous watering hole in deepest Africa, a place where more wildlife congregates than at any other spot on earth. Now let's go to Artie Schemmerhorn at the south end of the water hole."

"This is Artie Schemmerhorn from the south end of the watering hole. So far I have seen three red ants not more than ten feet from where I'm standing. That's all for now. Back to Wally Ballou at the north end."

"'y Ballou here at the north end of the watering hole, the one place where more wildlife can be seen than any other spot on this globe. Things have been rather quiet. I did see two sparrows fly past about ten minutes ago."

So it went, back and forth between 'y Ballou and Artie Schemmerhorn, neither seeing anything more unusual than one might find on a June trip to one's backyard in Oklahoma. It was funny, imaginative, vintage Bob and Ray.

May Ray Goulding rest in eternal joyful laughter.

I Left With All the Firmness of Will of a Jellyfish

May 1990

A vocation to the priesthood, especially the diocesan priesthood, was not something one took in by breathing the tradition of Christ the King Parish in Tulsa in the early 1940s.

Some had gone away to join religious communities—Steve to the Jesuits, Tim to the Benedictines and Manuel, a Marquette High School classmate of mine, who dropped out of sight after his sophomore year when he entered the Augustinians. But those happenings seemed removed from us high schoolers of the time. And the diocesan priesthood wasn't represented.

Nevertheless in the spring of 1945, as World War II was rushing toward an end, the vocation-to-the-priesthood question was intruding regularly on my thoughts. It was more of a bother than anything else, a nagging pest repeating: What does God want me to do?

Looking back, I suspect Father Cecil Finn had more than a little to do with the question. He didn't say much about it. He simply presented a daily joyful model of a priest's life. All the youngsters at Marquette, our parish high school, admired Father Finn. (Once a wise Benedictine nun asked a group of us why this was so. Our best and only response: Because he didn't smoke.)

Then Charles Skeehan popped the first olive out of the bottle. Charles, also a classmate of mine, was in ascending order of importance a second-class clarinet player, a serious fellow and a guy with the gutsy power to decide. Charles signed on with

Bishop Eugene McGuinness to go to a diocesan seminary the following fall term.

Charles's decision surely upped my concern about the matter: What does God want me to do?

From forty-five years away, it's hard to remember specifics, but I do have two recollections of related events. While serving Mass I, who am a musical ignoramus, was moved by the music. Apparently I decided right there, I'm going to do it.

I walked home to 1317 South Newport. My mother was in the bathroom. I shouted through the bathroom door, "Mom, I'm going to the seminary."

In the angelic Book of Odd Happenings Among the People of God that might rank right up there in the category of Announcing to One's Family One's Vocational Choice.

Came late August and Charles and I found ourselves on a platform at the Tulsa railroad station. Surrounded by clumps of family members and friends, we waited until the Frisco's Meteor came thundering through, hissing and snarling to a stop. We boarded, I with all the firmness of will of a jellyfish. The Meteor pulled away and beloved mother, Pythias-and-Damon friend Joe Dillon, and the gleaming towers of Tulsa were left behind in the night.

Saturday morning Charles and I arrived in the vast blackened cavern of St. Louis Union Station. We checked in at a hotel on Grand Avenue and Lindell Boulevard; we were due at the St. Louis Preparatory Seminary on Sunday afternoon. That night, God decreed it's time for a touch of comic relief. We went across the street to the Ambassador Theatre and saw Danny Kaye in Wonder Man. We laughed so hard, I almost forgot I was scared.

On Sunday, we took a cab to the seminary. We rolled to a stop in front of "the pile as a whole" (as described in the seminary brochure) which cost X number of millions and rang the front door bell.

Shortly afterward we were made aware that a seminarian never, ever used the front doors of seminaries unless he is carrying the suitcases of a visiting bishop. (This ground rule may have been abrogated by the shrapnel of Vatican Council II.)

We were led to a large L-shaped dormitory on the second floor. Someone had made the dubious decision to place all the boys from St. Louis in one arm of the L-shaped dormitory and all of rubes from the hinterland in the other arm. It was a formula that spelled w-a-r.

Metal beds with U-shaped mattresses in the L-shaped dormitory were lined in two long rows in each wing. The bed next to me was occupied by a lanky kid named Louis Rost. He is now a Maryknoll missionary in Taiwan.

Vincentian priests operated the seminary. We were shortly introduced to Vincentian Father William J. Winklemann. He informed us that to thank God World War II had ended all of us would wear coats and ties that year. It was the first broad hint that we would be ruled by edict. No votes.

So we began Year One of seminary life. The schedule was rigid. The rules were tight and some downright silly. Many of us struggled through the rough seas of homesickness. We adapted to a different culture and made new friends. Some of us became super pious. Others of us balanced piety with practicality as Don Murphy who closed his missal and took a nap during the offertory every early morning.

And at night, I would look out the window of the common bathroom at the outlines of the major seminary, Kenrick, about a mile away. I wondered if I would ever possibly make it that far.

Girl B Runs up Staircase to Appeal to Supreme Court

July 1990

tantrum n-s [origin unknown]: a burst of ill humor: a fit
of bad temper

Thus does Webster's Third New International Dictionary define
the well-known phenomenon of childhood, baseball managing
and basketball coaching.

Not so long ago I was an eye-witness of a tantrum. In fact, it
happened at my feet.

While visiting in a nameless family member's, home, I sat
quietly in the living room reading the second volume of William
Manchester's biography of Winston Churchill. The subtitle of
the book is "Alone." I was not.

On the carpet in front of me two young girls were playing
Monopoly. Girl A, the elder sister, was bored and under those
trying circumstances apt to be full of the Old Ned. Girl B, the
younger sister, didn't realize she was racing toward a painful
collision with a jagged reef of capitalism.

"I'll sell you Park Avenue for $500," says Girl A. "Okay," Girl
B replies. She counts out the payment and hands it across the
playing board. Girl B takes the Park Avenue card from Girl A,
looks at it and realizes she has been overcharged.

"I want my money back!" says Girl B.

"Oh, no! You agreed to pay that price," retorts Girl A with
a smirk.

"*I want my money back!*"

"You agreed to pay that price!

"I want my money back!"

(The perceptive reader perhaps can feel the outer fringes of a tantrum.)

The dialogue escalates from yells to screams to howls to shrieks.

The old bachelor relative grasps his book with both hands and reads Winston Churchill through the same door five times over. Each second seems an hour. Each minute a century. He is too rattled to think of dialing 911.

Girl B is no dummy. Even in her rage against life at the Monopoly board, the center of her mind is rational. She jumps up, runs out of the room and up the staircase. She is on her way to appeal the case to the Supreme Court. Girl A follows approximately .3 of a second behind.

The Chief Justice of the Supreme Court presumably is seated in his chambers mulling over the wisdom of Edmund Burke, John Marshall and the like when the litigants burst through the door.

"Dad, ____ cheated me," cries out Girl B.

"I did not!"

"You did too!"

"I did not!"

The story tumbles into the Chief Justice's lap. There was a sale of property, but not for the price on the card. The Chief Justice patiently tries to explain to Girl B that a deal is a deal. In the future, Girl B must carefully consider what she is agreeing to do.

This judgment is met with true revolutionary spirit. Girl B comes pounding down the stairs. The Chief Justice orders, come back here!"

There is no stopping. Girl B dashes into the living room. The cards, the little red property markers, the play money, the dice and the board are thrown in all directions. It's nihilism in practice.

But the Chief Justice has cast off his robes of fair play and has become the Chief of Police seeking to restore order. Girl A is commanded to leave the area. She does. Girl B is told to begin picking up what she has cast to the four corners of the room.

There is hesitation; there is arguing; there is pouting; but she does it.

"I'm mad at you, Dad!" says Girl B. "I'm really mad at you, Dad." The Chief of Police-Father allows that her anger is evident. The tension begins to drop. The tantrum is blowing itself out. The old bachelor relative begins to unwind, although he goes through the door with Churchill a sixth and seventh time.

The old bachelor relative wonders if the Chief Justice—Chief of Police—Father should be beatified by the church right then and there.

Later the old bachelor relative remembered instances of his own tantrums. According to family tales, surely more exaggeration than reality, he was known as a boy for throwing himself on the floor and crashing his heels down to show displeasure. And there were other stories about slamming his fists against household walls when things didn't flow his way.

Then there was the father of the old bachelor relative, that is, the great-grandfather of Girls A and B. At certain periods in his adult life, tantrums swam very close to the surface. If somehow the wrong signal was given, Boom! He would stomp out, slamming the door behind him.

Perhaps that background explained why the old bachelor relative had a certain combination of fear, empathy and amusement for such as the terrible tempered Tommy Bolt. He had seen Mr. Bolt stride down the fairways at Southern Hills in Tulsa, aglow with the harmony of the world, as he swept all before him in winning the 1958 U.S. Open Golf Championship. And he had seen, via Life magazine, two years later in the same tournament, this time in Denver, when Tommy had flung his driver as far as he could throw it into the pond fronting the eighteenth tee.

In life, there's not a great distance from the mood that all is well to the madness that all is hell.

The Official Asks,
"The Purpose of Your Visit?"
"Cerveza!"

April 1990

When Msgr. John Higgins was informed of one of his later priestly assignments, he said, "'All I ask these days are two questions: What is the TV reception like and is the water good?"

Is the water good? It better be. Every living thing outside my window, as well as gurgling I inside, depends on this H20 stuff for our greenness.

Some of the facts about water are spooky. Our inland minds are boggled by the data, for example, on the Pacific Ocean. The biggest pond is about 64 million square miles in area with an average depth of 13,000 feet—larger than even WhiteWater. But the scary part is how comparatively little is the amount of fresh water on the Earth (3 percent of all water is fresh and most of that is frozen around the two Poles) and, even more so, the much tinier barrel of pure fresh water for the human family.

And we Americans use this water prodigiously—168 gallons a day per person according to the American Water Works Association. (If you wondered who was the man wearing the raincoat and holding the clipboard in your shower with you this morning, now you know, an employee of the AWWA updating the association's data base.)

For generations now, we Yankees have taught our children that if they venture beyond the borders of the 'United States Don't drink the water!

I scrupulously follow this health habit principle. For example, if I pass into a Spanish-speaking territory, I whip out my one-word Spanish vocabulary: cerveza (beer). It works although I get some peculiar looks.

The following have probably happened.

When I enter a country, the immigration official asks, "What is the purpose of your visit?"

"Cerveza!"

At the hotel, the distinguished manager inquires, "When would you care to be awakened?"

"Cerveza!"

And the same gentleman may try again with, "Do you have valuables you wish to deposit in our safe?"

"Cerveza!

Or a person on the street may study this figure in the seersucker suit and wearing a Roman collar and ask, "What is your religious affiliation?"

"Cerveza!

But no stomachaches.

One memorable day, I was cooling my heels in a waiting room of the Oruba Palace in Cairo. Our group was going to have an interview with President Hosni Mubarak.

Cairo is perhaps the western Capitol of Queasy. At any rate, the least stricken U.S. journalist at this event felt as though a pack of gerbils were loose in his or her gastrointestinal tract. Others, more desperate, edged away from the center of the room, as Ricky Henderson might from first base, ready for a frantic dash to the water closet.

At this point, a suave Egyptian diplomat stepped into our space to remind us: "That he who once has drank from the Nile will return to drink again." Nobody upchucked, but it was a close call.

I failed to learn the Arabic word for beer.

The reference books define water as a pale-blue odorless liquid or limpid liquid or the liquid which descends from the clouds and is odorless and tasteless.

These definers certainly did not live in blessed Oklahoma City, a mile and a half west of Lake Hefner, at least during certain parts of the summer. I just strolled down the hall and ran a glassful of Lake Hefner water out of the tap. It is limpid. It is tasteless. It is odorless.

But wait, ol' buddy, definer. Round about the first of August, Lake Hefner will do a flip-flop, the algae will kick into gear and the water will don the costumes of cloudy, medicinal in taste and breathtaking. It is entirely possible that the first creation of the word Yuk! came during a shower bath in my area during the algae season.

By the way, Msgr. Higgins spent the last six years of his active ministry in Oklahoma City. The television reception was excellent; the water...

Veteran Golfer Unnerved by Opponent's Payless Shoes

August 1990

If the eyes of the golfing world had not suffered a corneal abrasion from a sprig of gorse during the British Open, they certainly would have focused the following week on Shangri-La's Blue Course. Golfdom's most bitter rivalry briefly flared along the shores of Grand Lake on July 24. Yes, it was the 1990 renewal of the lifelong contest between J. McGlinchey and D. Monahan.

J. McGlinchey, ever the crafty one-upman, arrived at the scene wearing new but extremely economical athletic shoes purchased at a Payless Shoesource. D. Monahan, sporting a fresh pair of Footjoy golf shoes furnished by an observant and generous nephew, was hurled into emotional confusion. What if he lost to an opponent wearing $10 Payless treaders? Oh, the shame!

The shock was compounded when the man behind the cash register in the golf shop blithely announced that green fees were $52.50 a day. That figures to $2.92 a hole for a round. No doubt the price worked on each players' subconscious during the competition at hand. A birdie on a par 3 meant $1.46 per swing! While a solid 8 reduced the cost to a more reasonable thirty-seven cents per attempt.

Speaking of eights, there were to be six of them, equally divided between the man in the Payless footwear and the other geezer in the Footjoys.

On to the first tee!

The first tee at a golf course, any golf course, is a study in self-conscious preening, self-conscious attempts to appear carefree, self-conscious teasing of opponents, and self-conscious commenting about one's ineptitude as a golfer plus remarks that "This is my first round since Eisenhower was president." Underneath all this folderol are timeless cold slabs of fear.

For first shots, D. Monahan managed a screaming line drive that came to rest on the left edge of the fairway but behind the overhanging limbs of a tree, while J. McGlinchey smashed a long high shot into the nearby eighteenth fairway. An onlooker was reminded of Vasco da Gama sailing forth to find a new route to India.

The two grizzled foes played as if they were strangers to the game, for example, nary a par between them on the first nine. There were, however, some rare happenings along their twenty-seven-hole way.

Take the 375-yard thirteenth hole, for example. On a person's drive on 13 the fairway is uphill so that the second stroke, for us short knockers, is a blind shot. D. Monahan fired his second up over a midget evergreen, swung and looked up to see the ball nearly on course. At the green he discovered his ball resting in a bunker just to the left of the putting surface, perhaps 30 feet from the hole.

With Gomer, his unfaithful sand wedge, he descended into the trap. His first swing moved lots of sand but the ball merely flopped forward a few feet. He swung again, caught the ball cleanly and sailed it not only over the green but 30 yards beyond. From hole high on two, he had managed to make it 90 feet removed from the green in four. It was, said D. Monahan, an example of his SGS (Short Game Stinks) System. He marked an accurate 8 on his scorecard.

Then again, the McGlinchey-Monahan duo performed rarely on the ninth hole. The ninth is a par 3 where one fires at an elevated green 180 yards away through a narrow alley bordered by thick woods. Our heroes played the ninth twice in their twenty-seven holes (reducing the price to $1.94 a hole, by the way).

On each occasion, all tee shots were struck radar-like into the trees. Disdaining to chip out into the center clearance, they chose to fight their way up the hill through the trees. Again. history-oriented spectators reflected that it was similar to Grant and Lee caught in mortal struggle in the Battle of The Wilderness.

Par for two players completing the ninth twice is 12. D. Monahan and J. McGlinchey admitted to twenty-one swings between them.

But, pray tell, who won?

At the end of the 27 D. Monahan was declared a 1-up victor. As is usual in this courteous war of the dregs of golfing, the match was as tight as George Washington's smile. Neither man had more than a two-hole advantage at any one time. Medal plays scores were J. McGlinchey 149, D. Monahan 150.

Thus matters were settled as the sun lowered in the sky on July 24. But came a recount on August 5. An error is discovered! On the eighth hole in the morning D. Monahan soared to an 8, while J. McGlinchey carded a 6. Yet the hole was somehow awarded to D. Monahan. On being informed, the United States Golf Association, the Royal and Ancient, and the Putt-Putt American Alliance awarded the cup, if there was one, to J. McGlinchey 1-up.

A downcast D. Monahan stated at a press conference, attended by the *Sooner Catholic* newspaper, that "it is unfortunate these days that too much emphasis is placed on winning."

Agents of the two old fogies said later that tentative arrangements have been made to play 1990 Part II in October.

An Odd Duck in a Pond of Many-Hued Protestant Birds

September 1990

To be a life-long Catholic in a state where one met only two or three fellow Catholics per 100 citizens walking toward you on a given sidewalk should produce memorable adventures. That is the point of this column.

I'm somewhat embarrassed to report that I cannot recall any heroic tales nor tight moral squeezes occasioned by the fact that I'm an odd religious duck, a wee creature flying the papal colors in the midst of a pond of bobbing many-hued Protestant birds.

But there have been instances.

The Traband brothers and I were across-the-street neighbors. We outlasted the long summers with hundreds of gun battles. Darting behind a tree here, scooting around a corner there, always with weapons in hand, we blazed away at one another. The sounds of violence flew between our lips—tuh, tuh, tuh our tongues squeezed off "pistol shots" against the roofs of our mouths or the rapid huh, huh, huh, huh, huh of machine gun fire. (Mr. Curly Camblin around whose home these battles frequently raged later confessed those sounds nearly drove him to a psychiatric ward.)

The point is the Trabands and I spent a lot of outdoor time together. Then one hot evening they informed me they knew a joke but their mother had told them not to tell me because "You're a Catholic."

I was on the outside, somehow barred from this sharing because the Monahans were members of Christ the King Church.

On another twilight in another neighborhood, I was surprised to learn I was the only boy on my block who favored Gen. Francisco Franco and his rebels over the loyalists in the Spanish Civil War.

I had never heard of the cruel Fascists on Franco's side nor of the daring International Brigade including Americans risking their lives for the "freedom" of Spain with the loyalists. The other guys in the 1500 block of South Evanston did not know of the communist menace of the loyalists nor the help provided that side by Moscow.

This weighty discussion took place during a game of catch in Bob Arnold's backyard. Nobody's feathers got particularly ruffled. It was just one of those accepted differences between Catholic school kids and their public school counterparts.

Perhaps I had a secret sense of superior knowledge. After all I was a regular reader of the Young Catholic Messenger and in each issue Gen. Franco tenaciously bombed his way closer to victory.

The summer of 1944, between my junior and senior high school years, I worked 54 hours a week at Wheatley Pumps and Valves along the Sand Springs Line west of Tulsa. I am moronic about things mechanical but I can be taught to perform repetitive functions with mechanical parts.

John, my foreman, trained me to assemble large oil pipeline valves. Then he motivated (read: terrified) me into perhaps the fastest-moving valve assemblyman in the entire 48 states. I was a 600-minute daily blur of efficient activity for the glory of God, the stars and stripes, and John. My mother would never have believed it possible.

Back in the valve assembly area things were mostly grease, noise, sweat and expletives. From time to time though there were bits of conversation. Many of the workers there had been citizens of Arkansas which they referred to as the "Old Country." One gathered that the Catholic Church did not rank in their personal Top Tens.

Once, with me standing by, one gray-haired fellow said to another, "Dave here is going to be a priest or a lawyer."

The second, solemnly staring straight ahead through lids almost drawn shut and jaw disfigured by a plug of tobacco, finally broke the silence with, "Best be a lawyer."

End of conversation.

Years passed. I walked out of the stadium at the University of Oklahoma having just witnessed a slam-bang football game between the Sooners and Notre Dame. The Fighting Irish won 13-7 with a heart-stopping fourth quarter goal line stand.

Although a summertime graduate at Notre Dame then, I rooted for Oklahoma. And I had worn a big OU button on the lapel of my black suit coat which, in turn, was crowned with my Roman collar. None too joyful over Oklahoma's loss, I joined the flow of the crowd out of the stadium. On the sidewalk outside suddenly I was eyeball to eyeball with a scowling old codger. He took a long look at me, obviously intent on the Roman collar but missing the pro-Oklahoma button. His succinct sour remark: "Pretty lucky!"

More years fell down the tube of time. An evaluation of McGuinness High School was underway. The spine of the North Central Association's evaluation committee at McGuinness was composed of a cadre of kindly, courtly and somewhat ancient gentlemen from the Oklahoma State Department of Education.

As the institution being evaluated we had managed to work ourselves into a collective case of nerves. But the evaluators hastened to calm our fears. We expected microscopes; they used casual glances through bifocals. We were geared to please; they were struggling to understand this Catholic thing.

On the last day of the evaluation, I visited with an elderly gent in my office. His hair was white as pure cotton. A gentle soul was he. He leaned toward me beaming honest benevolence.

"I knew a Msgr. Gavan P. Monaghan who was a Catholic educator," he said softly.

"Oh, yes," I replied. "He was the superintendent of Catholic schools here."

"Was he your father?"

"No."

Charlie and Me: The Story of a Painful Collision Course

October 1990

This is the story of Charlie and me or how a highflier and a lowflier were set on a painful collision course.

Not all that many months ago, I sat in my usual semi-comatose state staring at the evening news. The news item concerned the alleged attempt by a savings-and-loan mogul to influence the votes of five United States senators through their love of mammon.

Reporters pushed microphones into the face of a tall solemn-faced man. The conversation went something like this:

Reporter: "You have been charged, Mr. Keating, with trying to buy the votes of five senators. What do you have to say about that?"

Tall solemn-faced man, with great emphasis: "I certainly hope I succeeded!"

"Keating? Keating? Charles Keating?" The name jiggled through the bad memory connections in my brain. "Charles Keating? Keating? *Keating*!" The connected name opened the floodgates to a fateful day in the 1960s.

A wealthy Oklahoma Catholic man had decided to wage war on pornography, war on a sexual revolution. The sexual revolution had erupted in America. Hugh Hefner had slithered Playboy magazine into the mainstream. The sexual revolutionists were happily poisoning traditional morality and cultural practices.

The wealthy man determined to fight. He arranged for a judge from Pennsylvania and a tough pornography fighter from Cincinnati to come to Oklahoma for a week's blitz. He enlisted the aid of numerous Oklahomans who had good cause for alarm at the rapid erosion of sexual mores. One of the enlistees was the gentlemanly Bishop Victor Reed, my boss.

I was given to understand that the bishop wanted Mr. Keating, the anti-pornographer from Cincinnati, to address the students of McGuinness High School. As principal, I had misgivings about this venture but I agreed to go along.

Came the day. I met Charles Keating, a second man, an anti-pornography attorney from California, and the befurred wealthy man's wife and escorted them into the high school auditorium.

Keating was a fine specimen of a human male – better than average height, trim and radiating confidence. He was introduced as a former U.S. Navy pilot and an Olympic-class swimmer or diver.

He launched into a fervent attack on pornography with particular force aimed at Playboy. Keating's style was reminiscent of a 1940 retreat, heavy on the fear angle, perhaps something he had picked up at some point from an overwrought retreat master.

In any event, I was uncomfortably aware that this approach was not going to be swallowed docilely by the high schoolers seated behind me. (Mrs. Big and I were perched in the front row.) Oh, well, thought one, only fifteen minutes to go, we can make it. But then…

When Keating stopped and asked this roomful of bubbling puberty if they had any questions or comments, my anxiety measurement needle flipped to "Extreme." In my abdomen a voice shouted: "All stomach acid valves full open!"

A senior young man sprang to his feet. "I think you are all wrong about Playboy! It has some good articles by respected writers."

Keating fired back. The youngster answered him. The old Navy pilot shot another zinger. Two other boys stood up to have their say. The guest speaker's face was turning angry red. A nun stepped forward to spread calming oil on the waters. Another student playfully tossed a verbal match in the oil. Keating strafed the junior and senior classes with rapid fire denunciations of the comments he had elicited. The kids went to their antiaircraft guns. The bell rang to end the fighting. The principal crawled out from under his seat.

On the way out of the auditorium, Charles Keating said to me, "That was disgraceful in a Catholic school!" I thought: "How many Catholic high schools has he been in? Two?"

Then, probably from some masochistic urge, I blurted, "Would you like to stay for lunch?" Yes, improbably said they—Keating, the attorney and Mrs. Big.

The McGuinness faculty dining room, in those days, was tiny and the decor was storeroom plain. Into this tight wedge, we compressed Keating and his party together with our teachers, still tense from the assembly. The equation spelled d-y-n-a-m-i-t-e.

The McGuinness faculty then included a cherubically innocent man with possibly a slight mean streak who taught religion. His name was Peter. Having just achieved his master's degree in theology, he, of course, knew all the answers, even to questions which no one had asked.

Peter waited about 8.2 seconds before he stated in a loud clear voice, "I thought the judge's theology of marriage in his talk last night was the worst I've ever heard." This referred to the Pennsylvania judge who had come to Oklahoma, at the same time as Keating, to purify us.

Thus the Lunchroom War began. Voices rose. Blood pressures rose. Stress rose. Agape it was not. Teachers caught in the firing zone began to squeeze their way between the chairs toward the door and safety. Husky cowardly coaches straightened their ties and stared at the ceiling as they sidled to the escape hatch. The principal's entire gastrointestinal tract tied itself into a square knot. Mrs. Big, whose fur coat had added a heretofore unknown note of elegance to the faculty dining room, looked on in shock.

By this time the attorney had opened his briefcase and was tossing out handfuls of pornography to prove that pornography did exist. Peter and Keating wildly zapped arguments at one another.

Somehow a merciful Gods providence brought the catastrophe to an end.

Twenty-five years later I'm seated here in my office looking at a photo of a handcuffed Charles Keating being lead to a bail hearing, indicted on forty-two counts of criminal fraud in connection with the collapsed Lincoln Savings and Loan of California.

Charlie, maybe you should have stayed in the high school speech business.

Golf Games Melt in Water at Fall Match Play Classic

November 1990

An apt image of the 1990 Fall Match Play Classic was footprints in the mud of Rowlett Creek below the bridge on the path to the fifteenth hole at Chase Oaks. The first print was two inches deep, the second four inches, the third eight and the final one a good foot and a half into the gumbo. 'Twas the sign of disaster, the kind of total catastrophe into which the golf games of J. McGlinchey and D. Monahan wetly descended during their November 12-14 confrontation in North Dallas.

The shame of it all was compounded by the fact that for the first time in the lifelong McGlinchey-Monahan international competition, there was a trophy at stake. A Ms. Dorothy Hardesty, Tulsa connoisseur and patron of elegant sporting events, presented a suitable memorial in August. The trophy is a framed sketch depicting a fierce deity scowling from the clouds at a mortal golfer bending down to move his golf ball by hand from its position behind a tree to a better lie. Ms. Hardesty revealed she purchased this priceless article at a garage sale. It will be known hereafter as The Hardesty and will be in the possession of the biannual winner of the McGlinchey-Monahan combat.

The settings for the 1990 Fall Match Play Classic were the Indian Creek Lakes Course in Carrollton, Texas, and the Sawtooth Course at Chase Oaks north of Plano, Texas. These courses were, of course, most carefully selected—the first on a tip from the manager of the La Quinta Inn on 1-35 at Lewisville and the second from an ad, on page nine of The North Texas

Golfer, which included the intriguing phrase "play where the people who know, play."

On the first day at Indian Creek, the starter declared that J. McGlinchey and D. Monahan would play with Hurst and Tom. (The uninitiated should be aware that on crowded public links, citizen golfers arriving by ones and twos are assigned at random to make up foursomes. First names are exchanged at the first tee.)

"There's a lot of water on this course," Hurst said. "And a lot of it you can't see when you are hitting the ball."

Water. Hidden water. Neither J. McGlinchey nor D. Monahan was reminded of their baptisms. In fact, thinking was not their reaction. Fear was. The kind of fear that raises heads too soon when swinging a golf club, the kind of fear which progresses from peeking to panic to kerplunk to primitive purple pronouncements. Water was to be the nightmare factor of the Fall Classic.

At sunset of Day One, D. Monahan held a five-up lead.

Day Two found our heroes paired with Kent and Ed, a son and father team.

Again water was an ever-menacing presence. Take the sixteenth hole, for example. A lake licked its lips to the left of the fairway. D. Monahan drove down the right side of that fairway. No trouble here, thought he. In a carefree manner, D. Monahan smashed a 5-iron. The ball hit an oak tree and ricocheted at a right angle across the fairway and into the lake. Incredible.

As Day Two closed in shadows, D. Monahan claimed a gigantic eleven-up lead.

What happened at Chase Oaks on Day Three was, to put it delicately, sickening. Rowlett Creek played the role of the serpentine monster voraciously swallowing golf balls of all makes and colors—Ultras, Top Flights, Hogans, you name 'em.

On the sixteenth green, a tired J. McGlinchey looked at a tuckered D. Monahan and said, "I'm here in seven."

"And I'm here in thirteen," croaked a blushing D. Monahan. Final scores for the whole were ten and sixteen.

Astoundingly, J. McGlinchey picked up hole after hole. Heading for the eighteenth tee, D. Monahan led the Fall Classic by a scant one-up. The eighteenth, a 545-yard par 5, was a fright. From the tee box, one could see only the first half of the hole which ended where Rowlett Creek made one last crossing of the fairway. The second half of the hole proved to be a slightly rising fairway to a green bordered tightly on one side by a lake.

J. McGlinchey's first drive struck the trees on the left. He hit a provisional ball which also tailed into the trees. D. Monahan skittered his tee shot down the middle. When the exhausted competitors finally managed to putt out, the score written on the card was D. Monahan 6, J. McGlinchey 9. Thus the first winner of The Hardesty was....

But wait! After the tee shots, J. McGlinchey had found one of the two balls he had swatted. But was it the first one or the second? He wasn't certain. If the first, it meant he was playing his second shot. If the second, he was playing his fourth stroke. Having assumed it was his second ball that he found and that the hole and the match were lost, he made only a lackadaisical attempt at a short putt, which he missed. Hence the possible outcomes were: Monahan won two-up, Monahan won one-up, or the match was a draw.

There was nothing to do but to refer it to the Fall Classic's Rules Committee. The Rules Committee's three members are Charles, Prince of Wales; Pee Wee Herman; and Minnie Pearl; plus honorary but deceased members Humphrey Bogart and Claude Rains.

The Rules Committee met in emergency session on November 16. On November 17, J. McGlinchey and D. Monahan received registered letters with the decision: "Play it again, Sam." Supernatural interposition is suspected.

The Hardesty has been returned to storage awaiting the 1991 Spring Match Play Classic.

School Boy Happens upon a Delightfully Bloody Book

December 1990

The late Msgr. James Rooney on a former Oklahoma bishop who was great on the doing side but rather thin in the thinking department: "Sure and the man never read a book! Never read a single book! "

The celebrated British author Graham Greene on meeting Pope Paul VI and being congratulated by the pope on the excellence of one of his novels: "But, your Holiness, that book has been put on the Index of Forbidden Books!" "Who did that?" asked Pope Paul. When Greene told his famous fan which cardinal in the Roman Curia had been responsible, the pope replied, in so many words: "That figures."

Daniel Patrick Moynihan, upon meeting his fellow Nixon administration member John Ehrlichman in a hall at the White House: "Achtung, Herr Ehrlichman! It wouldn't hurt to read a book now and again, John."

D. Monahan, sitting in his reading chair with three stacks of books, each stack about 18 inches high, at his right hand and smaller piles of books marching westward across the carpet: "Let's hear it for Johnny Gutenberg and Brother Book!"

My life hasn't been exactly as exciting as Chuck Yeager's, but it would have been as dull as West Texas without books. It's hard to imagine life without books.

My reading career began as a little squirt in Tulsa. Sometime before First Communion, I recall lugging around a copy of a yellowed book on the sinking of the Titanic. The book had pen-

and-ink sketches of the stages of the disaster. This volume was a fixture of our household scene. I can't remember how much I read of it, but its images survive even in my leaky memory.

While climbing the elementary ladder at Tulsa's elite Marquette School (tuition $1 a month), I happened upon a delightfully bloody book, "Mangled Hands." It was the story of Isaac Joques, a French Jesuit, who was martyred in North America during the middle years of the seventeenth century.

"Mangled Hands" fascinated me. Tulsans of those days witnessed this near-sighted boy with face in book stepping into space off curbs and colliding with trees as he wandered away from school under the spell of this yarn of heroism. The description of the saint having his thumbs chewed off might get a thumbs down today from the local PTA, but it was an adventure then for this kid.

When Grandma Connolly died, the Monahan home inherited a complete set of James Fenimore Cooper's books – a raft of them, all bound beautifully in green. Motivated by the movie, "The Last of the Mohicans," I set to work on the task of reading them all.

Seated in bed in my back bedroom under a powerful sixty-watt bulb in the ceiling, I struggled along the rough route of the Leatherstocking series—"The Deerslayer," "The Pathfinder," etc.—but suffered a serious collapse of willpower and limped back to comic books. One insight into human nature was gleaned, no one in our family had ever read Cooper's books. The pages had to be sliced open as I went along.

At the same time as I had a secret sense of superiority to others my age because of my clandestine reading of Cooper, I was voraciously chomping my daytime way through every Poppy Ott and Jerry Todd book I could find (at thirty-five cents a throw for new hardback copies).

Then the inimitable Aunt Kate gave up housekeeping and took to staying, a month at a time, with her four nieces, one of whom was my mother. This transition occasioned the transfer of some of Aunt Kate's possessions to each of the four households.

The Monahans received an elegant longish cabinet filled with artifacts and rows of more books that nary a soul had ever read. (One of the unusual items in the cabinet was a rolled up skin of a python bagged by Uncle Wells in Borneo while searching for oil. As I recollect, the snake skin was twelve to fifteen feet long and a real conversation starter when it was unrolled on rainy afternoons.)

A handsome set of books in the cabinet was the entire output of Alexandre Dumas, the creator of "The Three Musketeers," "The Count of Monte Cristo" and "The Man in the Iron Mask." Later, in the seminary, I discovered that Mr. Dumas's works were lock, stock and barrel on the church's Index, even before Mr. Greene made the exclusive list. My mother would have built a bonfire in the living room if she had known.

Out of all of this, I became a reader—not the world's best-read reader and certainly not the fastest reader, but a fellow who enjoys plugging his way through a good book.

Where else would I have been so well introduced to the likes of Abraham Lincoln, Winston Churchill, Harry Angstrom of "Rabbit Runs" etc., Gus McCrae of "Lonesome Dove," Douglas MacArthur, Hazel Motes of Flannery O'Connor's "Wise Blood," Sam Houston, Ulysses S. Grant, Martin Luther King, tough and lovely Dorothy Day (who read Dickens when she was melancholy), Ivan Denisovich of "One Day in the Life of...," P.G. Wodehouse's "Oldest Member," Jim Chee and Joe Leaphorn from Tony Hillerman's "Navajo mind, "The Headmaster" as sketched by John McPhee, Vinegar Joe Stilwell as revealed by Barbara Tuchman, and even Chuck Yeager as he casually rocketed through the sound barrier out of the pen of Tom Wolfe in "The Right Stuff"?

CHAPTER 15

1991

Is It the Fault of the Irish that Catholics Can't Sing?

January 1991

"Why Catholics Can't Sing" is the title of the book. Thomas Day, the author and obviously a brave lad, has set forth his theories relative to the title of the book in a straightforward manner. The problem with Catholics and singing, Day writes, is the Irish. At least, one gathers that from a book review by Msgr. Charles Diviney in the December 22 issue of *The Tablet*, Brooklyn's Catholic newspaper.

To have printed publicly that the Irish are the nodules on the collective Catholic larynx is a chancy business, Thomas, perhaps foolhardy or even bordering on stupid. Especially in Brooklyn. And repeated on page twenty-four of *The Tablet* where the three advertisements at the bottom of the page have been commissioned by the likes of Michael Connors & Sean Grogan, James A. Reilly and William J. Keegan, all attorneys at law. Do you think for a moment, Thomas, that Michael Connors own father was not an Irish tenor whose sweet voice could charm Waterford crystal to Liquefy happily into its original elements?

To be fair to Thomas Day, it needs to be said that he did not arrive at his musical conclusions after decades of driving a bus. He is an organist, who holds a doctorate in musicology from Columbia, and presently is chairman of the music department at Salve Regina College.

And his thoughts about the Irish and singing are based on history rather than on his perception of their lack of talent. Dr. Day is of the opinion that the secretive and hushed worship of the Irish, during three or four centuries of English religious persecution, produced a tradition of muffled liturgy which was carried to America and eventually became the American Catholic standard.

Ah, so.

Humbly confessing—*mea culpa, mea culpa, mea maxima culpa*—my own shortcomings, failures, sins, peccadilloes and wretched transgressions against the canons of decency in church singing, I proceed nevertheless to offer other possibilities of Why Catholics Can't Sing.

The Conspiracy or the Ellis Island Theory

Immigrants to the United States in the latter half of the nineteenth century and the earlier decades of the twentieth were not exactly greeted with bands playing, champagne receptions and six-course dinners. There were quaint American sobriquets sprinkled on the newcomers—Irish Need Not Apply, Yellow Peril, wops, spicks, Polacks, krauts, etc.

Is the rumor true that the apples given to the immigrants at Ellis Island contained a drug which contracted their vocal chords so they couldn't sing in church? Those Know-Nothings were a miserable lot but would they stoop that far? Most likely.

The Catholic Schools' Terrorism Theory.

According to this school of thought, every Italian child could sing at least as well as Pavarotti or Sinatra and every Irish lad was the likes of the immortal John McCormack until they went to Catholic schools where the music was scared out of them.

There are some problems with this theory. One, it is held only by those who still believe there are guns stored in the basement at St. Joseph's Old Cathedral and/or that the present pope was born with 666 tattooed on his left big toe. Two, there is the testimony of Jimmy Breslin, New York Daily News columnist, that Catholic schools taught him to punctuate correctly and to be terrified only of anything to do with sex.

The West of the Hudson Theory

This theory is firmly founded on the well-known fact that citizens living east of the Hudson River have a skewed view of most of the United States of America. (One notes that Dr. Day's place of employment is Newport, Rhode Island, which is but a solid tee shot from Killarney.) Persons east of the Hudson think the Shootout at the OK Corral took place on the outskirts of Harrisburg, Pa., and that Lewis and Clark felt their way along the Monongahela River until they discovered the steel mills at Pittsburgh.

A critic of American Catholic singing, who resides in such a shrunken atmosphere, is liable to have severe sound distortions regarding the greater part of the church in this nation. For example, Dr. Day probably never had the pleasure of hearing the magnificent voices at St. Theresa's in Luther, Oklahoma, swelling to an a cappella crescendo in "Now Thank We All Our God" for the two hundred and fifty second consecutive Sunday.

The They're Americans Theory

Have you ever noticed that Americans as a whole can't sing? "Let's join with the Natrona County High School's marching band as we sing our national anthem!" bellows the announcer. The band toots and pounds the drums, but nobody sings. Think of the last time you were at a football game. Did the guy on the right of you sing? Did the gal on the left warble about the rockets red glare? Did you sing? The answers are No, No, No. Sure, a few people sing—choir directors, drunks and other incorrigibly uninhibited types, but not many. We Americans don't even do well with the Happy Birthday song, for crying out loud.

So, this theory correctly holds (American) Catholics can't sing because Americans can't sing. The truth will out.

After Forty-Six Years in the Rough, a Golfing Game Reborn!

April 1991

Golf critics may argue over the appropriateness of the timing. Should the resumption of golf competition between J. McGlinchey and D. Monahan have been scheduled during the month of the Masters? Was it out of place for the non-masters of the ancient game to step on the golfing stage as the drama at Augusta was about to unfold? Would the sometimes startling exhibition in Oklahoma distract N. Faldo or G. Norman in yonder Georgia?

In any event, the post-Easter match play golf tournament between J. McGlinchey and D. Monahan took place April 2 and 3 at the Texoma State Park Golf Course. The course is located on the north shore of sparkling Lake Texoma.

First, the ambience of the Texoma layout. There are ample evidences of Good ol' boysness and Good ol' galsness at the joint. There is a kind of refreshing laxity whether groups start play at the first or tenth tees. And one notes local rule 8: "Foursomes only during peak play unless approved by pro-shop personnel." "Unless approved" would be thought a ghastly feature at English links courses, but for a good ol' boy in Little Dixie "pro shop personnel" need a legal way to nod Yes to the other than foursome. So be it.

As to the actual physical course, the Lake Texoma venue is short on grass but long on wind. And the occasional rocky patch on the fairways adds an unusual challenge.

The competitors agreed to meet at the golf course at 10:00 a.m. on April 2. D. Monahan found J. McGlinchey in the golf shop at the appointed time standing straight as a drill sergeant with a confident smile on his face. "Buy a seniors' green fee permit" was the wise counsel of J. McGlinchey.

Outside the winds were blustery and chill. The distraction of the weather flustered D. Monahan to the point that he did not immediately discern a new, and perhaps ultimately decisive, element in the biannual competition. J. McGlinchey had arrived at the scene of battle with a new set of clubs!

No longer did he carry the pitiful assortment of golfing sticks which some claim predated Henry VIII. No longer did he possess the deadly but scarred putter which had drilled putts of all levels of difficulty while striking golf balls from the successive golfing eras of the feather ball, the gutta-percha and the Titleist.

"Who gave you the new clubs?" inquired D. Monahan.

"They were an anonymous gift," responded J. McGlinchey.

(My informants said there was no truth to the rumor that the new golfing sticks had been handmade by an aged Scotsman working secretly in a hidden Libyan complex under the personal direction of Col. Qaddafi.)

Playing with J. McGlinchey and D. Monahan was P. Bryce, a celebrated sportsman of the royal and ancient game. P. Bryce was appointed to the 1991 Spring Classic by the rules committee. His role: to see that the rules of golf were more or less observed and to prevent fisticuffs at tense moments of the match between the bitter rivals.

The match.

Declaring themselves Good ol' boys, the contestants teed off at the tenth hole. Pars were made. Then they settled into their golfing grooves—bogies, double bogies and but one more par between the two through the back nine.

One hole featured unusual scoring, the amazingly short par 5 thirteenth hole. The configuration of the hole is such that it must be played with irons. The green is approached up a steep hill. D. Monahan deftly sent his approach shot whistling over the green and into the woods behind. J. McGlinchey took a 7, D. Monahan an horrendous 8.

The other nine went like this: J. McGlinchey—par, bogey, bogey, par, double bogey, double bogey, double bogey, par and bogey. D. Monahan—triple bogey, bogey, par, par, bogey, bogey, triple bogey, bogey and bogey. D. Monahan had a one up lead at the end of eighteen. The two old-timers each had a round of 92. The entire display was the essence of inconsistent golfing mediocrity.

The second day. The first nine belonged to J. McGlinchey. He evened the match on the first hole and was three up after the eighth.

Then came the turning point. Between the eighth green and the ninth tee, D. Monahan was seized by the inspiration that if he watched the ball while he swung at it things might go better. Lo and behold, he parred the ninth.

The back nine belonged to D. Monahan. Victory was clinched at the seventeenth with a par.

After forty-six years of chasing the little white ball through the rough, D. Monahan's game had been born again! Keep your head down. Watch the ball. Elemental rules of the royal and ancient sport which will have been forgotten once more before the next McGlinchey-Monahan joust.

Note: The Hardesty, the treasured trophy of the Match Play Classic was not awarded to the victor following the contest. Inadvertently the treasured trophy had been left leaning against a wall of D. Monahan's room at the Archdiocesan Pastoral Center. A private presentation ceremony will take place in Room 110 of the Pastoral Center during the Masters tournament. A news release complete with glossy photos will be made soon for the benefit of the apathetic public.

ANTI's Motto: Nothing Good Will Come of It

April 1991

I've been known to be a little sour on the wonders of technology.

Like the other day, I listened to this veteran pilot describe the first fully computerized commercial airplane. According to its designers and makers and a major airline which has purchased a fleet of these marvels, if a human being can manage to move one of the flying carpet computers out to the runway and aim it in the right direction, a simple press of a button will send the thing zooming away with no involvement by species Homo sapiens until the aircraft has landed at the end of the flight. That's what the veteran pilot said. My understanding was that the thought of the technological super plane gave the veteran pilot heartburn.

The veteran pilot explained that the fully computerized aircraft could refuse to let the poor sap wearing the captain's hat override its computer even in moments of emergency. Humans err, we don't, reasons the computer. One of these delightful fully computerized aircraft not long ago landed a mile or so short of the runway, said the veteran pilot. Assuming a lot of non-computerized people were killed in this crash, one could imagine the surviving computer at the next morning's press conference explaining that the runway was not where it should have been because of the usual miscalculations made by stumblebum human beings.

Depressed by listening to the veteran pilot, I was in a blue funk for days until I read a passage in a book which offered a ray of hope. The book was "The Secret Pilgrim" by John le Carré, the master of the spy novel.

On page 179 of his late about British intelligence spooks, le Carré has his protagonist think the following: "Registry was in its last days before computerization, and could still find what it was looking for, or know for sure that it was lost." God's blessings on John le Carre, thought I. The passage made for a good night's sleep.

While I realize it's probably some newly discovered sin to be hostile toward the "miracles" of technological progress, I have to admit that when I see signs of the human family stoutly rebuffing the onslaught of technology, I feel a sense of pride in our obstinacy.

For example, the other day I read in a newspaper that it takes thirty years to get a telephone installed in Ghana and twenty-two years in Argentina and Jamaica. "That's the spirit," I whisper under my breath. "Stand firm, you Ghanaians! Foul the system, you Argentineans and Jamaicans!"

As a matter of fact, in the clutter of my two-room apartment there sits one of the older telephones in North America. Color: black. Style: dial. Furthermore, my telephone is not shaped like a football, nor Mickey Mouse, nor Madonna but like the squat ugly black machine it has always been.

Another report, this one out of Libya, lifted my spirits. There the esteemed Col. Muammar Qaddafi has declared meteorologists to be carbuncles on the complexion of our time and summarily stricken them from the television screen in his fiefdom.

Here at home the ever-present Doppler radars scan our skies, interrogating every cloud to see if it may be in an angry mood. As a surly anti-technologist, I pay scant heed to the reports. That was exactly my stance when I heard the warnings on the night of April 29, 1970. The fact that my house was scattered over the surrounding area a few hours later I attribute to a lucky guess on the part of a weary seer of the radar screen.

Given my peevish attitude toward things technological, it may not surprise you to learn that I have chosen to use my vast financial resources to found ANTI (Americans Negative on Technology Institute).

ANTI's motto is *"Nihil boni de eo evadet"* ("Nothing good will come of it"). Our symbol is the mastodon. Our battle cry: "Viva, the surrey with the fringe on the top!"

It's possible you have not heard about our board members. After careful consideration the following were chosen to impose the ANTI board: Peter the Hermit, William Jennings Bryan, Clara Bow and Shoeless Joe Jackson. I, of course, am the founder and chair.

At our initial meeting on April 1, the board debated and listed the five major threats to humanity. They are, according to the consensus:

- computers
- telephones
- the horseless carriage
- aluminum baseball bats
- and the Guinness Book of World Records

On a more positive note, the ANTI board called on Congress for a series of acts designed to lessen the technological intensity of US society. This legislative agenda includes:

- the reintroduction of "dead" baseballs in the major leagues
- the re-establishment of streetcars as the primary mode of urban transportation
- the mandatory use of only cotton, wool or burlap in manufacturing clothing
- the reinstitution of the three-cent stamp
- and a congressional resolution that spats are back in fashion

The board meeting ended in confusion as the members were unable to agree if the site of the next session would be Anticosti, Canada; the Lesser Antilles or Antisana, Ecuador.

More later.

I Looked Up and Wondered Who That Elderly Gentleman Was

June 1991

Long ago this writer drove to Will Rogers Airport to pick up a few priests arriving for a funeral. One of these priests was a portly man wearing a cherubic face with a seraphic smile. Minutes earlier he had stolen a cocktail glass from American Airlines. The glass, actually made out of silicates with nary a drop of plastic, rested in a pocket of the black suit of the portly priest.

It so happened that the horizontal dimensions of the priests being transported were a challenge to the width of my car. The priest with the stolen glass was the last aboard, squeezing his bulk into the front seat of the automobile with me at the steering wheel and another fellow in the middle. The thief with the seraphic smile slammed shut the car door. There was the distinctive sound of glass breaking. A second or two of silence. Then the calm voice of the larcenous cleric intoned: "Jesus always wins!"

So it was at the utterly ut Westcourt in the Buttes resort on the outskirts of Phoenix this past week. I was there for the annual convention of the Catholic Press Association.

The devisers of Westcourt in the Buttes seemed not to have considered meditation on eternal life as a major goal in their planning efforts. Their concentration focused on providing a thousand and one earthly pleasures: waterfalls, swimming pools, Arctic air in the desert, whirlpool baths hidden among the rocks, cacti, pleasant stewards (bellhops, maids, desk clerks, waiters, waitresses, telephone operators, maintenance men, bartenders etc.) and a great view from atop our butte, on which, to which, in which and around which the resort clung.

From the lobby level I took the elevator five floors down to my room level. In my room, 6309, the bed had been constructed to the size of a standard handball court. The management had succeeded in lining up six pillows—three stacks of two each—across the top of the bed.

Westcourt in the Buttes is definitely a place to avoid during Lent, thought I. Those kinds of ruminations together with garden-variety guilt feelings at the wretched excess of it all accompanied me into the dressing and bathroom area.

I was brushing my teeth when the awful avalanche of reality came crashing through. I looked up and absently wondered who the elderly gentleman was whose rear view I was observing – a pitiful balding figure of sags, bends, flab, slack, wrinkles, pouches. One obviously not long for this world. Then came the rush of recognition, as the prophet Nathan said to an earlier David: "You are the man!"

The dressing area had mirrors on three sides of the room. Westcourt's mountain of merriment and mirth contained in its core the message: "Remember, buddy, you are dust and unto dust you shall return, in fact, you might be swept out by the maid in the morning."

Jesus always wins.

Tony Hillerman, the celebrated mystery writer, arrived on the scene of the convention at Thursday noon. He was there to speak to the assembled as a writer to writers, or more accurately, a writer who is a Catholic to a collection of Catholics who hope they are writers.

Tony is quick to say he hails from Sacred Heart, Oklahoma, that tiny non-speck in southern Pottawatomie County where Sacred Heart Abbey once stood before history scraped it from the land.

The creator of Jim Chee and Joe Leaphorn spotted Sister Martha Mary McGaw in the crowd in the dining area. "Do you mind if I eat at your table?" he asked. So it was that the Oklahoma delegates proudly broke bread with Tony Hillerman.

He was bright-eyed, affable and modest as a luncheon guest. It was pointed out to other people at the table that Tony's brother Barney Hillerman processed the *Sooner Catholic's* film. "He's my older brother," Tony said. "You know how that older brother thing is. The relationship never changes." He grinned at the idea of it.

When it came time for his talk, Tony made his way to the front of the room, got behind the microphone, scratched his nose once or twice and proceeded to lay out a beautifully clear explanation of his appreciation of the Navajo people. He got into ethnology and myth. To a question from the floor, he said, "I'm a lot more comfortable in a Navajo trading post than at a Manhattan cocktail party." Afterwards he autographed books for a swarm of Catholic editors and writers.

An endangered species was spotted by me at Westcourt in the Buttes. This endangered species' representative was observed in the dimly lit hallways, at the elevator and once seated in the restaurant. It was a rare view of one of the few extant gray-haired, mouth-moving, breviary-reciting priests. (In the olden days young men preparing for ordination were taught that when one privately prayed the Liturgy of the Hours, one was required to form the words silently with one's mouth in order to be on the up-and-up.)

The sightings were images to be savored and treasured by an old priest priest-watcher as I. My guess is there will be no general movement among the populace to save the gray-haired, mouth-moving, breviary-reciting priest from extinction.

This Moses on I-40 Didn't Wear a Long White Beard

July 1991

Let the word go out. J. McGlinchey of Tulsa, Okla., thrashed D. Monahan of Oklahoma City, Okla., in the June 1991 revival of their lifelong golfing classic.

The coup de grace was fired by J. McGlinchey on the seventy-fifth hole of the 90-hole match at the University of New Mexico South Golf Course in Albuquerque, N.M. The debonair Tulsa left-hander, playing in his custom-made Payless shoes, slid his par putt into the cup on the tricky par 3 thus reducing the hapless D. Monahan into a parched heap of blue funk.

J. McGlinchey's official winning score was 16 and 15, a rout previously unheard of in this memorable series. Rumors are afloat in the golfing world that D. Monahan may have at last reached the end of his less than mediocre career. Old devil age may have caught up with the veteran linksman. It is well-known that J. McGlinchey is the junior of the two by a full 24 hours.

Reached in the clubhouse after the awful experience, D. Monahan lavished praise on his longtime opponent. "He done good." Pause. "But he was lucky."

"If my foot hadn't been sore...if the sweat hadn't gotten on my glasses...if I hadn't been frightened of rattlesnakes...if it wasn't so hot...if I hadn't lost my 7-iron...if my shoes had been broken in before the match...if I hadn't contracted an acute case of the heebie-jeebies...if I hadn't 3-putted forty-six times... if I had practiced before the match started on Thursday...if I hadn't practiced so long before we played on Friday...if I had occasionally kept my eyes on the ball when I was trying to hit it…if I had been born with a different name like Tom Watson or Nick Faldo…if the air hadn't been so thin…if the ball had stayed in the fairway a few times following my tee shots…if the course superintendent had been decent enough to mow the rough more often…as you can see, he was lucky. "

The venues of the tournament were the University's South Course, a gem of a public course, and the newer Cochiti Lake Golf Course. The University's layout measures 6,480 yards off the regular tees and 7,253 yards from the back tees. A long sucker. And the rough is the golfing equivalent of a rain forest. When one rolls or bounces a ball off the fairway, even a little ways, one inevitably finds the white sphere buried in three to four inches of thick grass.

The Cochiti course was built by the formerly wealthy Hunt brothers of Dallas as part of a development southwest of Santa Fe. It has been ranked as one of twenty-five best public golf courses in the United States. It is now owned and operated by the nearby Cochiti Pueblo. Business is excellent.

One of the charms of playing on public courses is the characters you meet.

Playing as a twosome, J. McGlinchey and D. Monahan found themselves toiling across the golfing tundra on different days with Tom and Babe, Pilot Bob and Blaster Bob, and Big John and Young Doctor John.

"Where are you from?" asked Tom, doing a fair imitation of Grumpy the Dwarf. Told that J. McGlinchey lived in Tulsa and that Tulsa was D. Monahan's hometown, Tom replied: "Tulsa is the most miserable place in the world." Asked which miserable place he called home, Tom barked: "Tulsa." Having completed his act, Tom settled down to be Mr. Nice Guy. His wife, Babe, soothed tensions with languid Mississippi talk.

Pilot Bob had taken his World War II training as a flier at Cimarron airport southwest of Oklahoma City. Pilot Bob's son,

Blaster Bob, is a graduate of West Point and a captain in the field artillery. Blaster Bob swatted his tee shots a fur piece, unfortunately not always on target. Sixty-eight-year-old Pilot Bob played down the center. He was the best golfer the Oklahoma twosome met during the week.

Big John, a gimpy-legged former soccer professional from England, stirred breezes with mighty swooshes of his clubs. The results were both spectacular and ridiculous. Young Dr. John, an anesthesiologist packing a beeper on his hip, corkscrewed his lean body into slashing swings at the ball. He could whack them a long, long way (example: a pitching wedge at a 150-yard par 3), but often off course.

Miscellaneous notes:

- Shot of the match. J. McGlinchey rolled a fifty-foot rainbow putt squarely into the hole for a birdie on the tilted par 3 eleventh at Cochiti. Even the hotshots in the group ahead turned and applauded.
- Greatest discovery. While searching for an errant J. McGlinchey shot on the next to the last hole of the tournament, D. Monahan found in rapid succession three Titleist #4s, plus a Hogan, all in mint condition. A merciful God rewarded the ancient player in His own fashion.
- The Longest Day. Yes, June 21 was it, but in spades for the golfing pair from Oklahoma. The twosome arrived at Cochiti at 12:30 p.m. and staggered away eight hours later—two hours of practice and six hours of playing time. The longest day also proved to be the driest day— no drinking water available on the back nine. Cotton mouths provided such speech as "Wha yuh tak las whol?" And "Ishent thish funt?"
- The climb to the top. The University's South Course is set on a hill. Starting off number 17 one is at the bottom of the hill. That 343-yard stroll is a horseshoe trek upward.

Breathing deeply one strikes one's drive off the eighteenth tee and wobbles forward ascending constantly along an S-shaped fairway toward the green some 500 yards away. Players still conscious after putting out on the final green then struggle to the clubhouse some seventy-five feet above the last hole. They say it's a test of character.

- Final humiliation. Cruising east on Interstate 40, on the way home, D. Monahan idly wondered what the emergency lights behind him meant. He learned they meant $40 to Judge Haven Dysart, Justice of the Peace, Potter County, Texas, for the "alleged speed" of seventy-three miles per hour. The arresting trooper's name: "Moses." He did not wear a long white beard. But he did wear a long black gun.

Center of Guatemala City Offers Rich Variety of Noises

August 1991

Guatemala City streets are populated by young men preparing for careers in stock car racing. Especially at night. So my ride from the city's modernistic airport to the non-exclusive Plaza Hotel was both brief and thrilling. Moved the old pump in the chest to pound a little harder. No tired blood on these streets on July 24.

At my post-10:00 p.m. arrival, the desk clerk at the Plaza answered my questions accurately and succinctly: No restaurant open, no bar open. for a man who had promised his entire gastrointestinal tract that nary a drop of water would pass his lips until the return landing in Dallas, this was a shocker. No restaurant and no bar spelled n-o b-e-e-r.   And beer was the stein of life on this safari.

I compressed my parched lips and thought: What would Lawrence of Arabia do in this situation? Answer: Go to his room.

I looked at my key. Number 991. But the building ahead of me was only three stories high. A note of mystery. This old journalist found his way to the second floor. Strange hotel. Nobody around. Few lights on. Around a bend in the hall Room166 came into view. The old journalist thought, Ah ha! He turned the key over. Eureka! Room key #991 had become 166. He tried the key. It opened the door. Déjà vu raised its pinhead. I had stayed in this very room a year ago. It was, of course, the luxurious Monahan Suite.

The Monahan Suite at the Plaza is the Southwest Airlines of hotel accommodations. No frills. There is a bed. In the Land of Eternal Spring air-conditioning is spurned. Room 166 is hot. There are no screens on the windows. The room is compact, the bathroom possibly larger than the bedroom. Following a nearly universal hotel practice, the lighting is feeble. Modernism has crept into a corner in the form of a television set.

The old journalist reconsidered the situation. Stiff upper lip, he said to himself. Make the best of it, he mumbled. We all have our little crosses to bear, he thought. He turned on the TV set.

Once the screen filled with colored images, amazingly room 166 in Guatemala City catapulted back to the United States. The relentless sports reporting of ESPN was right there in front of me. I watched the evening's baseball scores.

I lay down on the bed. It was a kind of topographical bed— highlands to the north and west, an alluvial plain across the broad middle, a tropical lowland to the extreme south and east.

The old journalist imagined various odors being released in different sections of the bed. When his nose touched the highlands it was…chili peppers? When the nose moved toward the east…the fragrance of old cigars? He longed for the fine flat bed in Room 110 of the Pastoral Center. Stiff upper lip, he repeated to himself.

With the lights out in the room, the old journalist's sense of hearing sharpened. One in Room 166 of the Plaza need not have the hearing acuity of a bat to become aware that the near center of Guatemala City offers a rich variety of nighttime noises: automobile engines running, tires squealing, trucks growling, horns honking, music playing loud, music playing louder, music playing loudest, music playing repetitively, voices talking, voices shouting, sirens wailing, popping sounds (that an old journalist nervously translated into gunfire), and, incredibly, a few brave birds singing.

If Guatemala is the Land of Eternal Spring, then the Plaza is the Inn with the Eternal Din. Nevertheless the old journalist soon leapt into the Land of Nod with a stiff upper lip.

Well past midnight the sound of rushing wind reached the sleeper's ears. The sound climbed the decibel scale until the sleeper's eyes flickered open. Still the fearful noise increased. Jet engines. The roar intensified and doubled once again. Earsplitting.

The old journalist thought "that airplane is crashing into this hotel." It didn't. The sound to, in a sense, end all the night sounds passed over and faded away.

Came the dawn.

The old journalist, who made it through the clamorous night, has awakened as the old priest. Breviary in hand he sat in a lawn chair near the hotel pool. Between verses of the psalms his tongue felt its way around the inside of his mouth. He had just accomplished a "dry" brushing of his teeth. The thick taste of Crest filled his mouth. No doubt my tongue is pale green, he thought.

"You are a Christian?"

The questioner shone with vigor and amiability.

"I'm a Catholic priest," said the old priest.

"God bless you!"

The hearty soul explained he was a southern Baptist from Georgia who was preaching salvation in the Guatemala City market.

If this guy has the guts to do that, thought the old priest/journalist, I ought to be able to have a stiffer upper lip on noisy nights in Guatemala.

Testimony of One Lured by Siren Call of Sweet Sleep

August 1991

There have been ugly rumors making the rounds that some people sleep in church.

As a matter of fact, a present-day Oklahoma priest when asked, "How large is your church?" responded thus: "It sleeps about 200."

This writer can verify that even—gasp!—the clergy sleep in church now and again. Take the case of the Lethargy on Lindell Boulevard.

'Twas an early morning Sunday Mass at the Cathedral in St. Louis. The good monsignor was being assisted at Mass by a permanent deacon. A sprinkling of worshipers were here and there present in the huge cathedral

The deacon preached. As I recall it was a decent homily. The monsignor, chin in hand, appeared to be soaking it in.

When he finished speaking, the deacon made his way to the side of the presider's chair. Several know-it-alls anticipated the recitation of the Creed by standing. But the monsignor sat still, chin on hand, apparently reflecting on the deacon's words.

The deacon stood, and stood, and stood. Some of the less certain know-it-alls sat down. The deacon continued to stand. The monsignor continued to sit. More of the know-it-alls sat down. Only a few Olympic-class know-it-alls summoned the gumption to hold their ground.

After several centuries of waiting, the deacon bent slightly from the waist and tapped the monsignor on an arm. The old fellow jumped.

The report circulated along Lindell Boulevard that week was that the monsignor had—ahem—dozed during the sermon.

Sleep. Nap. Slumber. Somnolence. Catching some z-z-z-zs. Crash.

From expert practitioners as Rip Van Winkle and Ronald Reagan to contrary types as Roger Guy English (who in 1974 stayed awake for 288 consecutive hours to win a place in the Guinness Book of World Records), we share the experience of sleep.

We write about it. Some are enthralled about sleep.

"The poor man's wealth, the prisoner's release." Philip Sidney.

"Balm of the bruised heart." Bartholomew Griffin.

"Nature's soft nurse." William Shakespeare.

Others take a grimmer view.

"Immoderate sleep is rust to the soul." Thomas Overbury.

"Sleep is the twin of death." Homer.

"Up, sluggard, and waste not life, in the grave will be sleeping enough." Benjamin Franklin.

"Get up! Get up! You're going to be late! " Mothers of the World.

This writer can bear witness to the Siren call of sweet sleep even within the hallowed halls of the seminary...perhaps especially within the hallowed halls of the seminary.

It seems like only yesterday that we were sitting in that classroom on the second floor of Fitzgerald Hall at St. John's Home Missions Seminary. The afternoon was a quiet warm early autumn one, steeply slanted toward the slippery slope of lassitude.

Inside the classroom nothing moved except the lips of the Scripture professor. Those lips pronounced each perfectly formed word with care but devoid of all passion. The words rolled smoothly like wavelets gently touching a beach over the ranks of young men dressed in black cassocks. The class was sliding toward mass hypnosis.

"Ya-ooh! " A front-row student leaped to his feet with this cry. The assembled psyches snapped to open-mouthed attention. They stared at their classmate. He looked around, batting his eyes for comprehension of what had happened. At last, he said quietly, "Excuse me. I fell asleep and was having a dream."

He had answered the Siren call of sweet sleep.

The Siren call of sweet sleep appealed to me with irresistible charms in that philosophy class labeled Metaphysics. To be utterly candid, I slept through the course. I don't mean I closed the book and put my head on the desk as class started. It was infinitely more agonizing than that. I tried to stay awake. Firm resolutions were constructed. But 10 minutes into the lecture by Father Abstraction my head was bobbing followed by my elbows slipping off the desk to jar me into twenty seconds of attention before the head bobbing began again. In boxing it would have been a technical knockout.

The problem, of course, wasn't me, it was metaphysics. We labored over Aristotelian metaphysics, not what often parades today as metaphysics and encompasses everything from ghosts to monkey business with crystals. The latter might have kept me awake, but Aristotle's *ens qua ens* (being as being) kayoed me every single afternoon's fight.

If it had not been for Dan Hogan, seated immediately behind me, I probably would have been the first under Father Abstraction's tutelage to have fallen completely out of his desk and to have crashed onto the floor. (I can see another seminarian standing over my body counting 6…7…8…9 as Father Abstraction stood in a neutral corner). Dan Hogan saved me by periodic jabs in the back once he saw my head start to bob.

Such is the charity found among Christians.

"I'm from Oklahoma!" She Yelled to New York Cop

October 1991

A passel of useless fretting, high anxiety and glum predictions about the guest of honor's behavior and stamina preceded the big event. Some imagined an absolute refusal to put in an appearance. Others supposed an out-of-sorts presence in the midst of hollow good cheer. Different theorists feared the unexpected shock of the surprise party would be too much for her.

The small woman in the elegant green dress foiled the prophets of doom. She went beyond that—she wowed 'em. Thus on September 20 did Aunt Agnes mark her 31+0 birthday.

Born Agnes Ann Monahan at Frontenac, Kan., six days after an assassin's bullet had made young Teddy Roosevelt president of the United States and while an ancient Pope Leo XIII continued his long tenure as successor of Peter at Rome, Aunt Agnes must have hit the ground running. Take it from her nephew, me.

If only some bearded futurist of the 1920s would have understood the coming importance of assertiveness, he could have described Aunt Agnes and had a best-seller a half of a century ahead of his times.

In the mid-1930s Aunt Agnes purchased an automobile. The car was a coupe with one bench seat. Having had only the most rudimentary driving lessons, she braked to a stop in front of 1225 East 20th Street in Tulsa.

Two more or less innocent children, my sister Helen and I, became Aunt Agnes's first passengers. We lurched away to the west. We lurched north. We lurched west again. We lurched south.

(Some fool had forgotten to invent the automatic transmission and our aunt was, shall we say, still honing her skills with the clutch and manual gearshift.)

Our last lurch had brought us into a line of traffic headed home after work in downtown Tulsa. The blasted car would start, lurch and die…start, lurch and die. People behind us began to honk. Helen and I slid down in the seat in a cowardly attempt to avoid identification.

Did all of this make Aunt Agnes blush like the setting sun and collapse under the strain? It did not. She leaned out the window, aimed her mouth toward the honkers, and hollered loudly, "I'm just learning to drive!" Helen and I sank even lower in the seat not realizing that our aunt was exhibiting a rare brand of gumption, "Don't Tread on Me" would have been an appropriate license plate.

That summer Aunt Agnes and two friends—fitted like oranges in a box across the only seat in the coupe—raced across the fruited plain to New York City. There they suddenly found themselves going upstream on a one-way avenue. A giant policeman whistled them to a stop. Aunt Agnes's shouted explanation: "I'm from Oklahoma!" That satisfied the cop. He held up one large hand to stop the traffic until my Oklahoma aunt executed a U-turn and went with the flow.

If spunky assertiveness is one side of Aunt Agnes's character, generosity is certainly another. Always delightful Christmas Eve became more so with the anticipation of Aunt Agnes's arrival. Santa Claus couldn't compete with the sight of her coupe gliding to a stop in front of our house on that blessed night. Somehow she always brought more presents than even a spoiled little boy expected.

She was the one who cared for her father and her mother until their deaths. And after the coldblooded management of Sinclair forced her into early retirement thus cutting in two her

pension payments, her response was to consider volunteering for
Oklahoma's mission in Guatemala.

The 31+0 birthday party had several sides:

- A Mass of Thanksgiving was celebrated at Christ the King
  Church in Tulsa. God was thanked for John Monahan
  and Elizabeth Burns Monahan and their progeny – the
  men all coal miners and the women muslin weavers –
  hungry 18th century Irish immigrants to Scotland.
  Prayers especially were sent heavenward for William
  Peter Monahan and Catherine Johnson Monahan, Aunt
  Agnes's parents. Aunt Agnes was born on her father's
  fortieth birthday.
- The peculiar gravity of the birthday party attracted
  a wonderful assortment of kinsfolk and friends. No
  less than six grandnephews and grandnieces appeared,
  traveling from Milwaukee, Edmond and Norman. And
  they brought their children who effortlessly filched the
  heart of the honoree.
- The reception proved to be a reunion of the working
  women of Sinclair's Tulsa purchasing department.
  Beulah Benham, whose name this writer has heard since
  he could first hear, smiled over old snapshots of herself
  on former vacations with Aunt Agnes – vacations which
  ranged from pre-Castro Cuba to San Francisco Bay to
  Norway to driving the wrong way on a one-way street in
  New York City.
- Two Sorrowful Mother Sisters, at least one of whom was
  vintage Bavarian – accent and all, had the bravery to bear
  across the room to Aunt Agnes a poster-sized photograph
  of her that she had always claimed to detest. The photo
  shows a lovely young Agnes Ann Monahan bedecked in
  1920s style featuring yards of beads. This time around she
  thought the photo was great. Think of that, the collapse

of the Evil Empire and Aunt Agnes's conversion to her flapper picture, all in the same year!

- The impresario for the 1991 Party of the Year was my better than good sister, Helen, aided and abetted by – her two comely daughters, Susan and Mary Helen. A toast to them!

Present at the End: The Story of a Woman's Death

November 1991

The telephone rang sometime past midnight. It was my sister, Helen. Her message was urgent: "Mom is dying."

The report shook me into full wakefulness. Death had been shadowing my mother for a long time. The news that the hour was imminent should not have stunned me, but it did.

I guided the Ford through the darkness of the Turner Turnpike. The ruler-like road was nearly vacant of other vehicles. The atmosphere was made for cairn reflection, but I doubt there was much of that. Inwardly I must have been a boiling pot of emotions. I hope there were some prayers. My mother, my mother.

Margaret Evelyn Connolly Monahan had bent under the burden of chronic bronchitis from the time she was a little girl. The bronchitis was her terrible inward cross. Incredible racking coughs continued by the hour, often leaving her drenched in perspiration and utterly exhausted. Twice she had broken ribs during awful paroxysms of coughing. Much of this happened during endless nighttime hours when she was completely alone. My parents had divorced two decades earlier.

Gradually her Connolly heart began to give under the extraordinary effort to breathe. The tired pump in her ninety-eight-pound body couldn't bear the strain placed on it. Doctors medically delayed the inevitable. Now phlegmy bronchitis was about to claim its victim.

I parked on Utica Avenue in front of St. John's Hospital in Tulsa. My mother's room was on the fifth floor in the old northeast wing, last room on the south side of the hall.

Outside the room I met the assembled sad and somber watchers: my father, Aunt Agnes, my brother-in-law, Bob Perrine, Helen and perhaps others. Father Ed Kelly had been there to anoint mom and to give her Holy Communion, they said.

Helen and I stepped into her room. Most of the details are fogged by time, but two specific events remain clear in my mind.

Our mother looked at us with affection even in her extreme weariness and pain. She began to talk about us. How God had blessed her with two good children who had never caused her any trouble.

This kind of talk, in my case at least, was not objectively so. But for Evelyn Monahan, dying, it was the truth, mother truth firmly set on a mother's love. Never mind that at one point, having discovered a handful of stolen valve caps in a pocket of my discarded pants, she had visions of an incipient Irish Mafia member in her household. In her final blessing, this woman with the rattling but tender heart spoke of a deeper goodness which only mothers are gifted to see.

Sometime later, as a wave of pain rushed through her body, our mother gasped aloud, "Jesus, help me!"

The deathwatch continued. A deathwatch extended is, in many ways, the worst of times. A watcher, struggling to keep his equilibrium on the thin wire of reason, is tugged in different directions—letting go, holding on as long as possible, surrendering to God's will, yearning for an unexpected victory even when the game is decided and the clock is ticking off the final seconds.

Staring out the windows, we saw night glide into the daylight of November 13, 1958. In this interlude, I may have recalled what was often in my mind as a small boy. What will I do when my mother dies? It was so awful to consider then that I couldn't except for short periods.

I decided to go down to the hospital chapel and celebrate Mass. We prayed for mom and for each other, no doubt, but I have no specific memories of that liturgy.

Afterwards I went outside to my car to get an electric razor. While I was there Mike Egan, a first cousin and real friend, came hurrying out the hospital doors. "You had better come quick," he said.

Evelyn Monahan was taking her last few feeble breaths. We stared in silence. Even the tiny intakes of air stopped. Her mouth remained open, her worn face absolutely still as if in a photograph. Thus our mother died after sixty-one years, five months and three days of life on this earth.

Helen and I hugged each other and the tears ran down our faces, another gift courtesy of our gentle mother.

When Pope John XXIII wrote his will, dated September 12, 1961, he included this line: "I await the arrival of Sister Death and will welcome her simply and joyfully in whatever circumstances it will please the Lord to send her."

My guess is that our mother awaited death in the same humble and trusting spirit. I still pray for her.

Up close no deaths are pretty, but some are beautiful.

Will Someone Please Call the National Enquirer?

December 1991

Things have changed. The last time I had been a patient in a hospital John F. Kennedy and Nikita Khrushchev had just gone eyeball-to-eyeball over Cuba with the Soviet gentleman finally blinking to end the missile crisis; Kevin Costner was seven years old; Grace Kelly was a gorgeous thirty-three; George Bush was a young Texas oilman with political ambitions but no office; and Joe Don Looney was ready to return the opening kickoff fifty yards against the Missouri Tigers. And Mercy Hospital was firmly situated on Northwest Twelfth Street.

A pain fanned out from the middle of my back as I finished a late dinner with the *Sooner Catholic* gang at Charleston's Restaurant on Monday evening. (Later the medical sleuths inquired, "Exactly what did you have for dinner?" I had to reply, "A martini, a cup of potato soup and a club sandwich. ")

When I got back to my quarters, Brother Pain was showing no signs of letting loose. I tried to relax with Monday Night Football but that didn't work. I walked about in my room. The hurt seemed to be spreading to the front of me. I pulled on my coat, got into the dusty Ford and drove north to the emergency room at Mercy Health Center.

There was no waiting. Kind people escorted me to a room and asked me to stretch out on a gurney. There were questions and a changing cast of nurses and physicians with stethoscopes, an electrocardiograph machine, blood pressure apparatus, and a needle or two in the arm. All went calmly and efficiently.

Then the Lord ordered up the first humiliation. The pain faded away. Well, thought I, even though I feel a little silly for having brought about all this hubbub, now I can go home and get a good night's sleep.

Not so fast, replied the Mercy health team. It's upstairs to bed with you. Tomorrow we'll run some tests. At 2:00 a.m. the old editor was rolled into Room 209, hooked to a heart monitor and muzzled with oxygen tubes.

It has been said that one of the nicest experiences in the world is to be a little sick. You know how it is you're the center of attention, others are scurrying to meet your every request, your only responsibility is not to fall out of bed, and all this with a .0001 degree of suffering.

I was a Horizontal King for thirty-six hours.

Nurses Mary Lynn, Michele Churchill, and Sharon tended to my physical needs, placated my whims, smiled at my "that-reminds-me" tales and overlooked my crotchety mumblings.

As good-willed as they were, these same nurses conspired to have me wear that most mortifying of all duds, the hospital gown. (Research into the origins of the hospital gown are inconclusive but it seems to have been the fiendish creation of one of these three: a) Oliver Cromwell after a poor day running down Irish people, b) the Inquisition, or c) the KGB when they had time on their hands at the Lubyanka.)

The pastoral services crew, led by Sister Modesta Weyel, was in Room 209 quickly and often to look after this sinner and to encourage a stiff upper lip even while in the clutches of the dratted hospital gown.

On Tuesday, modern medical science aimed all of its hailed investigative machinery at my 64-year-old frame. Various people stuck needles in my arms and thermometers in my mouth, carted away discharges from my body, listened to stethoscopes, ran ultrasonographic gizmos over my abdomen and X-rayed my innards. But only Michele Crawford captured my heart.

Ms. Crawford is the wizard of echocardiography. With her nimble mind and fingers at the controls of this science fiction device she took me on an intriguing inner space journey into my heart, a place previously familiar only to God.

As I watched the screen this shapeless pulsating blob appeared. It seemed to be made out of fur.

"That looks like something from a horror movie," said I.

"That's your heart," said she. "We're looking at the inside of your heart. There's your mitral valve. There's your aortic valve."

Oh, my gosh. The whole wonderful thing was in fluid motion, valves opening and closing, as it had been operating in perfect synchronization since it began in my mother's womb the summer of 1926.

Then the wizard added the sound effects: sshhshugg! sshhshugg! Each valve contributed its own musical note to the symphony: barrump! barrump! tootoot! tootoot! barrump!

The next morning a handsome Dr. Dominic Pedulla reviewed the test results and reported all was normal, or as near the norm as a senior priest could be expected to be. The doctor said the Monday night discomfort probably came from a small gallstone winding its mischievous way through my body. Dr. Pedulla's advice: take an aspirin every day. I think I can afford that.

Now for the final humiliation. These days when hospitals release one, the hospital insists on ferrying the releasee to the door of the building in a wheelchair.

My question (which is everybody's question): Does this have to be?

The answer: yes.

So I'm being pushed along the halls by a considerate volunteer. I'm holding a heavy jacket across my chest with one arm. A woman walking toward me blurts out as she draws even with my wheelchair: "Oh! I thought at first you were carrying a baby. "

Will someone please call the National Enquirer?

CHAPTER 16

1992

Is There a Man with a Pint of Old Crow in His Jacket?

January 1992

Will some future archaeologist unearth pieces of a ticket stub or a glob of gum stuck semi-eternally to a slab of seat bottom and thus reconstruct the scene?

The other day I drove by the vacant lot on the northeast corner of the intersection of East 15th Street and South Lewis Avenue in Tulsa. It was just that, a vacant lot – dirty gray grass and weeds, a plot for sale since the reign of Og, King of Bashan, one might think.

Except…except there was the faded red sidewalk on the 15th Street side which reminded old passersby that this was the site of the onetime Delman Theater. The Delman Theater has gone the way of Atlantis, lead soldiers and priests' maniples.

I must admit that as a stripling I was a regular at the Delman, rubbing elbows with its elite clientele.

To my eyes the Delman was a luxurious entertainment paradise. Its cool colors gave a note of modernity that set the Delman in a different class than the more ornate Ritz and Orpheurn theaters in downtown Tulsa. And the place seemed spacious. When a twelve-year-old boy paid his dues and found a seat he felt he had been admitted into a privileged inner sanctum.

That last sentence brings me to a moment of confession, a tale from the past which shows how narrowly skinny D. Monahan avoided a life of grand larceny and prison stripes.

I was twelve. In those days, at least, twelve was the dividing line between ten-cent tickets and thirty-five-cent tickets. The theaters' philosophy apparently was if you're old enough to be a Boy Scout you are old enough to fork over an adult thirty-five cents.

It was not unknown that a bit of fudging took place. Younger teenagers became magically eleven year olds at the ticket window. Some girls, it was rumored, had a 'movie dress" in their closet, a frock which transformed them into lisping children.

I had heard of these scandals. I also had heard of the Seventh Commandment. But this evening only thirty-five cents jangled in my pocket. If I bought a regular ticket there would be no popcorn, no licorice.

With shifty-eyed guilt written transparently across my formerly innocent face, I pushed my dime forward to the cashier.

"How old are you?" said she.

"Eleven," I mumbled.

Ticket in hand I stepped into the lobby. The ticket-taker took a quick look at my ten-cent admission and asked: "What is your birth date?"

"March 6, 1927," said I, realizing somewhere between the one and the nine that I was a gonner since the world's calendars had turned to May 1939.

I found myself outside on the red sidewalk in a state common to us sinners—confused, angry and humiliated. I paid the quarter, got an adult ticket in my hand, gave it to the triumphant ticket taker and slunk into the darkness of the theater resolved to go straight.

I fought the Second World War as I watched newsreels at the Delman. The remains of Pearl Harbor, Guadalcanal, Sicily, Anzio, New Guinea, MacArthur sloshing ashore in the Philippines, Stalingrad, D-Day, the victory march in Paris, the bombing of Berlin, Iwo Jima and Okinawa, Hiroshima—the whole bloody affair in the comfort of the Delman—for thirty-five cents a throw.

The funny thing is I can't remember a single particular movie that I saw at the Delman. I'm certain I watched the twitching face and sad eyes of Humphrey Bogart, heard the 'Yep' of Gary Cooper and laughed at the antics of hours of Donald Duck in the darkness of the Delman, but as to specific films my memory is a blank.

One thing that is well recollected is the appearance in the flesh of one Alano Doss. He was a seer of sorts, a dapper gentleman who stood on the stage, tossing a crystal ball from one hand to the other, and revealed "truths" about those in the audience.

"Is there a gentleman seated in the middle of the center section who has a pint of Old Crow in his jacket pocket?" Yes, there—hee-hee—was. And the woman in the green dress need not worry where she will get the money to make her house payments. And the gray-haired couple in the back need not fret—their grandson will soon be safely home from military service.

Alano knew it all or so he made it seem. But he never revealed a thing about the boy in the balcony who lived at 2125 East 20th.

One night I exited the Delman to begin my way home down Lewis Avenue. My route took me along a narrow path through a weeded vacant lot.

I tripped and fell forward to the ground. Looking back from my prone position I could see that in the dark I had stumbled over the legs of a sprawled man. I started running toward home, running as hard as I could. No thought about the needs of the poor fellow on the ground. Just get away. Maybe the movie had been an Alfred Hitchcock doozie.

The Delman. *Sic transit gloria* Hollywood.

Packed with 620,000 Batting Statistics

February 1992

Now computers are complicating life for another batch of Americans, the denizens of the Hot Stove League.

Here we are in midwinter but edging toward baseball's spring training, a time of year when baseball fanatics can sit back and leisurely trade dreams of what was or might have been or can be embellished to be by reams of statistics—semi-accurate, wildly exaggerated or simply invented to fit the need.

Suddenly into this season of contentment rushes Franklin Electronic Publishers with their $129.95 computerized Baseball Encyclopedia, an instrument designed to drain the joy out of yarn-swapping about the national pastime. The Baseball Encyclopedia, according to *Time* magazine, is "packed with 620,000 batting and 270,000 pitching statistics on every player who ever wore cleats in the majors."

Any bald, bifocaled, hard-of-hearing baseball fan worth his chewing tobacco knows that Tyrus Raymond Cobb is the all-time highest percentage hitter in baseball history with a .367 average. But, dad-gummit, now every whippersnapper with a styled hairdo will be sitting there with his electronic Baseball Encyclopedia rattling off Cobb's average year-by-year. It's a high-tech blow to conversational lying.

There are certain baseball truths which will elude this dastardly electronic facts vomiter.

For example, which player made a catch of a baseball falling from the highest altitude? Joe Sprinz, of course. The immortal

Joe, a tough catcher for the old San Francisco Seals of the Pacific Coast League, squinted into the sky for the ball on August 3, 1939. The baseballs were dropped from an airplane at approximately 1,000 feet over Treasure Island.

Joe's task was not for the timid. First he had to spot the speck of a ball, and then, with winds in the Bay moving the thing this way and that, he had to catch it. He missed the first four. But on the fifth attempt Joe had the luck, good or bad, to get his mitt on the ball. The force of the plummeting baseball drove the mitt into the catcher's face. He lost four front teeth…but he held the ball. That's how you get in the Guinness Book of World Records, but not among the 620,000 + 270,000 statistics in the electronic encyclopedia. All hail to gallant Joe Sprinz!

One way to check out the thoroughness of a baseball encyclopedia is to search for the information on one Charlie Wheatley, pitcher, of the 1912 Detroit Tigers. Charlie's won and lost totals for the Tigers that year, now eight decades removed from today, was one win and four losses. That also was Charlie's lifetime major league record.

However meager be the stats of pitcher Wheatley in the big show, the same fellow of yesterday holds an all-time pitching record: most wild pitches in one inning. That is, the last time I could find the record, Charlie, unlike the Babe in homeruns, was still the champ of the wild pitch in big league history.

Charlie Wheatley eventually settled in Tulsa where he became a prosperous businessman in the oil supply business. He was a friend of my father and contributed his share to the tales of colorful behavior by members of that group of oilmen.

I heard one about a time Charlie was in San Francisco. His room was ten or fifteen floors above the pavement. One morning he spotted a Catholic school across the street from the hotel with nuns watching their charges playing on the school grounds. Somehow this scene seemed to have inspired Charlie Wheatley.

The holder of the record for wild pitches changed a good sum of paper money into 50-cent pieces, returned to his room, and began to try and sling the coins out the window to land in the playground. The result was a sporadic shower of fifty-cent pieces landing in the street, on sidewalks and, perhaps, bouncing off cars.

The way I heard it, when the police entered Charlie Wheatley's hotel room, the sweating sidearmer was still launching the silver with the same happy enthusiasm he had displayed for the Tigers. "Am I going to be arrested," he reportedly said, "for trying to give away money?"

Historical statistics are part of what makes professional baseball attractive. But taken by themselves and dished up in cold slugs of 620,000 batting and 270,000 pitching numbers the statistics become about as charming as bat droppings in a cave.

When DiMaggio hit safely in fifty-six consecutive games, the story was not so much in the numbers as in the day-by-day drama of this stoical athlete' responding gracefully to the pressure. The best pitchers threw their wickedest stuff at him, and he answered with ringing hits. No doubt the electronic baseball encyclopedia will manage to reduce that magic time to gaunt lifeless facts. Maybe they will do that well.

That's the State of Things at 1015 Rosario Lane

February 1992

The perfect week off for this old fellow included leisurely breakfasts in the company of the *Los Angeles Times*, two rousing high school basketball games (one a genuine heart pounder), two good books with a third one in reserve, and all the while in the protective custody of dear friends.

This earth offers few greater pleasures than sitting at a breakfast table with a cup of good hot coffee in one's right hand, a bran muffin in the left, and the *Los Angeles Times* open for one's quiet study. All that and one other key ingredient: no deadline to stop reading. Man, oh man!

Reading the *Los Angeles Times* is like cutting into and savoring a thick slice of pink prime rib. And it doesn't clog your vascular system.

The front section of the Saturday, February 1 issue was twenty-six rich pages, written by thirty-some *Times* staff writers. Eight different staff writers covered the United Nations summit meeting the previous day. The articles were thorough, intelligent and with enough human stickum to keep one reading.

So it went page-after-page through the front section. Staff writers from Washington, Montreal, San Salvador, Moscow, Houston and the Los Angeles Police Department brought the world to 1015 Rosario Lane in Vista far more completely and clearly than any television presentation.

I found the obituaries particularly well done. (Father Tom McSherry would say it's only natural I would be drawn to the obits, that part of a newspaper he calls "the Irish sports page.") In the obituaries there were concise and precise tales of the passing of nine internationally renowned people.

For example, Arvo Yippo had died in Finland. Possibly some of your readers are unacquainted with ol' Arvo. You might think he was a rock star of the frozen north or a member of a famous Scandinavian comedy team called the Yippo Brothers. Neither. As they say on our side of the Atlantic, Arvo had the smarts. Arvo Yippo was a principal reason Finland achieved the lowest infant mortality rate in the world. God bless him and keep him.

On Wednesday, January 29, I was one of the lucky spectators packed into the gym of the Vista High School Panthers. The Panthers opponents were the more affluent and altitudinous lads from Torrey Pines High School. Vista had not one player taller than 6 feet 2. Nine of the Torrey Pines basketballers stood more than 6 feet 2 inches. And their center was a decent athlete who measured 6 feet 11 inches.

Torrey Pines was ranked first of all prep basketball teams in San Diego county, a county with approximately the same population as the state of Oklahoma.

From the opening tip, the Torrey Piners knew they were in a dogfight. The well-coached Vista boys played with tremendous intensity. They pressed Torrey Pines all over the court from the first second to the last. A casual observer might think the Panthers were playing eight men at a time. They were here, there and everywhere. They exerted extraordinary pressure on the player with the ball. Eventually they took the ball away from their taller California cousins thirty times that evening.

At the beginning of the second half Vista sank five straight 3-point shots to take the lead. For the game they scored 15 three pointers. Twice this year the Panthers have made 18 three-point shots in a game. No wonder their pep club is called the Bomb Squad.

In the end, the unequal height difference was too much for Vista. But just as the game appeared to be getting completely away from them, Vista rallied when my namesake, David Dillon, canned two long ones. The game was tied with less than 30 seconds to go. Torrey Pines won 81-79. Wow.

The books I read at 1015 Rosario Lane last week were the latter part of "Little Giant: The Life and Times of Speaker Carl Albert" and the first half of Pat Conroy's "The Prince of Tides." Each of them made me glad Sister Mary Andrew finally succeeded in teaching D. Monahan how to read.

Carl Albert's memoir takes our big-little hero from the rural school district of Bug Tussle, north of McAlester, to the period in the 1970s when Speaker of the House Albert was being guarded by the Secret Service as the next in the line of succession to the presidency of the United States. Along the line we meet characters as diverse as Ernie, Mr. Albert's tough coal-mining father, Professor Cortez A.M. Ewing, Sam Rayburn, the canny Howard Smith of Virginia, John F. Kennedy, Richard Nixon and Lyndon Baines Johnson.

The undamming of LBJ's energy as he succeeded to the presidency moved Carl Albert to describe his own situation as majority leader of the House "with Lyndon Johnson beside me, behind me, and seemingly all over me." The telephone seldom rested long between rings.

This slow reader has reached page 338 in "The Prince of Tides." To my tastes it is a delicious book. I've even begun to underline especially compelling lines. For example: "Coaches were simple creatures…who wanted all their boys to behave like rabid animals on the field and perfect gentlemen in the school hallways." Right on the nose.

One thing is for certain, the book is so much more complex and fascinating than the movie which I enjoyed a great deal.

My home away from home in California was the house on Rosario Lane, where Joe and Carole Dillon and their basketball-playing son are occupants. Get this: Joe and Carole vacated their own bedroom and slept on a pull-out deal in the living room so that their Oklahoma friend could sleep late undisturbed by everyone else who was up with the dawn to go about an honest day's work.

I noted these lines, a response to a Scripture reading, in my breviary:

"What joy to see a family united in love!
The blessing of God rests upon it."

That's the state of things at 1015 Rosario Lane.

Father Harold Never Heard about Passive Resistance

March 1992

There's courage and then there's courage. The moxie virtue comes in many different flavors. The decision to do or to endure in threatening times happens mostly unobserved like the blossoming of the tiniest wildflower in a crack of an abandoned road.

Courage is usually an everyday affair. And believe you me its deep red glitter can be seen in the most unlikely souls even those of the standard model priests. Take the examples of the following priests whose moment of fortitude has been passed down in our Oklahoma sacerdotal anecdotes.

Father Ed was a Dutchman. He sailed across the Atlantic in the first decade of this century as a missionary to join his elder brother, Father Tony, already working in the Diocese of Oklahoma. Father Ed arrived here bursting with zeal and good health. He was ready to give his all.

Not long after Ed's arrival, Father Tony suggested to him that they join a few other priests on a short fishing trip near the Wichita Mountains. Fine, said Father Ed.

So the group of clerics made their way to a fishing spot they knew and set up camp. The next morning Father Tony told his younger brother that they were running low on drinking water. Would he take this bucket and walk a mile or two through the woods to a farm where there was a well? Certainly, said Father Ed. Off he went lightheartedly swinging the bucket and thinking how blessed he was to be here with such good friends.

Father Ed had walked through the trees for 20 minutes or so, when quicker than he could observe exactly how, a half dozen armed men -Indians! – pounced on him. The captors were men of fierce countenance and they spoke a language unlike Father Ed had ever heard.

The Indians roughly tied Father Ed's arms behind his back. Then they bound him to a tree. They're going to kill me, Father Ed thought. I'm going to be a martyr, and I've only been here a week! He made an Act of Contrition. He forgave his killers.

A rifle shot rang out in the woods. And another. And still another. As the firing continued Father Ed watched his assailants spinning and dropping to the ground as the bullets apparently struck them. Then Father Ed caught sight of his brother and the other priests running toward him, firearms in hand.

In seconds the priests had reached Father Ed and untied him. "You've saved me! You've saved me!" he cried out through his tears as he embraced his brother. But he noticed the Indians were getting up from the ground and they were grinning. And the priests were laughing. Soon the captors and the rescuers were clapping each other on the back and roaring with laughter.

Thus it was "Welcome to Oklahoma, The Land of the Red Man" for Father Ed.

Father Joe's opportunity for courage came about as a result of his first assignment as a priest. He was named assistant to a legend, Msgr. S, but a legend with a hair-trigger temper capable of Mount Vesuvius class eruptions.

Father Joe was afraid of the monsignor. More accurately, he was terrified of the old boy. Once he had simply walked into a room where Msgr. S was reading a newspaper. The monsignor snapped down the paper and bellowed, "Father, what are you doing, sneaking around like a damn spy?"

One day, Msgr. S's blood pressure reached the boiling point. He had a stroke. While the ambulance screamed through the streets toward the rectory, the assistant priest was summoned to anoint the unconscious man.

Father Joe, vial of the Oil of the Sick in one hand and ritual book in the other, hesitated before he entered the room of the prone and dying Msgr. S. What if the fearsome pastor awakened in the middle of the anointing? What if, when he entered the room, the monsignor sat up and tongue lashed the assistant in a new height of anger? What if…What if…Father Joe sucked in his breath, bolted into the room, anointed his nemesis in record time and left. A victory of courage.

Father Harold probably never heard the term passive resistance, but he was a practitioner. Perhaps he failed to realize the implied courage in passive resistance. He was 35 years old when he was ordained by Bishop Francis Clement Kelley. His assignments were small country parishes – out-of-the-way places, few parishioners, lots of opportunities for loneliness, the kinds of spots where one tended to grow in decreasing appreciation of the importance of paperwork from the chancery office.

At the same time the chancellor of the Diocese of Oklahoma City and Tulsa was Msgr. D, a man who prized the value of accurate records and who had the gumption to demand in extremely clear terms that reports be forthcoming on schedule. Msgr. D's signature warning of danger ahead for recalcitrant pastors was indicated by certain key sentences or paragraphs in his letters being typed in red.

Father Harold failed to send in an annual report.

Msgr. D's response was (in red) "Send the report posthaste."

Father Harold ignored the command.

Msgr. D zinged another message west (in red). "Report must be in by Monday or there will be serious consequences."

Nothing from Father Harold.

"If the report is not in this office within three days of the receipt of this letter, you will be suspended as a priest of this diocese," wrote Msgr. D in red and underlined.

The story ends with Bishop Eugene McGuinness examining priests' files when he first arrived in Oklahoma. When he came to Father Harold's packet and had read of this battle between the chancery commander and the passive resister, he noted one final cryptic note attached to the file by Msgr. D. The note read: "The little _____ never did send it in." (Being a family publication we judge it best not to include the missing word even though Webster's carries it but warns that the word is usually considered vulgar. We can say the missing word rhymes with "art.")

The bishop, we have heard, laughed until tears ran down his face.

A Sudden Onset of Eire Ire in Front of Cathedral

April 1992

You will be among the first to learn the news: the Monahan family bears a genetic flaw, usually non-fatal. It will be labeled in scientific tomes as Eire Ire (or more commonly known as Irish Temper with symptoms of highly flushed face followed closely by a rush of bitter words).

I suffered a sudden onset of Eire Ire late this morning in front of Our Lady's Cathedral. A good man had died and I had taken part in his funeral Mass. Following the liturgy I had walked to the sidewalk outside the front doors of the cathedral. Pious thoughts and sentiments of goodwill bore me along. The funeral procession rolled away toward the cemetery. I was about to leave when a gentleman asked me a question.

The questioner and I passed friendly comments back and forth until the conversation jumped, at the gentleman's choosing, to the subject of Father Stanley Rother. Father Rother was killed in Guatemala, the gentleman said, because he had been recruiting people for the guerrillas.

These words triggered an Eire Ire reaction. Gallons of blood rocketed to my head, blood pressure zoomed to alarming measurements, and words cast in molten steel came flying out of my mouth. The more understandable part of my verbal outburst sounded something like

"Stanley Rother did not recruit guerrillas!" When the gentleman politely demurred and cited his 19 years in intelligence work for this nation as a kind of proof of his knowledge, my sweetly

reasoned response was, "I don't care if you were in intelligence for 119 years, *you don't know what you're talking about*!!"

"Love is patient; love is kind...love is never rude...it is not prone to anger...there is no limit to love's forbearance," teaches the Apostle Paul.

The Eire Ire apparently has little common ground with Gospel love. When generations of ashamed, bowed-heads Monahans appear before the Lord on Judgment Day we can plead the Eire Ire genetic defect or we can throw ourselves on the compassion of the All Knowing One. Science can be hanged at that point, I'm throwing myself on the mercy of the Judge.

Readers of delicate emotions may think it an unseemly topic to pick about among one's progenitors for evidence of the Eire Ire, but perhaps it will prove to be instructive.

My father, Frank P. Monahan, was a man of charm and wit and a taste for good times. But we of his household came to understand that he too suffered from the errant gene. Festivities would be bouncing along on Christmas morning when *boom!* the dreaded Eire Ire exploded in our midst. House-rattling slams of doors might follow, and our father would be propelled away on a jet of Eire Ire. We loved him.

My father's sister, the lately departed and beloved Aunt Agnes, definitely was afflicted by Eire Ire. In fact, mischievous grandnephews, cool counselors-at-law they, discovered certain code words would infallibly trigger an eruptive reaction from her even in the ninth decade of her earthly life. They would toss "Reagan" into Aunt Agnes's psyche to warm up her wrath. This might be followed by "Nancy" and/or "Japan." And the dishes on the table shook from the ensuing storm.

I didn't know my paternal grandfather well, but I recall as a youngster witnessing an eruption of Eire Ire on the part of William Peter Monahan. His bald head shone with a coal-red that reminded devout onlookers of the fiery griddle upon which St. Lawrence was thrown.

How did this genetic anomaly originate? Did it first exist in John Monachan, 18th century coal miner of County Ayr, Scotland? Did distant grandpa John suffer this genetic blip after being brained by a hard-nosed Scot overseer for rashly requesting 12-hour work days just six days a week? Or was it a half-starved shepherd Monachan on misty Irish hills who feasted exclusively on local weeds who passed the trait to his raging descendants?

Whatever be the case the Monahans are solaced in their genetic crippledness by exhibitions of others who apparently suffer the same condition. Take the case of Robert Knight, basketball coach, who gives splendid displays of the symptoms of Eire Ire as his athletic teams perform. (There is a school of thought that Eire Ire is epidemic among gentlemen of the basketball coaching profession.)

Then there was the incident of former Secretary of Defense James Schlesinger and his son. When Mr. Schlesinger reported for work one morning at the Pentagon, his right hand was heavily bandaged. "What happened, sir?" "Oh," shrugged the secretary of defense, "my 16-yearold son got out of hand last night and I had to deck him." If not Eire Ire it might have been the related disorder: Germanic Goad.

There's always the hope of gene therapy. The day may come when Monahans will be the recipients of cloned genes from the likes of Prince Charles or Peter Jennings, AAAA+ specimens of unflappability. When that bold moment comes we Monahans will answer sneering taunts and unexpected jarring statements with cool aplomb – then most likely we will smile and kick their sayers in the shins. The kingdom of perfect genes isn't made in a day.

Not So Fast, New York!
No First for You
August 1992

The Catholic News Service's lead sentence on a July 29 article read: "A New York woman has announced plans to establish what she believes will be the first Catholic art museum in the United States."

Not so fast, New York! St. Gregory's Abbey and College have been home to a Catholic art museum for perhaps four times as many years as Miss Christina Cox, the "New York woman" in the newswire piece, is old.

I ought to know. I've slept in it. Sorta.

The Catholic museum at St. Gregory's had its genesis in the soul of a circus band musician. Robert Gregory Gerrer was the cat's meow as a clarinetist and a flutist. But he ran away from the circus to join the Benedictines. That was 1891 at old Sacred Heart Abbey. He was twenty-four years old.

At the abbey another talent surfaced. The young man could paint. He had the gift. The leadership at the abbey decided to send Brother Gregory to Rome for world-class art training. He left Oklahoma in 1900, was ordained a priest on Sept. 19 at Buckfast Abbey in England, and finished the year in Rome.

Four years later, Father Gregory won a competition and was tabbed to paint the official portrait of Pope Pius X. In the latter months of that same year the finished work was exhibited at the World's Fair in St. Louis.

Over the hills and through the valleys (and across the oceans) of the remainder of Father Gregory's life, the monk-artist collected a great number of paintings, statues and artifacts for his home abbey.

By the time of Father Gregory's death in 1946, he had assembled the stuff of which museums are made. But there was no separate building at St. Gregory's which was designated as The Catholic Museum of Oklahoma.

There was a room on the east end of the main building, as I recall, which was jammed with displays. There is no doubt that the room's main attraction, especially for Oklahoma kids (whose only culture was agriculture, according to one observant priest), were the two genuine Egyptian mummies.

Somehow my only recollected images of the mummies are that they were short and their withered little feet stuck out of the ends of whatever they were wrapped in.

The net result of possessing all this stuff of which museums are made and of not owning a separate structure to house the collection was the whole main building at St. Gregory's became a museum.

I remember making a retreat there in 1952. My assigned room was on the first floor of the main building. The walls of the room were covered with paintings.

The last sight I saw at night were paintings in front of me, behind me, and on both sides of me. And the first view I got in the morning was Sunset at Pompeii, Still Life at the Antwerp Zoo, Napoleon Smokes a Corona Corona at Elba, or some such. Frankly, it was spooky. The experience moved me to resolve to give up sleeping in museums.

Time passed. St. Gregory's evolved as an educational institution. Extensive remodeling was the order of the day. What to do with all this stuff of which museums are made?

Minds whirred. Sessions sessioned. Mental gymnastics were performed. The decisions: store the stuff or, better yet, loan the stuff to a public museum in the Big Town. A lot of the stuff of which museums are made was trundled west to the Big Town.

More time passed. An art-loving abbot was elected at St. Gregory's. He inquired as to where was our stuff of which museums are made. In a public museum in the Big Town, his fellow monks replied.

The art-loving abbot wondered about the state of the art. His intelligence sources reported that the St. Gregory's art pieces were busy growing coats of mildew in a warehouse. Furthermore, said the sources, a few of the choice items had found their way into the office of a Mr. Big of Big Town. The art-loving abbot gnashed his teeth.

The art-loving abbot was no dreamer, but a man of action. Hearkening back to the Middle Ages, he hastily formed an abbatial strike force. The abbatial strike force, dressed – you guessed it – all in black, roared away from Shawnee aboard the official strike-force truck.

The Dutiful Dozen first hit the public museum. They marched into the museum's storage area, seized their rightful properties, mummies with withered toes et al, and stalked out. They raced to Mr. Big's office, entered it, lifted the proper art work off the wall and left open-mouthed secretaries in their wake.

It wasn't long before the art-loving Abbot Robert Dodson saw to it, with a bit of help from his friends, that a proper building housed St. Gregory's art museum. The modern Mabee-Gerrer Museum sits on the south side of St. Gregory's property facing north, looking toward the main building where this scribe slept in a roomful of paintings. Go see it and know that Ms. Cox's Catholic museum in New York will definitely not be a first. But silver medals count too.

On Eating Breakfast Regularly with the Wizard

September 1992

During the summers, I eat breakfast with Ozzie Smith nearly every morning. That is, after a run-through of the headlines on the front page of our beloved daily newspaper, I turn to the sports section and there focus on the baseball box scores.

This happens about the time my spoon goes to work on a big bowl of fresh grapefruit.

I locate the box score of the St. Louis Cardinals. The Cardinals' bottom-line report there has been so-so, at best, in the past several years. But then my eyes travel to the second name in the lineup: O. Smith. I check the number of times at bat and hits – usually one or two of the latter. More importantly I note who committed fielding errors in the game. Rarely, rarely, does the name O. Smith appear on that line.

Let's say it: Ozzie Smith is the greatest fielding shortstop ever to play the game of baseball. Stationed at the key defensive position in the game and playing on artificial surfaces where baseballs come at infielders like bullets ricocheting off steel plates, Ozzie combines the acrobatic spectacular with the robotic consistent. He has won more Golden Glove awards for fielding than anyone at his position. That's why in the baseball world there is only one player called the Wizard, or, for those of us who meet him regularly at the breakfast table, the Wiz.

On Thursday, Aug. 21, 1992, Helen Monahan Perrine, my sister, and I, in Helen's big red Buick, roll across a bridge spanning the Mississippi River into St. Louis. In the process of visiting our cousin Margaret Miller we drive by the site of the old Sportsman's Park. It has vanished.

Long gone are the roars of the crowds for Rogers Hornsby, Grover Cleveland Alexander, Frankie Frisch, the Gas House Gang, Stan Musial and Bob Gibson. Gone is that curiosity, the Pavilion in right field, over which the likes of Ted Williams, Mickey Mantle and even the Babe had swatted baseballs into or across Grand Avenue.

Future archaeologists, I think, will dig in vain to find evidence that games of beauty and dash and flaming human spirits were contested at this now drab place.

As we drive about St. Louis – the huge cathedral, St. Louis University, the metamorphosed Union Station – I casually mention that the Cardinals are in town. Tonight they play Houston, say I. Helen is game for the game. We stop at Busch Stadium and purchase tickets.

We become part of a parade of people making our way from a parking garage toward Busch Stadium. Musical entertainment livens the scene at the small park north of the stadium. Free Pepsis are being handed out. An old homeless fellow sits on a bench with perhaps half a dozen empty Pepsi cans at his feet.

The sharp cracks of batting practice are heard as we enter the stadium proper. Ushers scan our tickets and point to a distant area. We have seats in a "loge box," in our case that translates to the forward section of seats in right-center field.

An African-American family of five occupies the seats in front of us. Two Hispanic women sit to our left. Immediately to our right is a gap in the outfield seats where large equipment is apparently moved in and out. The drop into this concrete canyon is perhaps 30 feet from our spot in the stadium.

Helen's torture for the evening is to watch a little boy, maybe eight years old, playing along the rail above the canyon. His elders show no concern when he sits on the wall and without holding on leans back under the top rail, to see how things look upside down. I hold my scorecard in front of Helen's face so she can't watch the topple over the side. He doesn't.

The cardinals lope unto the field to start the game. For the first time in my life I see Ozzie Smith in the flesh. From my vantage point he appears to be approximately 2 feet tall. I halfway expect O. Smith to do one of his forward flips as he trots to his position. He decides against it. For warm ups, he fields a couple of gentle grounders from his first baseman and returns the ball with languid throws.

Ozzie singles to center in his first at bat. In the fourth inning, he cracks a double down the leftfield foul line and moments later scores the tying run on a hit by Felix Jose.

In the fifth inning comes the play which transforms O. Smith into the Wizard. A Houston batter smashes a ball past the Cardinal pitcher. The baseball is destined for center field, until... until this flashing figure snags it at the end of a full forward bounces to his feet, and makes a perfect throw to first.

While the event will not be sufficient to allow me to die in peace for having witnessed it, this pearl of a play assures me that quality of the highest kind can still be found in America.

Thank you, Ozzie. See you at the breakfast table.

Dick Descended Culturally from Chopin, Debussy, and Bach

September 1992

Only minutes ago I made my way to my office directly from the Church of the Epiphany parish picnic. It was a leisurely American Catholic affair: bits of conversation, children, hamburgers, music, people seated on blankets and folding chairs, ice cream with wooden spoons, southerly winds, stories, beer, sunshine, mommas and papas, coniferous shade, balloons, Frisbees, dancing, Coca Colas, pale blue sky, bubble-blowing kits, smoke, baked beans, trampled grass, cooks, asphalt, and dancing.

The parish picnic pushed my mind down the track of altar boy picnics, family picnics and seminary picnics. And the images of a seminary picnic carried me to Petit Jean State Park, just south of the Arkansas River and northwest of Little Rock, in the election year of 1952. Petit Jean is a forested mesa, the home then of Winthrop Rockefeller and the site that year of the annual picnic of the denizens of St. John's Home Missions Seminary in Little Rock.

There is a lake at Petit Jean State Park. My one clear memory of that picnic was a lone swimmer with a measured stroke moving slowly back and forth parallel to our shore. He swam on and on and on.

The swimmer was a young man by the name of Richard Buchanan. His swimming marathon as others munched hot dogs and swilled soft drinks and swatted flies was a symbol of the man.

Dick was an individualist, a finely cultured gentleman who had discovered his own star and was following it. For him life was serious business. He had as little regard for the opinions of others about his mode of life as anyone I have known. The exceedingly narrow strictures of seminary life in those years must have been a day-to-day hair shirt for him.

Dick entered the seminary in St. Louis as a veteran of World War II, a convert to the Catholic Church, and after extensive preparation to be a concert pianist.

He arranged for a piano to be moved to a loft in the main seminary building. Every spare moment he was there alone, practicing various exercises and polishing his artistry. It was as if some inner propulsion from his previous life in the conservatory would not let him stop three and four hours of practice a day.

Unfortunately Dick's relentless piano finger exercises were taking place immediately above the head of the seminary faculty member known to the students as the Mad Scientist. One day, not far into that seminary year, when the Mad Scientist no doubt was wrestling with Einstein, the endless finger exercises snapped the final cord of gentlemanly restraint. The Mad Scientist charged up the stairs, flung the loft door open, and screamed, "There are 235,000 compositions for the piano in the world, and you have to play the scales!!!"

Fortunately Dick did not logically argue, "Yes, I have to play the scales." He took the hint, disassembled the precious piano, and carried it piece by piece down many flights of stairs to a small room off the gym.

Time passed. Dick and I and a squadron of others found ourselves moving from the seminary in St. Louis to that in Little Rock. In that crowded place on North Tyler Street, we became roommates.

We were indeed an odd couple. Dick descended culturally from Chopin, Debussy and Bach. I was a product of DiMaggio, Lujack and Two-Ton Tony Galento. I've read St. John of the

Cross. I studied The Sporting News. Dick had literally been around the world, having done wartime service in India. I once had traveled as far as Denver.

Even our internal thermostats worked differently. In the winter nights, I would be buried under blankets in my bed, while Dick, in the bed by the open window, stretched on top of the covers wearing only underwear shorts.

As we shared this room, I learned more about this curious fellow. His father had been an undertaker in a small town in Illinois. One of his school classmates was James Jones, who had lived for awhile in the Buchanan home. About the time Dick was telling me this, James Jones was walking unto the national stage as the vagabond celebrity author of "From Here to Eternity."

Dick was petrified that Jones would include him as the basis of a character in his next novel "Some Came Running." I think he did.

In his Little Rock years, Dick Buchanan became what today would be labeled a fitness freak. He panted his way through a strict regimen of calisthenics. And he swam. And he swam. He began to roam the area west of the seminary property looking for swimming holes. In time, he swam in most of the farm ponds, creeks and, perhaps, swimming pools in the vicinity.

One time he got permission for an appointment in downtown Little Rock. Off he went. He hadn't returned by supper. At night prayers there was no sign of him.

When the clock got to lights out, Dick was nowhere to be seen.

Seminaries then were not exactly prisons, but not to return by bedtime was considered equivalent to a capital crime. For me it was a moral dilemma. What if my roommate had suffered an accident? Should I report his absence to the rector? I fell asleep.

In the morning's light there was Dick lying on top of his covers. What happened? After I had my appointment, I went swimming at the Y, he said. That moved him to eat a good meal. And he followed the meal with a movie. Logical, but….

Dick had a thing about cars. He scorned them as somehow degrading to human beings. So on his first assignment after ordination for the Diocese of Springfield in Illinois, he began to do his pastoral work on foot.

A thirty-five minute walk here and a forty-five minute walk there were viewed by the pastor of the place as decidedly inefficient. "Buy a car. Now!" suggested the pastor. Dick bought a car…a Thunderbird convertible.

I suppose he was in that convertible with the night wind blowing his hair and a Chopin nocturne caressing his brain when his car hit a bridge south of Jacksonville, Ill., on July 22, 1963.

The news of his death triggered recollection of a conversation Dick and I had had about dying, "I refuse to die in an automobile accident," he had said. 'It's not dignified."

"But, Dick, the choice might not be yours. It might just happen."

"I refuse to die that way."

All this from a parish picnic on a September Sunday.

A 100 Percent Chance of Rain during the Game

October 1992

Imagine this: two men in their middle sixties drive over 1,800 miles in an old Ford Tempo in a little less than 80 hours for the privilege of sitting stoically in the rain watching a football game for more than four of those hours.

It was great! Read on for the particulars.

I meet longtime friend Joe Dillon outside a United Airlines gate at Will Rogers World Airport about 1:30 Thursday afternoon, Sept. 24. We walk to my car, toss his suitcase in the trunk and leave for South Bend, Ind.

By late Friday afternoon, the Ford Tempo is nearing Chicago. I recall the massive traffic jam we sailed into the year before where several interstate highways intertwine like a ball of snakes on the southeast side of the big city. "Why don't we turn east on U.S. 30 and avoid that mess we ran into last year?" say I. Joe agrees.

An hour later, we are still stopping and starting through a near infinite series of stoplights and stop signs as we edge through Chicago Heights, East Chicago Heights, Dyer, Ind., Schererville and Valparaiso. Our new route has not been successful, just a different kind of automotive torture.

Before we left Oklahoma, someone had said to me, "If you can, go to the pep rally the night before the game." So we make our way to the Notre Dame campus, find a parking place and start to walk toward the Joyce Athletic and Convocation Center.

Soon we find ourselves two old guys walking north while 2,000 other people are walking south. We are a critical 40 minutes late.

The pep rally is over. We stroll into the empty convocation center, observe the seats where the team sat, stop at a restroom, buy a program for tomorrow's game and walk back to the car.

We leave the campus and drive to our lodging. It happens to be in another state, the Holiday Inn at St. Joseph, Mich., on the east shore of Lake Michigan. We hear the weather report during the ride. "A chance of some light showers tomorrow," says the radio voice.

The next morning I smear my face, neck, ears and hands with Photoplex #15 sunscreen, despite the fact the sky is overcast. By the time we get to our car, a very light rain has begun to fall. Our radio voice informs us that it is raining.

We park the Tempo at St. Mary's College across the highway from Notre Dame property and about one mile from the stadium. Rain equipment is donned – ball caps and parkas, not the best for this element but better than sweaters. We troop off with others across U.S. 31 and through the woods to the school that Father Sorin built.

An hour before the kickoff with the rain continuing, Joe and I enter the stadium. We are pleasantly surprised to learn our seats are at midfield in the eleventh row. We also learn that the wooden seats bear a sheen of water and that the water is deepening where our feet are placed. Joe chooses to sit on his $4 game program.

A cheerful voice from the bone-dry press box announces: "The weather forecast is a 100 percent chance of light to moderate rain showers during the game this afternoon." There is an implied Ha! Ha! Ha! in the voice. In the damp souls of the soggy fans already seated there is an almost silent bittersweet response of Ha! Ha! Ha! to you, sir!

The common experience of the rain creates a sense of camaraderie. The matron seated next to me has a yellow plastic plate tied to the top of her head to keep the raindrops off her glasses. I say to her, "You win the award for the most creative device to foil the rain." A younger man in front of us lugs a sack of cans of beer in one hand and a family-sized bag of pretzels in the other. He shares the pretzels with us.

The stadium grouch is seated directly in front of me. Neither Lou Holtz nor his massive legion of players do anything the right way, according to the grouch. The officials are worse. Each play is followed by a volley of complaints. This man was possibly the model for Oscar on Sesame Street. But at the end of the grouch's row is a distinguished white-haired gentleman in raincoat but no hat. He serenely wears the 128-page program, opened to the center, on the top of his head.

The game itself is, let us say, comfortable for us N.D. fans. There is not much doubt who will win although Purdue is plucky. In the second half, Tulsa's stocky Reggie Brooks runs wild. He takes a pitchout on an option play and goes 63 yards down the far sideline for a score. In a brief scene of racing bodies, Reggie is a Jaguar zooming past a fleet of desperate Yugos.

Later Reggie disguises himself as the ball in a pinball machine, bouncing off and zigzagging by Purdue defenders along the route of a 20-yard scoring run. Finally the man from Tulsa goes right and then left for 80 yards and another score. Keep your eyes on Reggie!

The game clock winds down. We make our squishy march from the stadium through the woods to St. Mary's, jump in the Tempo and head west. At the Wilbur Shaw Motor Plaza the vote in our car is 2 to 0 to stop and change into dry clothes. Everything is wet – shoes, socks, pants, shirts and underwear. We notice other people hurrying toward restrooms with substitute clothing in hand.

Later Saturday evening, we cut the engine for the night at the Ramada Inn in Effingham, Ill. I pay for my lodging with U.S. currency which is still wetly limp. The woman at the desk with a thumb and forefinger lifts a droopy $20 bill and says to her partner, "Gladys, we'll have to get out your hair dryer."

Of Intersection Thieves and Heavy-Footed Tailgaters

November 1992

Here's the scene: On a lovely autumn day several cars are lined up at all four stop signs at the intersection of North Pennsylvania Avenue and Grand Boulevard.

The procedure is civilized. First, one car from each side goes north and south. Then the pattern is repeated east and west.

I and my dusty Ford Tempo roll into the number one slot heading west on Grand Avenue. Cars from north and south, in their turn, move past. Then as I begin to glide through the intersection, I spy a second vehicle from the north attempting to steal a crossing out of turn.

In a millisecond, whatever causes rage, squirts into my system. My foot clamps on the accelerator; the Tempo gathers speed. I look right and see a flash of anger pass across the intersection thief's face. He hits the brakes. The Tempo and I miss the would-be intersection thief's front bumper by three inches.

If I had been Dean Rusk, I might have shouted in triumph, "We're eyeball to eyeball and the other fellow just blinked." But being only little I, I drove the next six blocks righteously smoldering.

A daily life drama.

Some days later, I was discussing this business of selfish drivers with a colleague. We matched stories and raised our blood pressures even in the telling.

She said one of the more rotten offenses is committed by the person who zooms by the long line of other drivers patiently waiting in their automobiles to move through a one-lane detour.

The no-good zoomer, flinging human concern to the winds, roars past dozens of cooperative citizens to the head of the line and then shoulders his way into the proper lane, thereby scandalizing those he has passed to the extent they would pay to see the offender strung up by his thumbs to the crossbar of the nearest signal light.

I replied that another variety of the cut-in zoomer is the dastardly shoulder zoomer. The shoulder zoomer is often spotted after football games at Norman. There is this massive traffic jam. All lanes of the road are clogged with automobiles moving ever so slowly.

The shoulder zoomer, in a spectacular burst of sheer egotism, whips his car onto the shoulder of the road and proceeds to barrel onward as far as he can go. This performance triggers a volley of prayers from other drivers and passengers. "Lord, let there be the biggest and meanest trooper in the history of the Oklahoma Highway Patrol around the next bend!" The shoulder zoomer would tempt St. Francis of Assisi to vote for the death penalty.

Let's shift scenes to the beloved Turner Turnpike. This asphalt wonder handles mega loads of traffic. Therefore it is an excellent locale to observe that ignominous species: the heavy-footed tailgater.

To attract the heavy-footed tailgater, one pulls onto the Turner Turnpike in a 1988 Ford Tempo and proceeds at a consistent 60 miles per hour in the right lane. This tactic occasions a tremendous rush of traffic whistling by on one's left – the liberals doing 85 and the conservatives 75.

The heavy-footed tailgater, be he long-haired liberal or red-faced conservative, comes racing up the right lane behind the Ford Tempo. He can't pass because of the stream of automobiles in the left lane, so he comes forward as far as he can without actually butting the bumper of the slothful Tempo. In some instances, the heavy-footed tailgater will hold this position for many miles. It's something akin to synchronized swimming in the Olympics.

The driver of the Ford Tempo mutters to himself about the heavy-footed tailgater having watched too many stock car races. And the heavy-footed tailgater curses the turtle-like old jerk ahead of him.

Finally, we arrive at the most pernicious of all the traffic monsters: the Northwest Expressway darter.

The Northwest Expressway, even before its ongoing face-lift, is a devilish series of sprints and stops. It has been designed only for those of steely nerves and stout hearts. And this roadway is the breeding ground of the Northwest Expressway darter.

The darter may be described fairly as one who covers as much distance side-to-side as he or she does straight ahead. A chart on the darter proceeding east from MacArthur Avenue to Meridian Avenue might go something like this: right lane, center, right lane, center, left lane, center, left lane, center, right lane, center, right lane, center, right lane, center, left lane, center, stop!

In the wake of the darter is vast cloud of incipient vengeance. The mildest of the human species is drawn to do something drastic to retaliate. The ultimate satisfaction of one in the wake is to pull abreast of the darter at the next stop light, turn and smile at the darter, then slightly nod one's head. This maneuver is called morose delectation.

Before Sending a Cat to a Jesuit, Read This

December 1992

Once more the Jesuits have proved they have more guts than others of the human kind. *La Civilta Cattolica*, a Jesuit journal in Rome, dared to publish (on the front page, yet) that human beings have more intrinsic value than other animals on this planet.

For such temerity, the Jesuit editors were subjected to an onslaught of barbed protests from the animal rights crowd. Animals, said one rebutter, are "loyal, unwasteful, rational and above all considerate to their own – something humans are not."

A present-day putative follower of St. Francis of Assisi declared the Jesuits were guilty of heresy in stating that animals can't really love in the full human sense. Naughty Jesuits. A priest, disturbed by the Jesuit stance, called on all of goodwill toward God's beasties to send a cat to each Jesuit.

All of the above was reported beautifully from Rome on Nov. 20 by John Thavis of the Catholic News Service. His article was titled: "Theology vs. zoology: watching the fur fly at the Vatican. "

But let's get down to brass tacks. Let me tell you the story of Donald the Cat. I present this account only in the interest of truth about animals.

Donald the Cat was a Siamese. (No slurs on the good human folk of Siam or Thailand, as we now call it, are intended.) His owner was a Catholic priest of the mystic order of associate pastor. Let's call him Father Purr. Father Purr's pastor was a tall, handsome, rugged fellow. Let's label him Father Strong. Then there was little I, a guest in the back bedroom.

Father Purr first put his paws on Donald the Cat, when the latter was the proverbial cute ball of fur – with precocious development of his claws. Sample monologue heard near Donald the Cat from passing-by innocents: "Pretty kitty! Pretty kitty! Oh, so soft and furry – *ouch*!"

That autumn our evenings were spent in the living room observing Donald the Cat shredding the furniture, the drapes and our – *ouch*!! – ankles. Father Purr saw this as Donald the Cat moving through his clawing phase...not to worry. Father Strong remained strong and silent, although with gritted teeth. The priest from the back bedroom rapidly developed a severe case of fear and loathing. Donald the Cat responded in kind minus the fear.

Donald the Cat adopted a window in my bedroom as his favored place for meditation. He sat there and peered into the great world beyond. Soon a dark streak or two appeared on the wall below the window. Shortly after that, I turned in bed one night so that my nose faced the window. Instantly my olfactory nerves confirmed my worst suspicions.

At my next opportunity, I grabbed Donald the Cat off the window ledge and hurled him down the hall, arguably an attempted caticide. Donald the Cat, of course, landed smoothly on all fours, shook the dust of my room from his fur, and swaggered haughtily into the next room. He would return often to my place on terrorist attacks, no matter what security measures were employed by me. More dark lines were added to the wall.

Time passed. I moved. Soon I was assigned to pastor a smallish parish. Following on my heels, at the bishop's request, was Father Purr and with him Donald the Cat.

This was a smaller house. Within 3.5 minutes Donald the Cat discovered my bedroom and...I need not lead you gentle readers through the sordid details, but, yes, my nose confirmed the fact that not Mac the Knife but Donald the Cat was back in town. Once more images of caticide troubled my prayers.

One sunny day, Father Purr casually remarked, "You know what, Donald hasn't been using his litter box lately, I think he is getting up in the attic."

I, who am by nature an irredeemable procrastinator, turned on my heel, strode to the telephone, called a carpenter and ordered him to cover every conceivable opening to the attic.

Donald the Cat probably overheard the conversation and used his influence. Soon Father Purr and Donald the Cat were on their way to another rectory.

Thus began the rectory-wrecking career of this malicious feline. As in Sherman's March to the Sea, Donald the Cat laid waste to a string of rectories or, more accurately, laid his waste in a string of rectories. The paths (and pauses) of Donald the Cat gave off odors so strong that skunks in the neighborhoods held their noses.

At one stop, a confident, take-charge, barrel-chested pastor made it clear by words and deeds that Donald the Cat was henceforth and forever barred from the pastor's section of the rectory. Donald the Cat's response was to steal into the forbidden space, climb upon the pastor's sparkling new electric typewriter, and, in polite terms, do his number.

A report was heard of a mild-mannered priest who adopted the reasonable policy of throwing Donald the Cat as far as possible upon every sighting and successful seizure.

One could imagine retreat directors at priests' retreats hearing repeated confessions of hollowed-eyed priests admitting to thoughts, desires and attempts of caticide. Probably confessors counseled, "Remember, perseverance is needed!"

Finally, Donald the Cat, exhausted by his horrible labors, passed from this life, but not to some ethereal rectory, I trust.

I'm buying a lifetime subscription to *La Civilta Cattolica* as soon as I brush up my Italian.

CHAPTER 17

1993

Father Hugo's Advice: For Venial Sins, One Alleluia

March 1993

Four decades back I, a timid greenhorn priest, ate lunch in the chaplain's dining room at the old Mercy Hospital on Northwest 12th Street. My luncheon host was Father Hugo, a giant of a man with a very bald dome. I admired the gusto which he displayed in devouring food. A man who appreciated life.

Father Hugo became my confessor by my choice, of course. I went to see him in the rather oddly-configured house used by Mercy Hospital chaplains. He lived on the second floor in a kind of confusion of furniture and bric-a-brac. There I poured out my peccadilloes, scruples, dilemmas, illusions, and, now and again, areal stinker of a sin.

For his part, Father Hugo regularly anointed my soul with absolution, humorous comments, anecdotes and sage advice. Sample of the latter: "If possible, don't live in the same city with the bee-shop!" (That was his distinctive Germanic-tinged pronunciation for a successor of the apostles.)

He had had his problems with his own bee-shop in a diocese somewhere to our north and had fled to Oklahoma in the mid-1920s. Bishop Francis Clement Kelley, in his compassionate way, accepted Father Hugo into the Diocese of Oklahoma.

At his chaplain's quarters at the hospital, Father Hugo displayed his St. Francis of Assisi side. He constructed a large bird feeder on the roof of the porch outside a second-floor row of windows.

He had a friendly relationship with a mixture of cats. They climbed a kind of cat-ladder built by Father Hugo to his second-floor level where he installed a hinged door allowing the felines to enter from the outside directly into an unused kitchen cabinet. Thus, when the mood moved him, Father Hugo opened the cabinet door and pulled out a cat. When the cat's time was up, the same big hand returned the animal to the cabinet.

Then there was Fee. Fee was a grossly overweight German shepherd, a sight to see when Fee and his master went for their evening walk.

According to Oklahoma priests' lore, one evening Bishop Eugene J. McGuinness unexpectedly dropped by the rectory of Our Lady of Victory Church in Purcell while Father Hugo was pastor there.

Father Hugo seated the bishop in the living room and went to the kitchen to prepare a pot of coffee. Fee, the dog, attentively watched his master. Suddenly Father Hugo's voice boomed out, "Fee, go kiss the bee-shop's ring!"

Bishop McGuinness, with his damaged, high-pitched voice, called back, "That's more than the pastor will do!"

Father Hugo had a certain amount of justifiable pride in the powerful, oversized body God had given him. He would pull up a pant leg to display the great knot of muscle in a calf and laugh at the sight.

It's possible, even probable, that his impressive physique was the point of conflict between his first bishop and himself. It seems a physician, upon seeing and measuring him, declared Father Hugo to fit the early 20th century medical definition of a "perfect giant. "

The good doctor is said to have prevailed upon the priest to pose, in his impressive birthday suit, for photos to be used in a medical textbook. Eventually a copy of the book found its way into the bishop's hands and that, in a manner of speaking, is when the biceps hit the fan.

The gentle German priest came semi-regularly to St. Francis of Assisi Church to help with confessions. These would be overload times – before Christmas, before Easter and once-in-a-while for children's confessions.

I can say this: he had speed. Confessional slides would pop back and forth, and doors would open and shut with amazing frequency.

Before we threw ourselves to the mercies of hundreds of Holy Saturday penitents, Father Hugo's grinning penitential advice to me was "For mortal sins, three alleluias! For venial sins, one alleluia!"

Wherever Father Hugo went in this state, his openness, his humanity, and his spirit of goodwill left behind a trail of admirers, especially among those who had had little contact with the Catholic Church. Stationed at Canute during national Prohibition times, it apparently was more than a rumor that hot and thirsty highway patrol officers knew his rectory was a place where one on a hot summer day could lean back with a cold bottle of home brew.

He had a penchant for punching holes in pretentiousness. At a formal dinner for Mercy Hospital, one person after another was beginning his/her remarks with a series of standard word salutes: "Most reverend bishop, right reverend and very reverend monsignors, reverend Fathers, venerable Sisters, eminent physicians, dedicated nurses etc."

When Father Hugo's turn came, he rose to his full majestic height, looked solemnly right and left and said, "Distinguished members of both sexes."

In God's providence, Father Hugo died in a fiery automobile accident in northern Oklahoma on March 22, 1964. He was still doing parish work at age 77.

And Now a Tribute to the Unknown Baseball Player

April 1993

This good woman was seated in a refrigerator indifferently watching a baseball game. Well, it really wasn't a refrigerator but it certainly was frigid...and dark gray...and one could tell tons of rain were suspended above by a thread. A dreadful day to watch baseball and she was there out of spousal loyalty, not moved by affection for the national pastime.

Ozzie Smith came to bat for the team wearing the cardinal red jerseys.

"My, isn't he small," observed the good woman. "He's so tiny."

The elderly gentleman seated to the left of the good woman, heard the comment and leaned her way. She picked up the sighting of a red nose, under an imitation St. Louis Cardinals cap, turning toward her. Her instant reaction was the odd shape of the cap made this man look like a veteran of the Lower Slobovian army.

"Ozzie Smith," rasped the old fellow, "is, by common consent, the greatest shortstop to ever play the position in the history of baseball! He may be small, but he's the man with the magnet hands! Thirteen straight Golden Glove awards!"

He didn't mean to preach or to chastise, only to clarify that those of us seated in this refrigerator watching this dreary exhibition baseball game at All-Sports Stadium on April 3 were in the presence of greatness as long as St. Louis Cardinal O. Smith, #1, stood on this playing field.

However, when the Social Security recipient turned the good woman's direction some minutes later, she had changed places with her husband. No doubt, she was relieved to be separated from the crank with the weird cap.

That's the way the 1993 baseball season started for me.

The proteins of professional baseball are the records. It's an enterprise of history with each generation of players trying to scale the majestic peaks of statistics.

Let us take O. Smith for example. My handy "Total Baseball" reference book (2,362 pages) tells us that Osborne Earl Smith was born Dec. 26, 1954, in Mobile, Ala. His dimensions are 5 feet, 11 inches by 150 pounds. Ozzie's major league debut was April 7, 1978, with the San Diego Padres.

The universe's unparalleled shortstop had played in 2,188 games at his position before the start of the 1993 season. Only Luis Aparicio, Larry Bowa and Luke Appling, in that order have played in more. If half goes well, the Wizard of Oz will pass all but Aparicio this season.

But enough of the great man. The remainder of this piece will lift up the non-famous among major league baseball players of the past, a sort of tribute to the Unknown Player.

The roster:

- Pound 'Em Paul Easterling struggled in parts of three seasons – 1928, 1930 and 1938 – with the Detroit Tigers and the Philadelphia A's. On good authority, he is said to have blasted the longest homerun ever hit in the old Sportsman's Park in St. Louis. A clue to his failure to stick in the majors is contained in the stats: 200 times at bat and 44 strikeouts. He toiled many years in the Texas League, at least some of that time with the Oklahoma City Indians.
- Joseph Patrick "Joe" Rabbitt. Joe had an abbreviated career in the majors – 2 games, 3 times at bat, 1 hit, a single – 'in mid-September, 1922, for the Cleveland Indians. But he is remembered by very old timers in Frontenac, Kan.,

where he played the grand game of baseball with the likes of one Frank Monahan.

- Sal Madrid. As a member of the Tulsa Oilers in the 1940s, Salvador was a spectacularly erratic shortstop. He had a grooved waist-high batting swing. Throw it in that zone and Boom! Throw it anywhere else and Swish! Sal played in eight games for the Cubs in 1947, batted 24 times, got three hits, and struck out six times. He was entertaining.

Delaney Lafayette Currence, of the South Carolina Currences, is a finalist in elegant names of American League left-handed pitchers. What's in a name? Not much in Delaney's case. He pitched in- two' games for the

Milwaukee Brewers. Results: won none, lost two, earned run average of 7.71.

Unusual and Forgotten Smiths. There have been 80 Smiths, excluding pitchers, who played in the majors. Some have been well-known as Ozzie is (and Al Smith of the Indians, Reggie Smith of the Red Sox, Elmer Smith in the late 1890s, and Lonnie Smith of the Atlanta Braves). But what of Klondike Smith who batted .185 in seven games for the 1912 New York Yankees (or was it the Highlanders)? Or Happy Smith of the Dodgers who got 18 hits in 76 at bats in 1910? Or Stub Smith with one single in three games for the Boston Braves in 1898? Or Paddy Smith with no hits in two at bats for the Red Sox of 1920? Or Bull Smith who played a total of 15 games for three different teams each of which was indifferent to Bull's talents? Or Skyrocket Smith of the 1888 Louisville team, a glorious career that burned out in one season? They also served.

And, finally, Fred Tauby. Fred had two cups of coffee in the big time – 13 games for the White Sox in 1935 and 11 games with the Phillies in 1937. Now and again Fred would lift a stein of beer in concert 'with one Frank Monahan of Tulsa, Oklahoma. Which explains how the shirt part of Fred's White Sox uniform got on the back of a skinny 9-year-old Tulsa boy in the blistering summer of 1936.

From Zero to Sixty in What Seems Like Eight Seconds Flat

May 1993

In *The New Yorker* magazine of May 3, 1993, on page 67, there sits a P. Steiner cartoon which is simultaneously simple, true as true can be, piercing, and very funny.

The cartoon depicts a man seated in an easy chair. The man is neither young nor terribly old. He wears a plaid coat and a sport shirt buttoned to the top; and he sports spectacles, a moustache and a double chin. The gentleman's feet rest squarely on the floor. His forearms lie along the arms of the chair, fingers over the ends. His mouth is slightly turned down, no trace of merriment. And the man is staring straight ahead.

The caption, in large print, under the cartoon reads: From Zero to Sixty in What Seems Like Eight Seconds Flat.

If the reader is, say, 66 years old, he bursts into laughter. A few moments later a small wave of sadness laps on the beach of his consciousness.

Speaking from the ranks of the waist's-expanding U.S. cohort now walking, slightly slower, through their seventh decade, I second the motion that the sixties arrive more speedily than anyone expects.

One inning a fresh-faced Mickey Mantle smashes a baseball on a pure low line straightaway over the center field wall at Comisky Park. In the next, he is a tired man with an old bag of memories looking out a window in Dallas.

Sophia Loren dazzles both sexes with her sophisticated beauty as she strides across the screen, but Sophia glances at her watch and is pained to learn there is only .22 of a second left before…

And it was only yesterday, that brash Lee Iacocca was certain this shiny Mustang could go stylishly from zero to you-name-it in seconds, and now…

Just last night, a nearsighted seminarian gazed out a second-floor window of Glennon Preparatory Seminary and saw the lights of Kenrick Seminary. He wondered if he would live so long to get there. That was four decades plus seven years ago.

Perhaps the greatest pain of becoming older is the solemn duty, required by the iron law of vanity, to face one's face in the mirror each morning.

From a male perspective, one sees circles being engraved under one's eyes, lines tugging down the corners of the mouth, strange upward grooves above the eyebrows working their way toward the scalp, and, seemingly all at once, the neck skin decides to go totally limp and one gets this gobbler effect.

Meanwhile the male's hair begins to abandon the scalp with amazing rapidity. The entire Oklahoma City sanitary sewage system is clogged with the strands of your hair. One's hair part moves farther to the left and the longer strands are called upon, as Adam's fig leaves, to camouflage the terrible nakedness of this era of the scalp.

The man of western culture may recall the aphorism of Vittorio Alfieri: "Often the test of courage is not to die but to live."

Men, who become deeply depressed by this morning gaze at their images, are encouraged to secure photos of the great English-American poet W.H. Auden in his middle sixties. The face of the greatest English language poet of this century became an incredible mass of wrinkles, a kind of world-class facial wreck. Auden confessed that his face resembled a wedding cake left out in the rain. A friend, the composer Igor Stravinsky, commented that soon we will have to smooth him out to see who it is.

Most of us, thank God, are not quite at that state yet.

Meanwhile I take my frequent strolls through Resurrection Cemetery, panting up the hill as I head west, feeling full of vigor as I accelerate down the hill toward the east, and all the time extending blessings to the many friends and kind-of friends whose bodies lie in their graves along the way.

A sort of quiet chorus attends me on these walks. "Remember, friend, your sagging body will soon be where ours are, but there's something infinitely better just over the horizon – beyond Council Road, beyond the line into Canadian County, and even on the other side of the remains of Eischen's Bar."

So, I go forward, living, lit life in my sixties while the calendar turns rapidly toward the year 2000. I lurch forward feeling half guilty as the United States Treasury decorates my life with Social Security checks. And I look toward eternal life while watching Frankie Avalon, himself not all that far from 60, peddle hamburgers as the pseudo-eternal teen-ager for Sonic. May we meet at the pearly gates, rather than the Golden Arches, Frankie.

The Oh-Dear! and What-the-Hell Schools of Kite Flying

June 1993

They were studying the wind.

That was the explanation received by the principal from the priest-catechist whose charges had been observed flying kites, lots of kites -maybe 30 of them – during religion class time.

As I recall, it was a balmy, moderately windy day. As the DP, designated principal, of the Woodstock Era at McGuinness High School, I sat uneasily in my principal's chair most probably trying to decide which hole in the western civilization's dike to attempt to plug that fine morning.

The assistant principal hurried into the principal's office. (Assistant principals historically have been cast in the role of the upholders of law and order, with an emphasis on the order. They care not a whit about the Miranda decision.)

The assistant principal, wild of eye and mouth agape, pointed to the west and opened his mouth but not a syllable issued. He tried again, still pointing to the west. "Father ___," he gasped. "Father ___'s class is flying kites!! "

Indeed Father ___'s class was flying kites. And despite the assistant principal's extreme agitation, he had pointed in the correct direction, west of the school's main building.

Of course his students were flying kites, said the accused Father ___. "They were studying the wind. "

"Studying the wind," repeated the principal with the workings of his left brain, while his right brain silently howled, "Why me, O Lord?" This was not what some call a win-win situation, the principal realized. It was, the principal instinctively knew, a classical Schopenhauer schlock, or a lose-lose-lose-lose-lose situation.

The kite season is upon us. As I walk about my assigned plot on God's earth, I see kites in the air over the Northwest Expressway. As I steer my car around Lake Hefner's sparkling waters, I spy kites dancing in the breezes.

In the olden days, the kites were of two shapes: the basic diamond configuration or the more bulky box job. My own Oklahoma Kite-flying License carried two limitations: "holder must wear spectacles while flying kites and must use only diamond design." In other words, box kites were out of my league.

In 1993 DCA (damnable computer age), kites have taken off in designs. They are winged shape; they flutter; they are guided by two strings; they swoop and zing like purple martins on pep pills; and they are only sold to persons with the cool and the hand-eye coordination of a Chuck Yeager.

Psychologically, the American Kite Association, a.k.a. A.K.A., assures us, all kite fliers are divided into two classes: the oh-dear! class and the what-the-hell class.

The oh-dear! class members stagger about with inhuman burdens of anxieties as they clutch their kite strings with their sweaty hands. Every distant telephone pole bears – "oh, dear" – the imminent danger of electrocution. Every odd movement of the kite causes – "oh, dear" – the alarm of a certain crash.

The what-the-hell kite fliers send their kites upward into the flight paths of local airports and add a new ball of kite string while holding a bottle of beer in one hand. B. Franklin of Philadelphia, Pa., is the first recorded what-the-hell kiter.

The Guinness Book of Records, old man's edition, has some great stats from the what-the-hell school of kiting. Those numbers are 35,530 and 56,457. They are respectively the height, in feet, attained and the length, in feet, of kite string used in a dramatic flight by 10 lads at Porter, Ind.

Those Indiana boys actually built a train of 19 kites in their seven-hour effort. The altitude of the top kite was calculated "by telescopic triangulation," a phrase which seems straight out of W.C. Fields' mouth. Was the height of the kite kited?

Outside of brother Franklin's pragmatic use of the kite in the 18th century, kites seem to have no practical use. They are fun things, leisure time business, trailing a tail of joy, even studying the wind.

There is, however, at least one application of kite flying which is both serious and fun for the participants. That is in the Occupied Territory of the West Bank.

If the practice is the same as five years ago, one can sit on a terrace above the Old City of Jerusalem in the late afternoon and see many, many kites flying over this ancient center where God took the human family as His. The kites bear the colors of the PLO. At the end of each kite string is a grinning, heart-pounding Palestinian boy, knowing that Israeli soldiers are running and looking for the persons holding the strings. Even soldiers, angry at the time, must laugh later at being foiled by this fool's play. Some day, God willing, those boys and those soldiers of today will share a round of beers and chuckle good-naturedly at this child's play of the past.

The Thing Was Called a Sentimental Journey

June 1993

The thing was called a Sentimental Journey. It was; but it was a lot more than that.

The 1993 Marquette High School all-school reunion featured a deep plunge into the past and a swim through an ocean of memories, as well as the pleasant arrival of a tidal wave of affection.

Marquette High School was never a large place. Its first graduation class in 1933 consisted of 17. My class of 1945 had 28 members. Later, in the 1950s, class sizes soared upward toward 70 or 80. The high school section of Marquette closed in 1960 as the much larger Bishop Kelley High School opened.

Some indication that there was a general satisfaction with the schooling received at old Marquette was the fact that more than 700 free Americans signed up for the reunion.

The kids at this reunion were 50. The mature people were about 80. All were full of life.

Our class, everyone in their mid-sixties, scheduled a social hour and dinner on Friday night. We stood there in classmate Joe Moran's elegant apartment on the fourteenth floor of 2300 Riverside, sipped our gin and tonics, gazed at the Tulsa skyline and felt, like Daddy Warbucks, that all was well with the world.

Dick Mocha, a Tulsa Holy Family High School grad who married a lovely Marquette lass, told me a cute story at the dinner. It indirectly touches Oklahoma's Lieutenant Gov. Jack Mildren. Jack Mildren's father, "Big Jack" Mildren, coached the

Holy Family football team in the early 1940s. I recall Big Jack as a large swarthy man with a reputation as one tough hombre.

The story that circulated at Marquette was that Big Jack determined his football lineup for the next game by the simple expedient of two lines of players running head on into each other with the last 11 standing designated as the starters. I told that tale to Dick Mocha.

Dick, in turn, remembered the pregame scenes in the Holy Family locker room. Father Charles Conley, the roly-poly assistant pastor, would be present with Coach Big Jack and his players. As the clock ticked down the final minutes before the game started, Big Jack would say courteously, "Father Conley, would you mind stepping outside the locker room?" When the door closed behind the priest, Big Jack proceeded to describe in graphic and colorful detail what he expected his team to do to the opposition.

Benedictine Sister Marie Mundell was not only present, she was a presence at all the common events. She sat there somehow both exuding dignity and warmly welcoming former students' approaches with good humor. She was described at the Sunday Mass as one whose commanding level look froze evil in its tracks. She also exhibited grace afoot as she glided around the dance floor Saturday night. In one sense, Sister Marie is the still living spirit of old Marquette.

My great friend Joe Dillon had an unusual experience at the Saturday night dance. He was sought out by a rotund gentleman who at one time had been a superior high school running back at Holy Family High School.

The former halfback told Joe he wanted to apologize for biting Joe's leg in a pileup during the 1945 Marquette-Holy Family football game. Joe said he knew someone had bitten him on a leg, but he never knew who the culprit was.

When I saw Joe he said, with a grin, "Can you beat that? An apology for biting my leg 48 years later! "

Obviously reconciliation was in the air.

In the course of the proceedings, I made a public statement that I was one of the few persons present who had gone to Marquette School for 13 years, having acquired a solid foundation of two years in the first grade for my later intellectual pursuits. Afterwards Joanne Markey, class of 1946, told me that she too was a two-timer in the first grade. Joanne's first year in the grade one was my second year at that level.

Strangely enough, Joanne later became principal of Christ the King School in Oklahoma City and I became principal of Bishop McGuinness High School. Obviously the Catholic school system wanted the presence of administrators who knew what it was like to suffer in the classroom!

Pat Fitzpatrick Mooney ran into her former jitterbugging partner, Dick Barbour. The upshot of this meeting was the recollection of Dick's penchant for bicycling from Tulsa to Skiatook where Pat lived at the time. The distance was some 20 miles.

This was not just any old bike ride. What made it interesting is Dick's bike had only one pedal. He tied a jitterbugging foot to that pedal and pumped away up state highway 11. Pure jitterbug devotion.

As I left the reunion I heard one old guy yell to another old bird standing in front of the Marquette school building.

"What are you doing?" hollered the first fellow. "Smoking on the school grounds," was the crisp reply.

But It Is Raining and Nobody Else Is on the Course!

August 1993

June 4, 1971. Four middle-aged American men are standing in a cold rain near the southeast coast of England. Their discussion revolves around the subject: "Are we going to obey the secretary or not?" Odd sight and sound, what?

Leave us add background to the scenario.

The four gentlemen are recently arrived tourists. They have had themselves transported via an aeroplane to a London aerodrome for the express purpose of playing the game of golf at courses which have served as battlegrounds for that event termed The British Open.

The gentlemen's names are C. Finn, J. McGlinchey, D. Monahan and W. Swift. In a letter of introduction to the management of the revered courses they have described themselves as "avid amateur golfers." Avid they may be, skillful they are not.

They have arrived at their itinerary's first legendary venue: Royal St. George's Golf Club. They have been told by the club secretary that foursomes are never allowed at Royal St. George's, only twosomes.

Avid American amateur: "But it is raining and nobody else is on the course!"

Club secretary: "Only twosomes, sir!"

"But obviously it won't make any difference! "

"Twosomes, sir!!"

And that is why the four are huddled wetly near the first tee. A decision is reached. Tee off here as twosomes, then become a foursome after the first hole. The Empire has conquered again (but the Irish covertly will strike back).

'It is the American chaps first experience with a links golf course. A links course is one built near the sea on sandy soil with innumerable hummocks, dunes, ridges, swales, potholes, and assorted other geological freaks.

The fourth hole at Royal St. George's serves as a good example of a links course. About 100 yards from the tee your vision is obscured by a ridge. In the side of the ridge facing you are two mammoth sand traps. No doubt, the Royal St. George's membership has named these traps. They should be called the Sahara and the Gobi.

If one manages to drive the ball over the ridge, one has not a single clue about the situation on the other side. If there is a fairway over there, one can be certain that it is a narrow, bumpy thing sided by rough high enough to hide a tribe of pygmies. Walking along a hole at Royal St. George's, a player must proceed on faith alone that somewhere there is a green ahead and other holes to play in the near vicinity.

The above were some of my memories from that damp day 22 years ago as I watched the 1993 British Open being played in the sunshine this past weekend.

If Greg Norman, the redoubtable Australian Shark, had been a paying customer on the final day of the Open, he would not have gotten his money's worth. (Only 64 strokes.) Our group did. Each of us had approximately twice as many swipes at the ball as the Shark.

One thing is certain, any one of us could have defeated John Daly then. John was only four years old.

Following golf on our Royal St. George's trip, we drove the short distance to Canterbury Cathedral. It is a place of great historical distinction – St. Augustine arrived there in the 6th century and the present cathedral was built some 500 years later; St. Thomas Becket was martyred there in 1170; Chaucer's pilgrims spun their tales on the way to Canterbury; and the cathedral is the seat of the Anglican Church's chief bishop.

As we walked onto the cathedral grounds we met a pale lad in rather formal clothing. He said he was a student at the cathedral school.

Someone said, "Is the archbishop often here?"

"Yes," replied the young man. Then, "I believe that is his grace over there."

We turned and saw a balding white-haired man in a purple cassock strolling across the lawn. This was Archbishop Arthur Michael Ramsey. We four Irish-American Roman Catholic priests, dressed in soggy golf clothes, approached the archbishop and introduced ourselves.

Archbishop Ramsey was most amiable. He immediately recalled the name of the Episcopal bishop of Oklahoma, Bishop Chilton Powell. At one point, the archbishop said, "Look at us, four papists and the archbishop of Canterbury! "

I'm looking at a photo of the event. Archbishop Ramsey, big smile on his face, is making an open-armed gesture and is pointing with his left hand. Three golfer-papists – W. Swift, J. McGlinchey and D. Monahan -are responding with laughter. C. Finn was busy with his camera.

Toward the end of our 10 minutes of conversation, Archbishop Ramsey, responsible for more than 70 million members of the Anglican communion, allowed, "Sometimes I would like to chuck the whole church and just have my own little diocese. "

D. Monahan, Oklahoma pastor of 75 members in Jones and 20 in Luther, knew the feeling.

Chomping One's Way through a Mountain of Junk Food

August 1993

In Mythology, Hercules Performed His Fearsome Twelve Labors. At World Youth Day, Monahan suffered his Seven Trials.

Firstly, there was the decision of how to get from here to there. And once in Colorado where to stay.

The Catholic Youth Office leaders graciously offered a seat on one of the 26 buses, plus a dormitory room at Colorado State University. The alternate choices came down to driving an aging Tempo (with fervent prayers to the patron saint of junkers) and/ or adding one more guy to the homeless population of Denver.

Monahan revisited in memory long-ago high school bus junkets with dozens of over-energetic teenagers. He chose the chancy Tempo option. But, Monahan thought, I am partial to sleeping in a bed. Therefore I will take the kind offer of the dormitory.

The Second Trial was not unexpected. It consisted of chomping one's way through a mountain of junk food. Monahan prepared for this confrontation with the McDonald's menu in the Mile High City by a practice meal the first night out from dear Oklahoma City. The menu: a box of cinnamon enhanced graham crackers from Love's Country Store in Watonga, followed some hours later by an ice-cream bar and a bag of red licorice purchased at the Jug and Loaf in Boise City. Farther down the road, having secured a room at the fashionable Mission Motel in

Clayton, N.M., Monahan's innards were reporting back to him their "feelings" about this moving meal.

During the format of World Youth Day, senior eater Monahan bravely ate and drank what McDonald's offered: bratwurst sandwiches, barbecue sandwiches, chicken sandwiches, Coca Cola, Sprite, cookies, potato chips etc., etc. Was it his imagination when he observed himself in the morning mirror, or were his ears actually turning into fleshy Golden Arches?

The return to a college dorm – 50 years later – became the Third Trial. In an ocean of youth, Monahan was the Old Man (not And the Sea, but At Sea). He reflected that he was probably the first inhabitant of the modern Westfall Hall to wear black bedroom slippers to the bathroom area. He was intrigued, but horrified by clearly identified "rape whistles" hanging by chains in each of the shower stalls. To his surprise, he slept well.

The Fourth Trial, the sing and sway mode, took place, thank God, in a dimly lit arena. The elderly reporter had determined to follow a Faith Group of six young women and two adult leaders during the daylight hours of Friday. In the afternoon we took part in a session termed "Life Teen USA – 100% Catholic."

Life Teen USA featured high-protein singing, crashing instruments and fervent preaching.

At times the 2,000 or so participants stood, joined hands over heads, and sang, while swaying from side to side.

If one can picture Don Knotts doing this, one can envision Monahan at this task. He, thought he, carried through courageously, until a young usher approached from behind and said, "Sir, would you please move out of the aisle! "

The paralyzing puzzle of suitcase and car became the Fifth Trial. Having deposited his stuff in the dormitory at Fort Collins, Colo., Monahan checked his car into a parking garage in Denver on Thursday and began to ride the Oklahoma buses back and forth from Denver to Fort Collins.

The paralyzing puzzle entered our hero's consciousness on Friday. He became aware that the buses on Saturday would run straight from the campus of Colorado State University to the parking area a few miles from Cherry Creek State Park. His plan had been to ride the bus with the whole group to the staging area near the park, walk to the park, stay there awhile, grab a media shuttle to downtown Denver, pick up his car at the garage, drive to a motel, stay there overnight, then catch a shuttle back to the park Sunday morning.

There were two slight problems: one, he would never be able to lug that heavy suitcase to the park in that jostling crowd, and, two, on Friday he had discovered that the garage, where the car was resting would not open again until Monday morning.

In the end, Monahan talked a good-hearted bus driver into taking his suitcase to the Motel 6 where the drivers were staying. And a taxicab provided the reporter's transportation to the bus drivers, the bag, and a room.

The Sixth Trial: survival in the madding crowd. Never mind 90,000 human beings pushing in and out of Mile High Stadium. Never mind downtown Denver streets where tens of thousands of young people constantly swirled for five days. Those are not madding crowds.

A madding crowd is a gusher of 100,000 worked-up juveniles suddenly spurting down West 14th Street following the opening Mass. A madding crowd is a quarter of a million pilgrims, elbow to elbow, toe to heel, tramping three miles in baking heat and rising dust on their way to Cherry Creek State Park. A madding crowd is 250,000 camped on a park hill wondering with a certain terror if it was possible to get a crust of bread to eat or a cup of cool water to drink, and, if so, how many hours one would have to stand in line to use a portable toilet.

"Are you doing OK, Father?" "I'm fine," the priest lied.

Hercules Twelfth Labor saw him plunge into Hades to bring back bare-handed Cerberus, the vicious three-headed dog.

Monahan's Seventh Trial was to drink barehanded sufficient Sprite to avoid being carried out feet first by military medics on Sunday morning. He made it with one gulp to spare.

Driving Down the Left Lane of Life in Merry England

October 1993

(Note: The author and his sister, Helen Perrine, recently spent two weeks in Ireland and Great Britain.)

The rental car agency's fresh-faced representative led us across the airport parking lot to the white Rover Metro. The young man formally introduced us to the stubby Metro, then pulled out his version of an animal trainer's whip, in this case a black leather attachment to the keys, and zapped a command. The Metro obediently unlocked its doors. It was the first intimation that Helen, my sister, and I unwittingly had hired a trick car in which to explore Great Britain.

Minutes later we, two genuine U.S.A. senior citizens, were lurching our way toward the entrance of London's Stansted International Airport. (The progress along the road is described as "lurching" because D. Monahan, the driver, suffered eye/hand coordination problems with the left-handed manual gearshift.)

The Rover Metro rolled through the Stansted gate and turned left in the left lane with great premeditation. ("Drive on the left; drive on the left," D. Monahan repeated to himself.) The turn was in exactly the wrong direction, but we were in the left lane.

We wished to drive to The North on highway M11. But we first went west. Stopped. Turned around. Drove east. Turned right. Drove south. Saw a sign. Turned west again. Found M11. Thus we began our long ride up the east side of England to The North.

D. Monahan has been driving automobiles for a full half of a century. Some of this driving had been performed previously in

England, Scotland and Ireland. He was rather certain of his skills. How quickly we forget our former sins.

He would have done well to recall the aphorism: "When the going gets tough, the pseudo tough panic." And so it happened. On this first day, when the Metro and its two occupants went hurtling into one of England's patented roundabouts (known elsewhere as traffic circles), D. Monahan began grinding gears, grabbing for the directional signal but turning on the windshield wipers complete with spraying cleaner, hurling epithets at the Metro and all its Anglo-Saxon builders, and generally behaving in ways unfit for an English gentleman, but tolerated when the culprit is unseemly Irish.

Sometime later that evening the Metro glided to a stop in the crowded parking lot of a wayside inn. The driver felt a surge of relief at being off the road. He locked the door and the security system went berserk: lights flashed, horns sounded, perhaps bugles blew also. D. Monahan finally zapped the contrary machine into silence.

That was the first of numerous such incidents. It was apparent that the Metro had been cleverly designed so that the security system sprang into its act only when a crowd of 50 or more were in the immediate vicinity to witness the fun.

On this two-week autumnal journey, "lost" was not our middle name, but it was our first and last.

One has to be different than the common herd to get lost while gliding along a six-lane superhighway, but we did it more than once. D. Monahan was labeled the "Turnaround Kid" for his dozens of turnarounds and trys in the opposite directions.

On the final leg of our British driving, we thought we had it made when we reached M40, a superhighway into the heart of London. Nothing to it from here onward, thought I. But then it was noticed the Metro was running low on gas. And signs began to appear along this wonderful road proclaiming "No Services on M40."

I couldn't believe it. As we barreled along it became more apparent that the signs meant what they said – no gasoline and no food on M40.

There were roads where one might exit, but no indication whether petrol was available along those roads. The first exit we explored was barren of service stations. The second attempt brought us to a gasoline pump. Hooray!

But there was no restaurant and we were hungry in this mid-afternoon. Following local instructions, we drove up this narrow lane and down that. Lo and behold, we came across The Belfry Conference Center, which seemed to be an adjunct of Oxford University. No, they could not provide us tea and scones, but they were willing to serve tea and biscuits, biscuits being cookies.

We accepted.

I can't close this column on driving in Great Britain without a further word about adventures in the roundabouts. Roundabouts occur on all types of British roads from the simple two-lane versions to the smooth and many-laned Motorways. It's their way of handling junctions.

As a driver approaches a roundabout, he passes a sign displaying all the possible exits off this traffic circle. There may be three exits and there may be six. If someone chooses the wrong exit, he flies off into the mist and likely is never heard of again. (Presumably the British government forwards a message of condolence to the nearest of kin. "Her Majesty's government regrets to inform you. that D. Monahan mistakenly took the incorrect exit on A1 near Charlton on Trent. His vehicle was last seen cresting a hill near Swineshead. He is officially listed as missing in driving action.")

Somebody, somewhere understands the theory of which lane one enters, when one properly changes lanes, and which lane one uses to exit a roundabout at the correct place. Rumor has it that the English physics genius Stephen Hawking is working on the problem. The certainty is I never solved it, as attested by irritated horn toots, squealing brakes, and lips forming something like

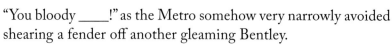

"You bloody _____!" as the Metro somehow very narrowly avoided shearing a fender off another gleaming Bentley.

As golf, driving in the United Kingdom is a humbling game.

The Day the Theory of Tickets Failed the Test

November 1993

The word from Notre Dame is that tickets for the Fighting Irish-Florida State football game are the most difficult to find since the 1965 Notre Dame-Michigan State contest. As in 1993, the winner of the 1965 struggle would be considered the overwhelming favorite for the collegiate national championship.

In Oklahoma, there had been developed after years of research and testing the Dillon-Monahan Theory of Tickets. The theory's central proposition read thus: There are always tickets available at advertised sellouts. The rationale behind the theory was the perceived psychological certainty of two modes of human inaction: one, people without tickets would avoid a sellout, and two, some people who had tickets would not show and their tickets would be available to the daring few who chose to travel to the site of the contest.

There was one other quasi certainty in our minds. Notre Dame University would never, ever keep Catholic priests outside its stadium at the big game of the year! It would be dangerously close to a sacrilege for them to do so, wouldn't it?

We were highly motivated because Tom Sullivan, a graduate of McGuinness High School, was scheduled to start as-an offensive tackle for the Irish. This was to be the crowning game of Tom's career, we thought. The big fellow had led the charge against Southern California the preceding week as Notre Dame smashed its way to more than 300 yards rushing.

As soon as we walked unto the South Bend campus the Theory of Tickets began to wilt. The closer we got to the stadium the more lifeless the theory became.

A ray of sun broke over the theory. Joe somehow got a band ticket. He didn't have to march in with the band, but he did have to wedge himself between tubas and tympani in the band's section of the hallowed Notre Dame Stadium.

Joe headed through the gate to the scene of the war. I and several thousand other rejectees, many surprisingly priests, circled the stadium in an agonizing quest for tickets. Some of us carried signs, others made pitiful verbal petitions. Outcasts collared outcasts in near tearful pleas for nonexistent tickets.

As game time neared, I found myself outside the tunnel which leads up to the playing surface. The locker rooms of both teams open into that tunnel.

As I watched the Michigan State door opened and the white and green Spartan giants poured into the passage. They had their hands taped, and those hands were lifted over their heads, thrusting in unison toward the ceiling as they chanted Go! Go! Go! Go! Go! The roaring chant was amplified by the tunnel.

Then the dark blue and gold Notre Dame team filed out into the tunnel and stood more quietly in place. Afterwards I wondered if the Notre Dame players might have been just a teence intimidated in that tunnel.

With the kickoff the stadium began to rock with explosions of crowd noise. I located a group of men listening on a transistor radio. We were in football purgatory, so close and yet so far away.

Between plays a gentleman said sadly, "I drove all the way from Elkhart for this." (Elkhart is 16 miles east of South Bend.)

I added, " I drove all the way from Oklahoma City." The others turned and looked at me with expressions of fear that they might be too close to a dangerous nut in a Roman collar.

One fellow, no doubt a Samaritan, said to me, "My wife's in the stadium. She doesn't know anything about football and doesn't care anything about it. When she comes out at halftime, I'll give you her ticket. We'll walk over to the Morris Inn and watch the second half on TV."

And that's how I, a probable actor in a future divorce case, found myself in a temporary, ground-level seat in the end zone for one half of a great football game.

Five minutes into the second half, I realized Notre Dame was outmatched. The Irish quarterback was not a good passer and Michigan State's defense overwhelmed the good guys' attempts to run the ball.

Our man Tom Sullivan, a really outstanding collegiate lineman, had the misfortune to play with Bubba Smith on his right shoulder and a more squat but amazingly mobile middle guard named Lucas, on his left. Behind them lurked linebacker George Webster (picked a few years later by Bud Wilkinson as the outstanding college defensive player of the century).

Notre Dame did not back away. The loud crashes of equipment as player smashed into player made one flinch. There was a fellow named Bill Wolski, I think, who returned a kickoff or two for Notre Dame from my end of the field. He caught the kicks about the goal line and ran straight ahead until there was a terrible Splat! Followed quickly by Splat! Splat! Amazingly Wolski managed to wobble off the field under his own power.

Michigan State won 10 to 3.

Dillon and Monahan returned home and threw their Theory of Tickets into the wastebasket.

That's the Way It Used to Be

December 1993

At St. John's Home Missions Seminary in Little Rock this was the yearly September scene: The tall kindly bishop stood on the sidewalk outside Morris Hall surrounded by ranks of seminarians in black cassocks.

In his rural Arkansas drawl, the tall kindly bishop said, "The seminary is like a laboratory." These words rolled slowly out of the tall kindly bishop's mouth like bottles of Dr. Pepper clunking to the bottom of a vending machine. The key noun was not pronounced lab-o-ra-tor-e but la-bor-a-tor-e.

There was a pause.

Then: "Why is the seminary like a la-bor-a-tor-e?"

Pause.

Finally the clincher: "Because the seminary is a la-bora-tor-e!"

More than 40 years later, this former seminarian replies: "The seminary was not a la-bor-a-tor-e." The seminary of the late 1940s was operated more like a medium security correctional institution for non-violent offenders.

When this nervous incipient seminarian arrived at St. Louis's Glennon Preparatory Seminary in the waning weeks of the summer of 1945, I was installed in the system. In classrooms, in chapel, in the dining room, even, at times, in walking down the hall, we sat, knelt, stood and walked in order by alphabet.

Gino Baldetti, the gentle class brain, always sat on the right side of the front row. Charles Zipperich inevitably was located at the end of the chain in the last row. Being a Monahan I sat in the middle.

Also toward the center was Hutchinson's desk. The fact that Hutchinson failed to show up for his entire first year of college in the seminary did not upset the system. The empty desk remained the seat of the missing Hutchinson for the whole academic year. Occasionally a priest-professor would inquire, "Who is missing over there today?" "Hutchinson," came the prompt choral answer. There was one rumor, possibly factual, that Hutchinson made a passing grade in science the first semester.

In those bygone Truman-Eisenhower years, when seminaries were crowded with students as diverse as pale lads who had not yet had the pleasure of shaving together with grizzled veterans of the Battle of the Bulge and combat tough ex-paratroopers, the same rules applied to all.

For example, the lights were to be out by 10 p.m. not 10:01 or 10:02, but 10 p.m. At Kenrick Seminary in St. Louis, the administration simplified procedures. Not even a light switch need be flicked by a student. All electrical power to their rooms was cut promptly at 10 o'clock.

An Oklahoma seminarian had been gifted with a statue which glowed in the dark, one of the first of its kind. Made giddy by possession of a light which even the administration could not darken, this young man took to the pitch-black halls, squinting to see figures of other seminarians stumbling toward restrooms. He jumped at these shadows while thrusting the statue in their face and whispering loudly "Boo!"

All went well in this game until the bilious-colored statue was stuck against the nose of Father Corcoran, the reigning Gregorian chant expert. A moment of terror for the statue-bearer was followed by immense relief, when this habitually exuberant priest said, "Pretty, isn't it!"

One might imagine that seminaries of that era did not encourage their students to travel frivolously hither and yon, and one would be correct. The permissive society had not yet knocked a large dent in seminary life, but explicit permission was what was needed to venture off the hallowed property or...!

At Kenrick Seminary, the gentleman who gave those treasured permissions was a priest known to the students as The Judge. In the very large seminary chapel, The Judge chose to occupy a seat in the choir loft. From his perch, The Judge issued solemn baritone statements on the approximate moral level of the student body's behavior.

One evening this frightening declaration was heard: "Gentlemen, the student body has been betrayed!!"

Two hundred brains wondered: Did the rector abscond with the soft drink account? Has the ancient spiritual director eloped with the cook? Has Pope Pius XII canceled the Christmas vacation? It was nothing as minor as those kinds of things.

This is what had happened. Joe Brown, senior seminarian, had requested and received permission to see a dentist. But, on the way back from the dentist's office to his seminary home, Joe Brown had been observed entering a theater! Perhaps secretly Joe had lusted to see the new flick "It's a Wonderful Life."

That's the way it used to be in the olden days. Thank God and Pope John XXIII for some healthy changes.

CHAPTER 18

1994

Wash Is Done...Gone the Socks...Down the Drain

January 1994

Today has been laundry day for this old sinner. The laundry room at the Archdiocesan Pastoral Center makes a kind of rectangle with my personal quarters. So I don't have to carry my dirty clothes very far.

As usual, the element of mystery enters into the laundry scene. What does happen to one's missing socks?

Folding my socks into pairs this afternoon during the Denver-Chicago football game, I came up two socks short, effectively widowing two other stockings. It was a sad event, an unexplained outcome. I now have 18 single stockings resting on the top of my dresser, each one bereft of its partner for life.

I repeat: what does happen to one's missing socks?

The only real theory I've heard about these missing-in-action hosiery is that they are sucked into the drains of the automatic washers. If that is so, a large part of the Mississippi River delta must consist of socks. I do not intend to go and to search.

Perhaps a more appropriate response, to borrow psychotherapeutic terms, would be to bring each sad revelation of missing dearly beloved hosiery to closure by singing this version of "Taps."

"Wash is done. Gone the socks, down the drain, down the pipes, ain't it rare!

"Three are lost. Boo-hoo-hoo! God knows where."

There are perhaps half a dozen of the human species still alive who recall a movie titled "The Man In the White Suit."

The fictional story was that of a textile inventor in England who managed to produce a white material which would never wear out. Furthermore if the material became smirched, a simple brush of one's hand removed the stain.

The inventor of this fabric imagined that the whole world would embrace his creation with an outpouring of gratitude. Instead owners and workers in textile mills as well as legions from cleaning and clothing establishments go bananas. While crazed hordes are chasing the poor inventor up one London street and down the next, the magical white suit begins to fall apart on its own.

While I don't want this leaked to those who might not understand, I think I possess the real McCoy of indestructible articles of clothing in three of my long-sleeve shirts. Doing the laundry today reminded me of that happy fact.

These incredible shirts were manufactured while John F. Kennedy was a member of the United States Senate. Pope Pius XII headed the Catholic Church at the time, but my best information is he did not own one of these long-lasting garments.

Only one of these shirts retains an identification tag and it hangs by a thread, although the shirt itself shows no signs of wear. The tag reveals it is a Banlon shirt.

These knit Banlon shirts have muted colors – kind of green, kind of gray, and kind of grayer. They are not necessarily fashionable. Although they have existed through so many eras of taste one would think they must have been in style at some point.

But they are loyal. More than anything else I own, these shirts have been with me – Banlons loyal to the last – as I traveled about this old globe.

Please don't tell anyone, unless it be officials of The Smithsonian, about my Banlons.

That brings us to my underwear, which at this moment is being dried next door. My underwear is basic white (some might say gray)—jockey-style shorts and shapeless T-shirts. These undergarments lack pizzazz and sexiness.

In an hour or so when I fold my underwear, my main concern will be to get the 32s on the bottom of the stack. You see, from time immemorial I have been the owner of a collection of 32-inch waist undershorts. My waist has not been as slender as 32 inches since John F. Kennedy first entered Congress, which must mean these articles of clothing are older than the Banlon shirts. A frightening thought.

By putting the 32s on the bottom of the stack in my dresser drawer, I postpone having to inflict their torture on my flabby waist. In fact, when I get to the 32s that's the signal that wash day will be the following Saturday.

Sad to say, there comes a time when even this underwear has to be decommissioned. In a short ceremony, a standard message of gratitude for years of faithful service is read to the retiring underwear, after which it is stuffed into a large bag to begin a new existence as shoeshine cloths

Afterword

In the column titled Present at the End (Chapter 15), the story of a woman's death, Monahan concluded: "Up close no deaths are pretty, but some are beautiful." I would add that some are even downright funny. Monahan's own death was a prime example. I know because I was present at the end. This is that story.

A holy vigil was taking place in the dimly lit room of the nursing home. Nurses came and went, softly tiptoeing to the bedside, checking vital signs and murmuring comforting words to me as I kept watch over my dearest friend. I had been there throughout the night, even though the nurses said it could be days yet. Instinctively, I knew better.

The nurses had also become my friends, for Monahan had been in their care for many years now. The Alzheimer's disease had been diagnosed a full eight years before. It was a very long good-bye.

After years of urging and coaxing him to eat, to open his mouth, the mouth is now open constantly but consuming only great shuddering gulps of air.

Soft music at his bedside played, "Holy Mary, mother of God, pray for us sinners now and at the hour of our death, Amen..." His family had put the recording on to play over and over in a continuous loop. I found the chanting and music annoying and distracting. I turned the volume way down but could not quite bring myself to turn it off, even though his family wasn't present.

Helpless in the face of approaching death, all that could be done was change out the now-warm cloth on his forehead for a cool one. "If we can get the fever to break, he will go quickly," the nurse said. So I kept switching the cloths.

But there was one other thing I could do. Remembering that hearing is the last of our senses to shut down as death approaches, I periodically spoke to him of all the things I believed.

"This is the day you have prepared for your whole life, David, and you prepared very well. God is surely pleased with you," I said to the comatose man as I held his hand.

"Soon you will be home again and your mother and father will be there waiting to greet you.

"Do you see the beautiful light, the light that radiates a love so powerful that you can't resist it? You can go to that light, David. It's okay to go.

And, "I will miss you so very much, but I will be okay. And some day I will join you."

These and many other things were spoken as they occurred to me. Many of them were repeated more than once. It occurred to me that it would have been a good time to add any amends, had there been regrets that needed forgiveness. But such was not the case. I could think of nothing that had been left unsaid or undone. I was very much at peace with all aspects of our long friendship. It was this peace which allowed me to let him go, to accept the fact that he was dying.

In the quiet interstitial space between his gulps of air, the softly sung words of the Rosary finally filtered through my thoughts and tears, offering now a surprising comfort in place of the earlier annoyance. It wasn't so much the words but the repetition of them, like a mantra, that now brought comfort.

Eventually, the space between breaths became extended, terrifying in their length, yet a welcome signal that the end of a long and difficult journey was close at hand. Intuitively, I knew when it was time. I whispered in his ear, "Just one more breath, David, and you'll be home!" And he did exactly that.

Amen.

About twenty minutes after his last breath, his niece breezed into the room, tossed her purse and coat on an empty chair, and surveyed the scene. All appeared unchanged to her. I was sitting in prayerful silence, still holding his hand, and listening to the now-soothing Rosary over and over again.

"Well, I've cleared my calendar," she said, "so I can stay for the duration. How are things going?"

"Oh, my dear, didn't they tell you at the front desk? He's gone," I said, somewhat surprised that she hadn't noticed that he was no longer gulping for air.

Moving now to the opposite side of his bed, she immediately lowered her voice and began speaking across him in hushed tones, as one often does in the presence of death. But I'm hard of hearing, and the hum of the air mattress pump made it all but impossible to hear what she was saying.

After having to ask her several times to repeat herself, I suggested she turn off that air mattress pump so I could hear better. She looked everywhere for an on/off switch but found none. Instead, she simply unplugged it.

Slowly, as we stood there transfixed, our loved one gradually disappeared into the folds of his bedding, sinking like a ship being swallowed up by the sea. We watched in disbelief as his thin, wasted body simply vanished before our eyes.

"Oh! Oh! Oh dear! Plug it in! Quick, plug it back in," I cried. Or maybe she said it. I don't remember. But the plug was found and reinserted into the electrical outlet. Immediately the noisy pump started pumping the air back into the mattress…and, magically, slowly, he rose up once again. This saintly man rose up, emerging from the depths of his mattress as if foretelling the resurrection of his soul.

We both burst out laughing. The laughter was so surprising in the midst of such sadness that we laughed even harder.

Once our mirth subsided, our faces wet with tears from both sadness and hilarity, we reflected on the many near-death stories in which people relate having hovered over their body, watching the scene below.

In this case, if indeed he was watching, I'm certain he was laughing too. He would have told and retold this story with great glee. And eventually it would have become yet another one of these delightful "For the Time Being" columns!

Given the author's many years as an educator in secondary schools, as well as his love of the English language and good writing, it seemed fitting that any and all proceeds from this book go toward a scholarship for aspiring journalists.

Thus the Reverend David Monahan Scholarship Fund has been established to honor his memory.

For further information about this permanent endowment, the scholarships or donations to the Fund, contact the Catholic Foundation of Oklahoma, c/o Archdiocese of Oklahoma city, Post Office Box 32180, Oklahoma City, Oklahoma 73123.

Other Books by This Auhtor

"*One Family: One Century*"—A Photographic History of the Catholic Church in Oklahoma 1875-1975, edited by David Monahan, published 1977 by the Archdiocese of Oklahoma City, c/o *Sooner Catholic*, P.O. Box 32180, Oklahoma city, OK 73123, 405-721-1810 or *http://archokc.org/history/history-books*.

"*The Shepherd Cannot Run*"—Letters of Stanley Rother, Missionary and Martyr (also available in Spanish), edited by David Monahan, published 1984, 2007 and 2010, by the Archdiocese of Oklahoma City, c/o *Sooner Catholic*, P.O. Box 32180, Oklahoma City, OK 73123, 405-721-1810.